COTTAGE INDUSTRIES

COTTAGE INDUSTRIES

Marjorie Filbee

David & Charles
Newton Abbot London North Pomfret (Vt)

British Library Cataloguing in Publication Data
Filbee, Majorie
Cottage industries.
1. Home labour—Great Britain
I. Title
658'.002 HD2336.G6

ISBN 0-7153-8286-1

Typeset by ABM Typographics Ltd., Hull
and printed in Great Britain by
Redwood Burn Limited, Trowbridge, Wilts.
for David & Charles (Publishers) Limited
Brunel House Newton Abbot Devon

Published in the United States of America
by David & Charles Inc
North Pomfret Vermont 05053 USA

CONTENTS

ACKNOWLEDGEMENTS

My grateful thanks go to the many craftsmen and women who took time to give me information about their work and help with photographs. I am grateful to the curators and staff of the Avoncroft Museum of Buildings, Bridport Museum, Luton Museum, the Maritime Museum for East Anglia, the Museum of English Rural Life, Oxfordshire County Museum, Truro Pottery Museum and the Welsh Folk Museum for all their help and advice.

My thanks also to the secretaries of the craft guilds who supplied lists and information about their members, enabling me to track down at least some of them.

Lastly, but certainly not least my thanks to my daughter-in-law Gloria Filbee for typing the manuscript, and to Patrick Filbee for his artistic assistance.

MARJORIE FILBEE

INTRODUCTION

Reports today from the Orkney and Shetland Isles in the North down to Cornwall in the South tell that cottage industries are alive and flourishing all over the British Isles. The traditional handmaking skills that kept the country supplied with all its needs until the Industrial Revolution of the eighteenth and nineteenth centuries are being revived and enjoyed by both those who practise them and those who simply like to watch others at work or buy what they make.

It is clear that many of these skills go back much further than one might think. Their origins are almost lost in prehistory—almost, but not quite. We now have so much archaeological evidence, especially for crafts such as pottery and basketry, which makes it clear that there is little new under the Sun and that materials, methods of working and the tools used in crafts being practised today, have changed but little over the centuries; only the social conditions are greatly different. Because of this ancient continuity of crafts techniques, it seems to me that the work of contemporary craftsmen cannot be fully appreciated without some knowledge of the history of their methods, and my book is therefore an amalgam of this history and an account of contemporary craftsmen and where their work can be seen.

Some articles such as those made of wood or cloth have not lasted to the extent that pottery has, but where artifacts were preserved, as in the wet, peaty soil of Somerset, we know from excavations at the Iron Age village of Glastonbury that over two thousand years ago lived a society of skilled artist-craftsmen, who made a high class of pottery, weapons, ornaments and textiles, as well as wooden bowls, tubs, spoons and ladles little different from those produced by craftsmen today.

There have always been two main categories of cottage industry and both are thriving at the present time. The first is still carried on today under much pleasanter conditions than in the past, and is what is strictly thought of as the true cottage industry. This is where one person in an area gave out materials to the workers in their cottages, mostly women and children, and then collected the finished work from them for sale either to a superior dealer or employer, or at local fairs and markets. The laceworkers, the netmakers, spinners, weavers, glovemakers, straw plaiters, smockmakers, buttonmakers, stocking knitters and even chain- and nailmakers were among those who all worked in this way until the introduction of machines. Then many of them either lost their livelihood and were ruined, or moved to the new factory towns for work. They were poorly paid, but even the little they did earn made all the difference between survival and starvation. Local authorities went to great lengths to keep them in work, often organising the schools that taught the children their craft. This was considered far preferable to them becoming a drain on their parish by ending up in the workhouse. If this dreaded fate did befall them, they often had to continue as outworkers.

Many cottagers lived and worked and brought up large families in most inadequate housing, often in one room of a cottage. The conditions for little children working at home were often even worse than when they later worked in factories. If there was little supervision in factories there was often none at home and parents were desperate for the pennies that the children could earn. It is not surprising that many travellers reported seeing cottage workers at their work outside, when the weather allowed, to obtain more light and space. In spite of the hardships, however, many workers preferred to work at home and did so for as long as possible.

The second category of cottage-industry workers were the village carpenters and woodworkers of all descriptions: the blacksmiths, leatherworkers, basketmakers and potters found in every village, who worked for themselves either alone or in small family businesses, often in small workshops attached to their homes. They were principally engaged in supplying the needs of their own particular area, working mainly to specific orders, or selling their wares at the great number of local fairs and markets that were then held. Most of these workers had a small garden, a smallholding or farm to provide them with food, especially valuable during economic depressions.

Both categories of cottage industries are dealt with in this book, showing their operation both past and present. I have tried to show what they made, particularly if it is still being made today, and those methods which have survived.

Individual craftsmen are included in the text, usually to illustrate a particular point, and a wide, representative selection are given in Appendix IIIB. Limitations of space made it impossible to mention more in the body of the book (as I would have liked to do), and I have not attempted to make Appendix IIIB complete for it would inevitably soon be out of date; but I advise anyone interested to get into touch with the craft guilds listed in Appendix I or to consult the museums in Appendix II. All such organisations are usually most helpful in supplying information about where cottage industries are active today—as often as not in or near your locality.

The social background to the cottage industries of the past as shown in these museums is very different today. While the work for those in the first category ceased at the end of the nineteenth century, the skills they had known were taken up again in this century as leisure pastimes for women at home, their children now safely occupied at school. Many women, however, are now earning their living at these traditional skills, either in teaching them to others in further-education classes or in turning their talents into successful businesses. When they find they have more work than they can undertake on their own, they are again working on cottage-industry lines, one woman obtaining the orders and marketing the work of others working in their own homes.

There is a more individualistic approach to cottage industries today. Workers are usually independent and no one is exploited through sheer poverty. In fact, most workers in the first category of cottage industries mentioned now work as those in the second category have always worked: where workers collaborate today it is usually to share premises and not to share work. There are an increasing number of groups of buildings around the country which are occupied by craftworkers, as are those on the Lockinge Estate at Ardington, near Wantage, Oxfordshire. Each of the old farm buildings from the dairy to the old watermill houses a different craftsman or woman, all working independently.

Without a dealer or agent to handle their goods they again have to handle their wares themselves, marketing them at craft fairs as in medieval times. There is an ever-growing number of fairs today and many craftsmen start out in this way. Often they have so much work that they do not have time to attend the fairs and rely on personal recommendation by one customer to another to provide them with work.

Making goods by hand is a slow process and if a high standard of work is to be maintained there is a limit to the amount of work that can be undertaken. In the past the various craft guilds which were in existence from the Middle Ages onwards controlled the standards of most of the main industries. Nowadays, craft guilds have been set up in each county to inform the public of the existence of the craftsmen in their guild through exhibitions of their work and, in the case of several counties, to provide lists of their members, often with a map showing their whereabouts as many cottage industries are tucked away in remote areas. The guilds of Dorset and Somerset are especially helpful in this respect as is the Western Isles Crafts Association. Many of the guilds set a standard of craftmanship which has to be reached before full membership is granted, so this is a guide to customers when commissioning a craftsman to make an article for them.

Strangely enough, the most modern of scientific developments, the silicone chip, is enabling people to work for industry in their own homes, in jobs such as computer programming. It may be that office workers of the future will stay at home with their computers and never visit the firm that employs them. By then, the cottage industry will have come full circle.

1
THE COTTAGE LACEMAKERS

Yon cottager who weaves at her own door,
Pillow and bobbins all her little store;
Content, though mean, and cheerful if not gay,
Shuffling her threads about the live-long day;
Just earns a scanty pittance, and at night
Lies down secure her heart and pocket light.

William Cowper (1731–1800)

A surprising amount of shuffling of threads and weaving of bobbins on pillows is carried out today in the cottages and farmhouses of England, 200 years after Cowper's lines were written. Some of the lace made now is produced for profit, much of it just for pleasure, but the methods and materials used have changed little over the years. The increase of interest in the craft has led to instruction classes flourishing and the formation of lace societies to promote interest and satisfy the need for further information. This includes lectures and visits to the Continent to see examples of old lace whose patterns first came to this country several hundred years ago and are still being made today.

One contemporary lacemaker is June Hunt who, after studying at the Chelsea School of Art and the Central School of Arts and Crafts where she specialised in fashion drawing, eventually moved near to Axminster and became fascinated by the local lacemaking industry. She learned to make Honiton Lace at evening classes and now devotes all her time and artistic efforts to making lace. She mounts her work in brooches, in small and large silver pendants, paperweights and designs for framing, as well as making lace for collars and handkerchiefs. Honiton Lace is especially suitable for using in small amounts as it is made in separate sprigs with a tradition of designs of wild flowers, butterflies and birds, which had originally inspired the seventeenth century Flemish immigrants (see plate 1). June Hunt sells her work at various craft markets or direct to customers who have admired her work when worn by others. The larger pieces of lace are usually undertaken only for special commissions.

In the middle of the sixteenth century refugees from the Netherlands, driven from their country by religious persecution, settled in comparative peace in the cottages of Devon and the Midlands. Many of them were skilled in lacemaking, a craft already well established on the Continent, and brought their knowledge of making pillow lace to their new homes. What had formerly been known as lace in England was really embroidery, either needle lace, drawn linen or cut work. Pillow lace is made in long strips supported on a pillow by the intricate weaving of bobbins with linen or silk thread attached; these threads are kept in position by pins stuck into holes in a parchment pattern on the pillow. The pins are moved into new positions on the parchment as the work proceeds, to form the pattern required. The net ground is usually worked at the same time as the design, which is outlined in a heavier thread called a gimp.

The many patterns formed reflect the original derivation of the word lace from the Latin *lacere,* meaning to entice or allure, and the rate at which lace became a popular item of apparel in Elizabethan times quickly fulfilled the meaning of the word, enticing many to wear it and to make it in their cottage homes.

Between 1563 and 1568 Flemish lacemakers settled around Cranfield in Bedfordshire, and around Newport Pagnell, Olney and Buckingham in Buckinghamshire. Within a short time there was a cottage industry in lace in many other counties including Northamptonshire, Somerset, Oxfordshire, Huntingdonshire and parts of Dorset. Lacemakers from Brussels found their way to the Honiton area and coastal districts of East Devon, where Flemish names are still found among the inhabitants, together with memorials to the earliest workers.

Plate 1 Detail of a section of a flounce of Honiton Lace made in about 1870

The early lace was known as bone lace. The makers used bobbins made from sheep bones and, where they were too poor to obtain pins, they used fish and bird bones to pin the lace to the pillows.

After the slaughter of Huguenots in Paris in 1572 and their persecution in France at the end of the seventeenth century, many Protestant lacemakers escaped to England and joined the Flemish workers in Buckinghamshire and Northamptonshire.

The Flemish immigrants were keen gardeners, and the flowers, ferns and foliage of their English cottage gardens soon appeared in the motifs used in their lace patterns. They brought with them the tools of their work, importing brass wire pins for themselves and for the English workers. Any other type of pin marked the lace. By 1626 a pin factory for their manufacture was established in Gloucestershire.

Spanish lace may have been introduced into England by the Spanish-born wife of Henry VIII, Katharine of Aragon. When she was in enforced retirement at Houghton House, near

Ampthill, Bedfordshire, in 1531 it is believed that she occupied much of her time in embroidery and taught some of the villagers around her. How much of her work was embroidery and how much bobbin lace is not known, but early bobbin lace was made in nearby Northamptonshire with a pattern known as Queen Katharine, and a stitch known as Kat Stitch, also found in Buckinghamshire, was said to have been invented by her. The story goes that when there was a famine in the area she burnt all her lace and ordered more from the local workers to replace it, providing them with work and saving them from starvation.

The most fashionable lace of the sixteenth century was displayed in the enormous ruffs edged with lace, supported by a wire frame, worn by Elizabeth I and her court. Stocking fronts made of lace were also fashionable.

The poorer classes bought their lace at local fairs. It became known as 'Tawdry' from the cheap and showy goods sold at St Audrey's Fair in Cambridgeshire.

In the early days of lacemaking men were involved in designing, making and selling lace. By the beginning of the seventeenth century some of them were finding it so profitable that they risked breaking the strict Sunday trading laws; if caught, they were brought before ecclesiastical courts. Lace was now worn more than ever: large lace collars took the place of the Elizabethan ruff, and rich lace formed the lining of high boots, with the tops turned over to display it. This fashion was discouraged by the Puritans, but from the restoration of Charles II onwards the industry flourished. In fact, Samuel Pepys regarded the wearing of lace as a necessity, not a luxury. The fashion extended to lace caps, aprons, gloves, petticoats, nightshirts and handkerchiefs. Cravats later took the place of lace collars, which, during the Stuart period, were often hidden under long wigs. At the end of the century William III and his queen spent about £5,000 a year on lace.

In the eighteenth century lace decorated all types of clothing and was worn in profusion at every event from birth to death. The baby daughter of the Duke and Duchess of Chandos was so overloaded with lace at its christening in 1778 that it died.

Lace frills became popular on shirts. The ruffles were called 'weeping ruffles' because they hung down over the hands. Beautiful lace decorated the fans that were so popular with eighteenth-century ladies, more often than not used to hide bad teeth and bad breath.

The cottage workers supplied lace for all these fashions over the centuries; at times they were protected by government import restrictions on lace from the Continent. By the end of the seventeenth century it was estimated that over 100,000 people, mostly women and children, earned their living by lacemaking.

The lace industry flourished later in Wiltshire, where in such villages as Downton, near Salisbury, which became one of the main centres for the buying and selling of lace in that area, lace was made by women and children in almost every house in the village. Business so flourished that tradesmen made their own lace-tokens to supplement the lack of small change in their transactions. Often lacemakers received no money for their work but exchanged it at the village shop for its value in goods. Although this practice was forbidden by law the lacemakers were still being defrauded in this way in the mid-nineteenth century.

The middleman would call at the shop to buy the lace from the shopkeeper, and take it to the lace markets which were held in London, at the George Inn, Aldersgate Street, and at the Bull and Mouth in St Martin's by Aldersgate, as well as in other towns outside the capital, such as Newport Pagnell. They would return to the cottages with silk, thread and patterns for the workers to make up into orders. The designs on the parchment patterns used on the pillows are often found marked out on pieces of old deeds or wills and were passed around a district so that various areas can be identified by the patterns for which they became famous, although pillow lace was always more individual in its design than the later machine-made variety.

The designs were first pricked out on cardboard, the lines of the main pattern having been inked in; then this was transferred to the pieces of parchment. They were usually about 14in

(355mm) long and the lace was moved carefully to the top of the parchment when the strip was finished for the design to be repeated. Lacemakers sometimes used two of these parchments at a time to avoid having to 'set-up' the lace again, a time-consuming process. These were known as 'eaches', sometimes spelt 'eke', a word still used today in the expression to 'eke' something out, ie, to extend it. The parchments often had linen ends (also known as eaches) to enable them to be fastened easily to the pillow.

The large variety of bobbins were made by the men in wood, bone, brass, silver, gold, pewter, glass and ivory, often inlaid and often carved (Fig 1). The variety was practical and necessary to enable the lacemaker to distinguish her bobbins more easily while working her pattern at great speed. Even working quickly it takes about an hour's work to produce 1in (25.4mm) of lace. Coloured beads were also fixed to the bobbins by wire for greater identification (they were often working with a hundred bobbins at a time) and groups of beads at the ends of the bobbins for greater weight to keep the threads taut.

Bobbins were the cherished possessions of lacemakers and many were given as love tokens on engagements and weddings or made and inscribed with a biblical text or to commemorate some historic event. At a wedding feast part of the bone from a ham or joint of meat might be saved so that a

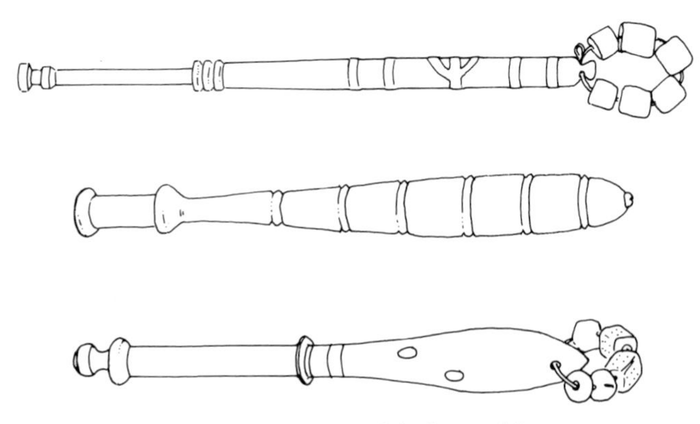

Fig 1 Bobbins used for lacemaking

bobbin could be made from it and inscribed with the wedding date. A lady from Leighton Buzzard had at the time of her death over 200 different bobbin designs in her possession, acquired over her 82 years of lacemaking. Bobbins could be ordered or bought at fairs or markets. They were often kept in oak or mahogany bobbin boxes, which had two compartments. One of these was for quills, bobbins which held all the thread; the other was for trollies on to which the thread from the quills was wound. Today bobbins are collector's items and, owing to the revival of interest in making pillow lace, makers of bobbins are again in demand. Bobbins which were lost under the floorboards are often found today when a cottage in a lacemaking village is demolished.

Some of the pillows were home-made, some made by families who specialised in making them. Certain shapes were popular in different districts. They were tightly filled with hay or straw and covered with hessian canvas, but they were covered again with a pillow cloth by the worker before pinning on the parchment (Fig 2). Another cloth, called the 'worker', was put under the bobbins when they were attached, and a further piece of linen called the 'draw' covered the finished

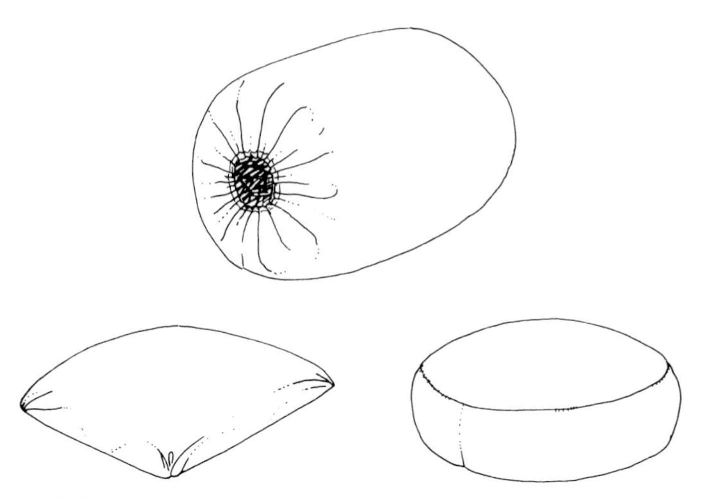

Fig 2 Pillows (left to right: flat square, bolster, round or Honiton) filled with hay or straw and covered with canvas on which the lacemakers supported their work

strips of lace as they were completed. Yet another cloth called the 'hind-cloth' covered the whole pillow when the lacemaker was not at work. All these precautions were taken to keep the lace white at all cost. To do this while working in a cottage with an open fire was not easy. Often a bag was made to match the pillow so that the completed lace could drop straight in. Smoke from the fire was a continual threat to producing clean work. A cloth was kept handy to wipe the worker's hands—keeping starch or flour nearby to dry the worker's hands was a practice much frowned upon.

Lacemakers in France using white silk often worked in lofts over a cow-shed where they kept warm by the heat from the animals to prevent smoke from darkening the lace. In England they kept warm with an earthenware fire-pot, known as hot pot or dicky pot, which could be filled with hot wood ash, obtainable from the local baker for a farthing if necessary, or perhaps a brass pot filled with hot charcoal, which they kept under their full skirts while working. A stool placed over the pot formed a comforting footrest. These heated pots were also known as shock pots owing to the habit of mischievous boys

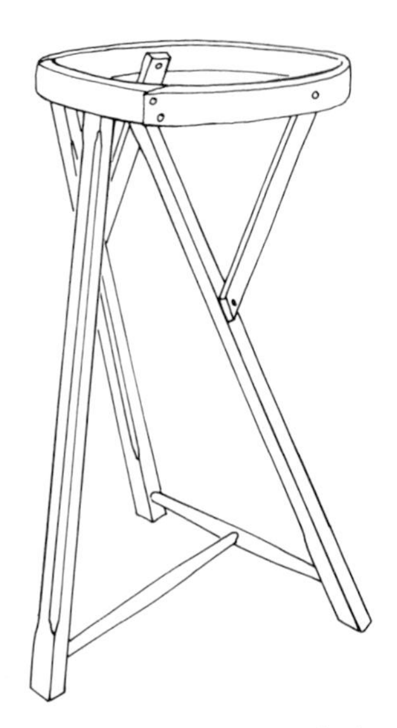

Fig 3 A three-legged 'horse' used to support the lacemaker's pillow

of putting chestnuts into them when the lacemakers left them unattended for a short time, and the exploding chestnuts giving a lively but unwelcome touch to their work. Three-sided box-type wooden footstools, with a fixed base and top with ventilation holes, could hold a small heated pot and are often seen in seventeenth-century Dutch paintings. These were imported into England from the Continent. Another type was four sided with a carrying handle.

The pillow rested on the worker's knees and could be further supported by a three-legged pillow 'horse', also known as the 'maiden' or the 'lady', a stand which sometimes had neatly turned legs, but was often homemade or made by the village carpenter (Fig 3). At the side of their pillows hung bobbin bags for empty and full bobbins. The remaining equipment was a small pair of scissors and, most important, a pincushion. All this could be housed in a special lace chest, an oak chest on a table-stand, the upper part for the pillow and a lower drawer for bobbins and patterns.

Many of the bobbin winders were also made at home by the men of the family (Fig 4). These winders were small wooden machines into which the bobbin was inserted, the attached thread being wound on to the bobbin by the turning of a handle on a wheel. There are several types of these winders, some made to clamp on to the table.

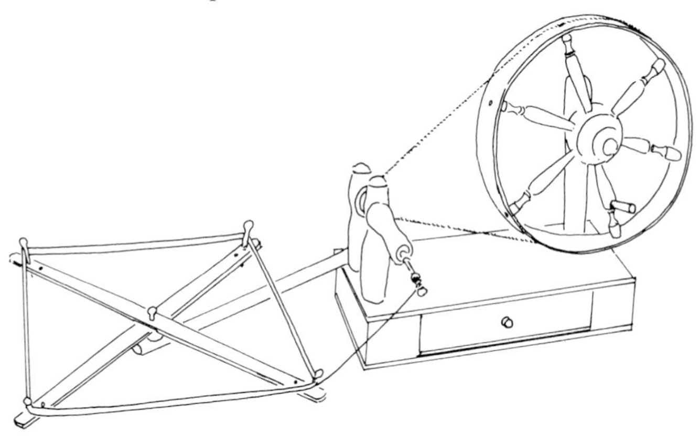

Fig 4 Bobbin winder, a small wooden machine into which the bobbin was inserted

Lacemakers started work at an early age. Many children from 5 years old upwards worked 4–5 hours a day and were taught either at home or in lace schools held in a cottage room. Here 20–30 pupils, girls and boys, sat in cramped rows on stools with their pillows in front of them supported on a form or on pillow horses. Older girls worked 12–15 hours a day. Their necks and arms were kept bare so that they could be slapped easily by the lace mistress; their hair was tightly plaited to prevent stray hairs from falling on the lace. Pauper children were taught lacemaking to enable them to contribute to their upkeep. The lace schools usually kept the first year's lace made by a pupil. Discipline was very strict. Girls were expected to stick ten pins a minute into their patterns and had to work extra time if they were as much as five pins short at the end of the day. While the children were supposed to receive some general education along with their lacemaking, this was almost non-existent, except for prayers being said at the start of the day's work.

They did learn rhymes, however, which they chanted to help count their patterns. These rhymes were called 'lace tells' heard as far back as the sixteenth-century in Shakespeare's *Twelfth Night:*

> O fellow, come, the song we had last night
> Mark it, Cesario, it is old and plain.
> The spinsters and the knitters in the sun,
> And the free maids that weave their threads with bones
> Do use to sing it.

The tells were not often cheerful songs and were full of references to coffins, corpses and storms, all too familiar in life a century or so ago. On the other hand, the lacemakers worked only their pleasures into the patterns they wove as the names by which the designs were known show: Acorn, Tulip, Great Running River, Beehive, Lovers' Knots, Wedding Bells, Primrose, Rose, Honeysuckle, Butterfly, Wheatear and Cornflower.

The conditions in the cramped rooms of the cottage schools were not healthy. The children were liable to suffer fevers and

Plate 2 A well-known Bedfordshire lacemaker, herself the daughter of a lacemaker, photographed in 1901 *(Museum of English Rural Life)*

consumption. They wore stay busks to support their backs while bending over their work which distorted their bones and contracted their chests. In spite of the hardships many lacemakers lived and worked to a great age (see Plate 2). One lacemaker, Nancy Berrington of Cardington, Bedfordshire, was still making lace in her hundredth year with her daughter who was 80. Many of her descendants now live in America.

Today lacemakers are more likely to learn their lacemaking at adult-education classes where teachers of the craft are in increasing demand, or at a lace school where conditions are very different from those of several centuries ago. The English Lace School at Tiverton in Devon was founded in 1979 to provide a centre for the study of lace and to teach the making of a large variety of laces. Residential courses in about fifteen principal types are held throughout the year, pupils travelling to the school from all parts of the country and from abroad. Each course lasts about 4½ days.

The school is under the direction of Mrs Susan Cox, with some of the most experienced lacemakers in the country taking the courses in their own particular speciality. The courses welcome beginners as well as those who are already experienced but wish to become more proficient, or perhaps to learn to design their own work, to identify the various types of lace or merely to learn how to care and preserve antique lace which they may own.

The school was founded to encourage a higher standard of workmanship and design, to publicise the qualities of handmade lace, to encourage patronage and commissioning of the art, and to make known worldwide the various types of English lace. A lace shop at the school is open to the public as well as to its students where all the necessary equipment for lacemaking can be bought. The school provides a centre for the local lacemakers in this traditional lace area to exchange ideas and information and to help establish standards for the craft. There are also classes in smockmaking, tatting and English quiltmaking. Children, who were the chief attendants of the early lace schools, have not been forgotten at Tiverton as the school firmly believes that this is the best time of life to learn the craft. Children's classes are confined to Saturday mornings while the rest of the time is devoted to adults and teenagers. The school holds a summer exhibition each August to which holidaymakers as well as lacemakers are welcome. Here lace can be seen in the making and completed for sale.

Plate 3 Jean Pegg at work on a piece of Torchon Lace, a bolder form than many types of bobbin lace, based on geometric patterns which are used to form edgings or insertions. It is suitable for use with heavier linen items such as traycloths and guest towels and is widely made all over Europe

Plate 4 Part of a lace pillow that belongs to Jean Pegg, showing Torchon Lace and bobbins. The bobbins were made by her husband and sons, some in ivory and some in New Forest yew, but all in traditional patterns

Jean Pegg is a lacemaker from Bournemouth in Dorset who is the English Director of the International Lace Society of the United States of America (see Plates 3 and 4). She teaches lacemaking at adult education classes and is both a writer and lecturer on lacemaking. She was a founder member of the recently formed Christchurch Lace Society and arranges exhibitions of lace at many craft fairs.

Lacemaking in the past must have been a much pleasanter and healthier occupation in summer than in winter, when, free of the need to keep warm and the effort of working in lamp-lit conditions, the workers could work much of the time out of doors. Eighteenth-century cottages were small, cramped and unhealthy. By the end of the century a few landlords were building better cottages. In Northamptonshire at the beginning of the nineteenth century the Duke of Grafton built some larger cottages for lacemakers with two or three bedrooms, a large living-room and a work-room for lacemaking, but this was unusual. Well into the nineteenth century a two-roomed cottage for a rural family was often living, working and sleeping place. Many tells reflect the lacemakers' anxiety about finishing their work before dusk:

> Nineteen miles to the Isle of Wight.
> Shall I get there by candlelight?

(Nineteen was a popular number during lacemaking.)

When darkness did come and the work for the day was still not finished, women and children would sit round a candle-stool or candle-block (Fig 5). This tall stool, measuring about 2ft (610mm) high, had a holder for a large candle in the middle adjustable in height, around which were four wooden cups which held flasks of water. These reflected the candle light on to the lace pillows enabling several workers to work by the light of one candle. Sometimes there were as many as two or three circles of workers. When not in use the flasks rested on straw in a basket made by the local basketmaker. Children often worked at their pillows at home after a hard day at school, and farm labourers did the same. Every few pennies

Fig 5 Candle-stand by which lacemakers did their work after dark

earned helped the family's small income, and when the cottage industry eventually declined, the loss of even these small sums caused great distress.

Women would work in each other's cottages, both for company and for the shared warmth and kettle for tea. To keep the youngest child safe, away from the workers and the open fire, while the mother worked, many cottages had a revolving post fastened to a beam and to the floor, with an extended arm with a wooden ring at the end into which the child fitted. Most cottages had a board across the door to prevent children escaping to the road outside. Today's lacemakers still meet together in farmhouses for instruction and company, although their children are at school and coffee is preferred to tea.

Every few weeks there was a 'cut-off' day when lace was removed from the pillow, taken to the lace-buyers, usually at the village inn and sometimes at the village shop, who eventually sold the lace to their customers at fairs and markets. These had been held in town and villages for centuries on saints' days and festivals. The lacemakers had several special days when some respite from their work was possible. St Andrew's Day, 30 November, known as Tanders, was one, and St Catherine's Day, 25 November, known as Catterns, was another. This latter date was kept originally in honour of St Catherine, the patron saint of spinners, but later the saint became somewhat confused with Katharine of Aragon. Singing and dancing took place at the festival, and special dishes were baked, such as Cattern cakes made of dough, sugar, lard and caraway seeds, and stuffed boiled rabbit 'smothered with onions', a favourite eighteenth-century dish.

In Buckinghamshire, St Catherine's Day was also called Candle Day as it was hopefully the first day when they needed to start lacemaking by candlelight. The candlestick referred to in the old nursery rhyme

> Jack be nimble! Jack be quick!
> Jack jump over the candlestick

is probably the one used by lacemakers and was one of the games played by them on festive occasions.

Although more lacemakers from the Continent came to England during the French Revolution, bringing still more varieties of lace with them, by 1809 John Heathcoat's bobbin machine was patented and the industrialisation of the lace industry began. The cottage workers could not compete with the low price of the machine-made lace, which flourished apace for many years. To make matters worse, the restrictions on the importing of foreign lace were lifted and the lacemakers petitioned Parliament not to 'endanger the security of this interesting and staple manufacture which has given employment for a period of 150 years to above 150,000 persons'.

In Nottinghamshire, Derbyshire and Leicestershire women

and girls were employed both in the factories making machine lace and at home on lacework of different kinds, such as embroidery and mending the fabric produced by the machines, or in drawing out with a needle the threads which joined together the single widths of lace when it came from the machine. All this work was poorly paid.

In time many people, including Queen Victoria, began to compare the machine-made lace with the more durable handmade product, which was seen to be less uniform, regular and flat, giving it an interest and individuality unobtainable by machine. The wedding dresses of Queen Victoria and several of the royal princesses were made of Honiton Lace, the work being shared by a hundred workers from Honiton and villages in East Devon.

Royalty has always supported the handmade lace industry, accepting gifts of it for weddings and births. Lacemakers from Downton contributed lace for the layette of the future Edward VII. They travelled to Malmesbury with their bobbins and stayed there for several weeks until the order was completed. Handkerchiefs trimmed with traditional patterns were accepted by the Princess Royal in 1922, and by the Queen, Princess Margaret and Princess Anne on the occasion of their weddings. A lace garter was presented to the Princess of Wales on her wedding to Prince Charles as a gift from the Christchurch Lace Society. It was made by Mrs Bertha Kemp who, at 72 years of age, put 60 years of lacemaking knowledge into the work. Mrs Kemp, who has made lace handkerchiefs for Princess Anne and the Princess of Wales, is the only remaining Downton laceworker. Downton Lace was made in the form of edgings and insertions and varied from ½in (12mm) to 4in (100mm) in width. The patterns peculiar to the area had such names as Duke's Garter, The Bean, Mrs Rolf, Eggs and Rasher, The River, The Grecian and, appropriately, The Princess. It is hoped that the knowledge of Downton Lace will not be lost as Mrs Kemp lectures on the subject both here and in the United States of America, where there is also a great interest in lacemaking.

The Great Exhibition of 1851 showed handmade lace from

the Midlands and gave it a new lease of life, although it was short-lived. In 1875 newspapers were complaining about 'the unreasoning preference shown by the public for foreign over native productions' and by the end of the century little fine lace was made by hand.

Only today is lacemaking again enticing a growing interest as a craft that can be carried on at home. At Eastbourne in Sussex lacemaker Isobel Kennett is one of the few lacemakers today making and selling lace as a full-time occupation. She has been doing this for the last 15 years since her family grew up, working from sixty to eighty hours a week, as well as teaching the craft. Her lace has gone all over the world, to America, Canada, Australia, Thailand, New Zealand, Hong Kong and India as well as Europe.

Isobel Kennett's mother was taught Bedfordshire Maltese Lace during World War I and started to teach Isobel crafts at the age of three, when she learned to knit with two 6in (150mm) nails and string. Such early training has made her an expert in all types of lacemaking, including Bedfordshire Lace. This is one of the earliest bobbin laces, said to be derived from Maltese Lace, and gives the lacemaker more scope for originality than some types. She also makes Torchon, Honiton, Swedish, French, Italian and Russian Lace, and lace patterns from many other countries, specialising in work with the finer threads of linen, silk and cotton, some in traditional patterns but some designed by herself.

Like many lacemakers she uses bobbins made by her husband and is also the owner of a large collection of antique bobbins. She is always willing to demonstrate her craft to callers if they telephone first, but to no more than six at a time. They can see her at work and purchase some of the lace items on sale, such as pictures, paperweights, handkerchiefs, mats, as well as lace by the yard—the products of sixty years' experience of lacemaking.

2

SPINNERS AND WEAVERS

The spinning of thread and the weaving of it into cloth must be one of the oldest cottage industries, dating back 9,000 years in the Middle East and 4,000 years in Britain, back as far as our Bronze Age; and, as we shall see, both crafts are still being practised today.

One of the earliest examples in this country of woollen cloth was found as a shroud in an oak dug-out coffin of the early Bronze Age in Yorkshire, which has long been well known as a wool-producing area. By the time Julius Caesar came to Britain the country was already famous in Europe for its woollen cloth, particularly for a woollen garment not unlike a duffle-coat. There was an ever-increasing demand for cloth as the centuries passed, and the making of it became one of the earliest cottage industries; moreover, as early as the fifteenth century it was one of the first to have some of the stages in its production mechanised. Weavers' guilds to control the quality of cloth and the conditions for buying and selling had been in existence since the twelfth and thirteenth centuries.

As well as wool, vegetable stem fibres, in particular flax, were among the early materials which were woven. Whatever the material used, spinning consists of drawing out and twisting fibres arranged longitudinally into a thin thread that can be woven on a loom. At first this was done by hand, the resulting thread being wound on to a stick. Then the twisting action was made easier by using a spindle, a tapered stick 8-10in (200-250mm) in length, weighted by a whorl of stone, hardwood or bone which had a hole in the middle. This helped to maintain the spin, producing a fine, even thread. Any weight—even a small potato—on the end of the spindle could help the spinning process. A large bundle of wool was held on a stick 3-4ft (900-1,200mm) long, known as the distaff, which was supported under-arm or in the spinner's girdle or belt. A length of fibre was drawn out from this and fastened to a notch on the spindle, twisted by the fingers while the spindle was rotated by hand and allowed to swing. Innumerable spindle whorls have been found on early archaeological sites, often buried with the women for whom they had been constant companions. In many districts spindle whorls were used as charms, such was the affection for them.

The fact that the spinner could spin while feeding the hens, herding sheep or cattle, making butter or going to market, probably accounts for the long period that this method lasted before the spinning-wheel took its place. The spindle was still in use in remote districts until the present century. That spinning was always a woman's work is shown by the expression 'on the distaff side', or the word 'spinster', which is never applied to a man.

Before the fibre reached the spinning stage a great deal of preliminary preparation was needed. Many cottages had a plot of land nearby reserved for growing flax. The crop was considered a difficult one to grow and needed much weeding by hand—again, woman's work. When harvested, it went through the smelly and unpleasant process of retting, being soaked in a pond, often near the cottage, to soften the stalks. Eventually the fibres could be freed by being beaten by wooden swords or mallets. This part of the preparation was usually done by men. The fibres were then combed with iron combs and were ready for spinning. Flax used today usually comes from Northern Ireland. Places such as Flaxpool, near Kingston St Mary in Somerset, indicate somewhere that originally supplied flax for the spinners.

If wool was used the preparations were just as long. If her husband had no sheep or money to buy a fleece a woman had to wander across the countryside, particularly in early summer before the sheep were sheared, collecting wool that had rubbed off passing sheep on to the hedgerows—'wool-gathering' in fact—or even begging wool from farm to farm.

From an old Saxon law of AD827 which forbade women to make clothes, card wool, beat hemp or shear sheep on a Sunday, it would seem that she first had to catch her sheep and then shear it before her work could start. The fleece of a sheep weighs anything from 5lb (2.2kg) to 14lb (6.3kg) and yields as many as 6 to 10 grades of wool; the best grades used for woollen cloth and knitting come from the shoulder, while lesser grades are used for carpets.

After the grades were sorted the wool was washed and dyed. The smell of the natural grease of the fleece could be strong and it was often dirty. Grease must be completely removed from a fleece for the dye to be absorbed. Rainwater was the most desirable water for scouring, with soap used to produce a good lather. The fleeces were washed gently to avoid the wool fibres becoming matted, then rinsed well and laid out in the air to dry quickly. In Wales for the production of flannels and blankets unscoured wool was thought to produce a closer cloth.

In many areas until this century the most common method of scouring was to soak the wool in a solution of one part urine to three parts warm water for two hours or more. The wool was then thoroughly rinsed, often in a basket in a running stream. Washing was still done in the river at Bradford-on-Avon as late as 1869.

Urine was collected from homes in casks on carts and taken to the mills where it was also used in fulling and dyeing cloth, as it had been since Roman times. It was said to leave the wool 'kind and soft to the touch'.

Where soap or soda ash were used for scouring, a wooden tub 3ft (900mm) in diameter and 3ft (900mm) deep was used, the wool resting on a false bottom with perforations, placed 6in (150mm) above the bottom of the tub. When the tub was agitated the dirt from the wool fell through the perforations and the wool could be lifted out on the false bottom to drain when it was clean, ready for rinsing.

Sorting the wool into grades was a highly skilled job which was carried out by hand by experienced sorters who were amongst the most highly paid textile employees. The wool, whose quality varies from sheep to sheep, grows in definite locks, known as staples, consisting of many thousands of individual fibres. These were prepared through different processes, which eventually gave employment to many cottagers as the wool industry expanded beyond the amounts of cloth needed for use in individual homes to supplying cloth for towns both here and abroad. It expanded under wool-masters who organised the work at first around their own homes and villages. These men became as essential to the villages as the blacksmiths and carpenters and from the Middle Ages onwards many became very wealthy. The beautiful homes they built can be seen today in the Cotswolds, in Norfolk and Suffolk, particularly around Lavenham. The attractive cottages that stand around them so picturesquely and serenely today in many a quiet village were both the homes and busy workplaces of the workers in a flourishing cloth industry. The villages were the industrial centres of past ages.

Originally, towns were principally the market and trading areas. The cottages housed workers who had such varied occupations as staplers, dyers, pickers, scourers, scribblers, carders, combers, spinners, spoolers, warpers, queelers, weavers, fullers, tuckers, burlers, shearmen, pressers, clothiers and packers. Today, many weavers' cottages can be recognised by the long windows which let in much-needed light for the weaver at his loom. Cottagers would not have been able to afford large windows in their homes unless there was a specific reason. Some cottages had extended roofs over spinning galleries where several women could sit at their wheels. A cottage on a southfacing slope where the sun could provide warmth as well as light was the ideal.

In the cloth-making district of Berkshire the cottage women with their spinning-wheels were visited every week by agents from the clothiers of Reading and Newbury. They arrived with their pack-horses laden with wool for the women to spin, and every week they left with their packs laden with yarn ready for the loom. It is difficult to imagine that many quiet, residential villages today, such as East Hendred in Berkshire, were once prosperous clothing centres, with every cottage engaged in some process of cloth production and with fulling mills and terraced fields where the cloth was pegged out to dry 'on tenterhooks'—a term still used to indicate a state of suspense.

One sixteenth-century clothier, John Winchcombe, known as Jack of Newbury, became a legend in his own lifetime. He was said to be the most successful clothier that 'England ever beheld', with 500 workers under his control. Ballads were written about him in wonderment at the extent of his business and prosperity. He was a master clothier who organised the production and marketing of cloth in all its stages. This system obtained in many areas—in the West of England, in Yorkshire, as well as in Wales. The cottage workers needed above all ready cash for the sale of their work, which made the difference between existence and starvation. Weavers could not afford to spend days, often walking, to get their cloth to fairs and markets, the chief of which was Blackwell Hall in Basinghall Street in London, and agents who handled the goods for them made their lives more secure. If a weaver had sufficient money to buy his wool or yarn and to exist until he could sell his cloth himself he was better able to maintain his independence; but he would be unlikely to have direct access to markets far from his home or abroad.

The clothiers, like their employees, were often farmers who were also part-time craftsmen. In times of recession in the textile trade, which were many, they had their land to support them, whether large farm or cottage garden. They had probably started with one or two looms in an out-house, worked by farmworkers or members of their own families during slack periods of the farming year. In the early days most farmworkers were hired for their textile abilities as well as for their labour. Gradually, as the demand for cloth increased, the out-houses expanded into factories, particularly after the adoption of water power if the farmer owned a mill. Steam power eventually forced many small clothing mills to close down, particularly those far from areas of coal. Weavers, who were the last of the textile workers to continue working in their own homes, were forced to move nearer to the factories to get work, and eventually worked in them.

Many textile workers were now obliged to take their wages in kind at a shop owned by their master, often at higher prices than elsewhere. With the coming of the Industrial Revolution the days of the part-time farmer who was also a part-time textile worker were over. In times of economic depression he no longer had his farm to support him.

Before it reached the weaver the wool was put through many processes. It was first disentangled before being carded, a process known as willying. Carding was done with two wooden cards, 9in (228mm) by 6in (150mm), with wooden handles. The cards were covered on one side with small metal hooks embedded in leather, by which the fibres could be stroked first in one direction, then in another and finally formed by the cards into rolls that made the spinner's task easier. This process is still used by hand-spinners today. The teeth were inserted in the cards by hand by women and children. The cardmakers were often also pinmakers.

If the wool had been scoured and dyed before carding, it was necessary during the carding process to replace the grease that had been removed to prevent the fibres from breaking and make spinning easier. Tallow, lard, butter or goose grease were the most usual fats incorporated, 8lb (3.6kg) of grease to 27lb (12.2kg) of wool, or vegetable oil (never fish) at the rate of 2pt (1.1 litre) to 15lb (6.8kg) of wool. At the cloth manufacturers of Thomas Fox, a Quaker of Wellington in Somerset, each worker was supplied with oil from a leaden cistern before they took their supply of fleece wool back to their cottages for combing.

In Scotland the carding was often done during long winter evenings to a background of Gaelic music and stories to ease what was a slow and tiring process. The work needed to be well done as the quality of the finished yarn depended largely on how well the task had been performed. When the industry expanded the supply of hand-carded wool could not keep pace with the spinners' growing demand for wool. As a result, this process was one of the first to be assisted by mechanisation. Carding mills, powered by water, appeared by streams and rivers at the end of the eighteenth century. Large revolving cylinders with teeth fitted into leather performed the same duty as the hand cards, straightening out the wool fibres, and incorporated more air into them than was possible by hand, increasing the cloth's characteristic warmth. In many cases the carding machinery was installed into already existing fulling mills or even existing corn mills, to which water-driven spinning equipment was soon added.

Spinning by spindle and distaff occurred in remote country areas until the last century. In this way a woman might spin 1lb (450g) of wool during a nine-hour day, or, if a less speedy spinner, 1oz (28g) an hour. With the use of the spinning-wheel the process was speeded up and, as it took four spinning women to keep a weaver occupied, this was something to be considered when the demand for wool increased. Today, many weavers who are in full production find it necessary to augment the hand-spun wool they use with machine-spun yarn.

The earliest type of spinning-wheel, common in England by the fifteenth century, was the great or muckle wheel, which could be made at home or by the local carpenter. It was in use in many areas until the early twentieth century (see Plate 5). The wheel was mounted on a stool and turned by hand; a band connected the wheel to the spindle, a thin rod ending in a metal point—the type of spinning-wheel on which Sleeping Beauty pricked her finger. The spinner stood to work the wheel, stepping backwards, pulling out and twisting the thread from a bundle of wool as she did so, then walking forwards reversing the wheel so that the spun thread wound on to the spindle. It has been estimated that she may have walked as many as 20 miles (32km) in a day's spinning. The later 'saxony wheel' took two forms, one with the wheel and spindle on the same level and one with the spindle directly above the wheel. These wheels were craftsmen made, in a variety of designs, the maker often carving his name on them and giving them touches of ornament. They have been handed down in families, not as artistic objects, however, but as articles of everyday use.

Today, it is still possible to buy a craftsman-made spinning-

Plate 5 Tom Griffiths using the great wheel at Solva, Pembrokeshire, in about 1928 *(Welsh Folk Museum)*

wheel in the Dorset village of Child Oakford (see Plate 6). These are modelled on earlier examples, with beautifully turned spokes, made in English hardwoods, oak, walnut, sycamore, yew and beech. They are sturdily constructed and finished with linseed oil and beeswax.

Spinning-wheels were not only used by cottagers and farmers' wives but by some of the greatest ladies in the land, from queens downwards. Everyone needed clothes and linen, and spinning and weaving by hand was for centuries the only way of obtaining them. It was in cottages, however, that the work became organised into an industry.

As well as the magical properties thought to belong to spindle whorls, superstition and fairy tales were also attached to spinning-wheels. If the band was left on the wheel at the end of the days's work it was thought that the fairies might use the wheel at night. Probably this caution arose to discourage bands being left in position when the wheel was not in use as the tension would be loosened. The thread would then snap when the wheel was turned, requiring it to be disentangled and rethreaded. In the fifteenth century the 'flying spindle' was invented allowing both spinning and winding to take place simultaneously. The later sixteenth-century wheels were turned by a treadle and the spinner could sit at her work, leaving both hands free to control the fibres and thread.

Throughout the eighteenth century spinning had afforded a remunerative occupation for women and children at home, but with the advent of mechanical spinning jennies and the eventual concentration of spinning processes in factories in the nineteenth century, it was these homeworkers who suffered the most, particularly in the rural areas, where the change caused grave poverty. The payment for their work may not have been great, but the removal of it brought disaster to many areas.

When textile families moved to the towns to obtain work children were employed in large numbers in the factories, employers believing that unless they learned the skills of the trade before they were 12 years of age it was too late. They said that they employed children under 4 years of age because the parents insisted that they needed their wages and also could not leave them at home alone. In 1833 came the first Factory Act limiting the age at which children could be employed to 9 years and restricting their hours to 48 a week.

After spinning, yarn or wool was wound into skeins on a winder.

The earliest looms on which the wool or flax yarn was woven into cloth were of an upright variety. The long threads, known as the warp, hung down from a frame and were weighted at the bottom by large weights to keep them taut, while the cross-threads, known as the weft, were threaded in and out by hand as in darning or basketry. This gives a plain weave used for flannel and most 'home-spun' cloth. Heavier warp threads could vary the texture. Like the spindle whorls the loom weights are found in large quantities on archaeological sites all over the world. A logical development of plain weaving was the twill or tweed weave, where the weft threads pass over and under two threads at a time, moving forward to the right or left at the same time, producing a heavier and denser cloth.

In Scotland this cloth came to be known as tweed, its name said to have arisen by mistake when a quantity of 'tweel', by which the cloth was originally known, was sent to London in the nineteenth century and the unclear invoice was read as being for 'tweed'; the recipient had associated the word with the River Tweed, an area for long well known for the production of woollen cloth.

The warp threads were prepared for the loom and arranged in the order required for a particular pattern. They were wound round pegs on a wooden framework before being attached to the loom. The process, known as warping, is still a hand process in the case of Harris Tweed, the warper needing to be highly skilled to prepare the warp of a complicated pattern.

In weaving tartan patterns exact records were marked on special warping-sticks, giving the number and order of the threads of each colour for both the warp and the weft threads. This enabled patterns to be reproduced exactly when required.

Early horizontal looms were narrow, enabling the shuttle holding the weft to be passed easily across by hand; large blankets had a seam down the middle to join two widths of cloth. When broadcloth was woven on a wider loom two weavers were needed to throw the shuttle from side to side. In 1733 the fly-shuttle, which could be thrown across a wider area of cloth by one man, was invented.

Looms were originally made of oak to individual specifications. The carpenter needed a good knowledge of weaving to get the balance of the loom right so that it was not too difficult to manipulate. It is still possible to buy an oak loom made by one of today's craftsmen. The cost would be prohibitive to most weavers, however, and modern looms are generally made of cheaper wood. Most cottagers could afford a spinning-wheel, but a loom was a much more expensive item, and eventually weaving became an occupation for substantial farmers who owned several looms. The boxwood shuttles also needed careful workmanship to make the weaving pro-

Plate 6 Jacqueline Sheriff, herself a spinner, making a traditional English spinning-wheel at Child Oakford, Dorset
Plate 7 Church Farm Weavers: John Lennon (in the foreground) and Talbot Potter weaving in the former cider barn at Kingston St Mary, Somerset

cess as smooth as possible, but handweaving was always slow compared with the speeds achieved by the introduction of machinery.

That small cottages in clothmaking districts contained few articles of furniture is not surprising for much of the space was taken up with the weaver's loom. There might be room for a board on a frame for a table, a few forms or stools, a bed and a chest, but most of the home was filled with the necessary cumbersome apparatus for the worker's trade, the clatter of the loom filling the small cottage endlessly.

The yarn was first wound on to bobbins, a job often performed by the weaver's children, and then transferred to the shuttles.

When eventually power weaving took over in the second

half of the nineteenth century the textile industry ceased to be one giving a variety of employment to people with a variety of skills, and became a series of processes of production by machines.

Sometimes yarn was dyed before weaving, sometimes the woven fabric was dyed. No doubt in early times the cloth was woven from undyed wool, giving white and black or a mixture of both; grey cloth was the most general, although it was not a popular colour with the gentry and royalty who associated it with the poorer classes and homespun tweed; they preferred clothes of brighter colours, particularly green and red.

Today, the wool from Jacob's Sheep, a breed that is popular with smallholders and those who wish to keep a few sheep for their fleeces, is usually woven undyed, the many shades of brown, cream, black and white in the natural fleece giving an individual touch to the garments made.

For the most part wild plants were used to obtain different colours. Many plants were especially cultivated to obtain a particular shade. The lichens produced browns and yellows; yellows were also obtained from saffron and from weld, a type of mignonette also known as dyer's rocket; oak bark and alder-wood produced shades of brown; blue was obtained from woad and from spindle-berries. In the Highlands of Scotland the colours of the vegetation could be seen in the cloth produced and gave distinctive recognisable colours to the cloth from different areas.

Where small quantities of wool had to be dyed it was easier to dye the raw wool and not the woven cloth. It was put into a pot with alternate layers of the plants selected for the required colour; each layer was sprinkled with a mordant to fix the dye and the pot was filled with water. Some plants with tough stems such as nettles and heather were first boiled on their own and the liquor used with the wool. The pot was then boiled until the right depth of colour was obtained, the whole process being a matter of skill and experience.

The same plants are used today by many home spinners and weavers for dyeing, the colours obtained being more subtle and varied than those produced by modern dyes. It is necessary, however, to dye sufficient quantities of wool at a time for a particular garment in order to achieve a uniform colour. The production of some dyes is a lengthy process.

John Lennon and Talbot Potter, the Church Farm Weavers, make cloth by hand at Church Farm, Kingston St Mary, near Taunton, Somerset, from yarn that is sometimes used in its natural white, black or grey or is dyed after scouring using plant dyes—heather, privet, weld, madder and walnut, among others (see Plate 7). These produce yarn of the most beautiful colours which they weave to their own designs and which is on sale at their workshop in an old cider barn. This is next to the lovely thirteenth-century church which owes its tower and decorations, appropriately enough, to the wealth in the area when it was part of the flourishing West Country wool trade of the fifteenth century. The altar cloth in this church was woven by the Church Farm Weavers, as are those for the church of St Peter and Paul at Longbridge Deverill, near Warminster, the Catholic church at Chippenham in Wiltshire and the church of St James at Winscombe, Avon. They have also made vestments for the church at Halse near Taunton and have produced 62yd (56m) of cloth for the Society of Friends, the Quakers, for each of fifty meeting houses to embroider one panel, the whole to be assembled eventually at Friends House in Euston Road in London.

It takes a good day's work to thread up the large looms and, after weaving, several days more for the cloth to go through the finishing and fulling processes. The cloth has to be checked for any knots or faults. After washing, it is set on rollers under tension and left to dry for three or four days to give a finished appearance. They also design and weave rugs, furnishing fabrics, wall hangings, stoles and blankets, but they find their work for churches the most rewarding.

At the Esgair Moel Woollen Mill, moved from its original site in Brecknockshire (now Powys) and reconstructed and in production at the Welsh Folk Museum at St Fagan's, near Cardiff, visitors can see dyeing done in large open vats heated with wood fires (alderwood being thought to give the best heat).

Dye vats and washing-tubs were made by local coopers. In fact, all the early equipment of the textile industry was made by local carpenters, coopers and blacksmiths, even the first machines used, until production of these became an industry in itself.

Before the use of alum and other chemicals as a mordant stag horn moss was used. Both mordants and dyes have been imported from early times.

'Fulling' to shrink the threads and give the material body was originally done by hand, or even by feet, by treading the cloth in large vats or working the cloth by hand on a table. In the Western Isles of Scotland this process was known as waulking, and in Wales fulling mills were described as 'walk mills' in documents up to the middle of the nineteenth century.

The cloth was laid the length of a board, 12-20ft (3.6-6m) in length and 2ft (600mm) wide, with grooves running lengthwise, which rested on trestles. After being saturated with ammonia, warm water and soapsuds, the cloth was worked vigorously by women sitting each side of the table, to the accompaniment of special waulking songs. When the process was finished the cloth was washed in a nearby stream, then rolled carefully on to a piece of wood to distribute evenly the tension of the weave. So important was the finishing of the cloth to the community that a certain amount of ritual attended the waulking, part religious and part superstition. It was a social occasion to be enjoyed by neighbours as well as the waulking women, with food that included oatcakes and barley cakes, chickens, whisky and crowdie, a mixture of toasted oatmeal and whipped cream, flavoured with rum or fruit.

Water-driven fulling mills which hammered the cloth into the finished state had been in operation for this process from the Middle Ages and fulling was the first stage in the production of cloth to be mechanised. In Wales especially, with its abundance of mountain pasture, sheep and streams—sheep being the mainstay of the economy of Welsh farms—small fulling mills were found on the banks of streams all over the country; the word 'pandy' (a fulling mill) in so many Welsh place names indicates their widespread distribution. This was typical of the Welsh woollen industry for centuries, with hundreds of small mills processing the wool for the farmers. The industry was never concentrated in specific areas as in Yorkshire, except in the second half of the nineteenth century when whole villages in the counties of Cardigan, Carmarthen and Pembroke were engaged in producing flannel—for which Wales is famous. Shirts and blankets were also produced for the fast-growing industrial areas of South Wales.

When dried and pressed the cloth was made fluffier with teasles, a plant still used for this purpose today. It has prickly seed-heads covered with minute hooks that loosen the fibres when drawn over the cloth. The teasles or 'fuller's thistle' had been widely grown for this purpose since the Middle Ages, usually by small farmers using family labour. Large quantities were grown in the basin of the River Severn around Tewkesbury and in the Curry Rival district of Somerset for the Cotswold woollen industry. In wet seasons the seed-heads were dried indoors, often in the bedrooms of small cottages. The cloth was then spread out to dry on tenterhooks either in the open air or in an indoor drying-room, and was finally sheared by men who were experts in this process.

At Esgair Mill in Wales many of the early clothmaking methods can be seen, including steam pressing by folding the cloth with sheets of cardboard or glazed paper between the folds. The metal press is placed in the grate over a peat fire, which gives a steady heat. The press is then screwed down for several hours.

The power looms and spinning machines introduced at the beginning of the nineteenth century brought to an end much of the work done in cottage homes. Even before steam power when the textile industry came to be centred near easily obtained supplies of coal, the use of water power had caused it to be centred near the larger rivers. In the Cotswolds where the cloth trade had made the area prosperous for centuries, resulting in much building and rebuilding, the trade declined in the first half of the nineteenth century; only Stroud mills went over to steam power. In the Western Isles of Scotland, however, the industry has prospered as a cottage industry through several centuries of change.

In Scotland well into the eighteenth century linen production was one of the principal home-based occupations. Scottish linen was considered to be the finest and a wealthy laird's son of the sixteenth century might own twenty-four pairs of sheets—many more than would be found in the home of someone of similar rank in England. Many Highland families still possess hand-spun and woven linen sheets beautifully made over 150 years ago.

From the eighteenth century onwards the production of woollen cloth in Scotland became more important, and all the skills previously lavished on linen production were turned to making woollen material. In particular, the weaving of tartan cloth in the Highlands and the tweeds of the Border Counties, together with the Harris Tweed of the islands, was the beginning of such cloth manufacture still famous today. In the case of Harris Tweed, the cottagers have always been anxious to keep as a cottage industry the production of this cloth, now in demand all over the world. This has caused problems since many of the cottage workers have crofts to run as well. They have therefore gradually adopted mechanical aids to keep up with the demand, particularly in the preliminary processes of production which are the most time-consuming, while at the same time maintaining the quality of a superior tweed, which is almost waterproof and warm in winter and cool in summer.

Some of the tweed is still produced by hand-spinning, hand-carding, hand-weaving and finishing to market to people who are prepared to pay the higher price for purely handmade cloth, but otherwise the industry has adopted mechanisation for all the processes, apart from weaving. The weavers are still self-employed and own their own looms, which are mostly semi-automatic domestic types with foot-operated treadles. It was decided that tweed produced in this way could be described as 'hand-woven' as the loom required the close attention and physical participation of the weaver. The 1934 definition of Harris Tweed decided which tweed could be given the official trade mark and stated:

> 'Harris Tweed' means a tweed made from pure virgin wool produced in Scotland, spun, dyed and finished in the Outer Hebrides and hand-woven by the islanders at their own homes in the Islands of Lewis, Harris, Uist, Barra and their several purtenances and all known as the Outer Hebrides.

The words 'at their own homes' prevents a concentration of weavers in a mill or factory producing the cloth.

The tweed so produced today has progressed from a cloth principally used for masculine clothes in a limited range of weaves and colours to a cloth in many varied colours, patterns and weights used by many of today's top fashion designers for women.

Lachlan Macdonald is an independent weaver who makes tweed on the Isle of North Uist from his own patterns, warps and weaves, although he does buy in the wool ready spun and dyed, and markets his own finished product. This finishing is done at the Lewis mills by machinery to produce a more sophisticated product than was possible in the past. Most of the weavers who work for these mills are either 'warpers', 'weavers', or 'finishers', and do only one part of the process, the mills usually marketing all the finished tweed.

On the other side of Scotland at Turriff, Aberdeenshire, the Russell Gurney Weavers have built up a small hand-weaving business over the last fourteen years, run from the 10-acre croft which David Gurney and his wife work to make themselves as self-sufficient as possible, exactly as the earliest weavers operated several hundred years ago. All the patterns woven are exclusive and never repeated, and the firm specialises in the production of cloth for both men and women.

They find there is a steady demand from people (mainly from overseas) to learn spinning and weaving and David Gurney runs courses, mainly in the wintertime, giving individual and intensive tuition. David and his wife welcome visitors to their croft to see them at work in this pleasant part of the countryside which is near mountains, woods and sea.

3

KNITTING BY HAND AND MACHINE

> Nothing is more common than to see the women trotting rapidly to market, with a most unconscionable load upon their heads, and with their hands, as if they were doing nothing else, actively and incessantly employed in knitting.
>
> *Tourist in Wales (1814)*

Groups of women still meet to knit for both pleasure and profit. In Wales they spin and knit in each other's homes, or outside in their gardens if the weather permits. They spin the wool, unwashed, from local sheep, as well as wool sent to them from the Shetland Isles. It is washed afterwards and, undyed, made into garments and shawls for sale.

Using the wool undyed in this way is very popular with today's knitters and those who buy their work. A surprising variety of shades can be found in the garments they produce. Fran Benton, who runs a group of about thirty-five spinners and handknitters in the New Forest at London Minstead, near Lyndhurst, travels as many as 1,800 miles (2,896km) from mid-May to the end of June, buying fleeces from farmers all over the Home Counties. She often helps at shearing time to obtain wool from a large variety of breeds of sheep. This enables the spinners to knit jerseys in shades of brown, beige, black and grey, as well as white, and also in mixtures from silver fleeces with black tips such as come from Shetland sheep—grey with black tips, grey with brown tips and honey-beige. The wool is spun in its natural state, which makes spinning easier. It is washed afterwards and hung up to dry in skeins which are weighted to straighten the yarn.

Plate 8 Spinners working at Fran Benton's studio in the New Forest at London Minstead *(Nick Carter)*

These spinners and knitters meet regularly to spin indoors and outdoors at Fran Benton's studio (see Plate 8), but for the most part they work in their own homes to specific orders and are paid, as are most home knitters today, per ounce (28g) of wool knitted. Sometimes they receive extra payment for a particularly difficult garment—what Fran Benton calls 'agony' money. A stock of garments is kept in various sizes and colours for casual sales and others are sold to top stores in London, where today hand-knitted jerseys are high fashion. So successful are these New Forest knitters that they hope to move shortly to an expanded workshop nearby that will also house a boutique for the sale of their products, many of which are made to the designs of a fashion designer.

Many of the spinners, who come from a large area around Minstead, were originally taught to spin by Fran Benton. She also sells spinning-wheels, some of them well-tried standard makes and some made by local craftsmen to her own specification. It is most important for a wheel to be either made or designed by an experienced spinner who appreciates the delicate balance needed in the construction for the work to proceed smoothly.

In Cambridge a group of about thirty-five hand-knitters work on specific orders, ranging from elaborate designs for pop stars to enormous sizes for outsize gentlemen. They are all experienced knitters capable of knitting garments from their customers' suggestions, without a pattern if necessary, in any size, although many customers produce both wool and pattern, having failed to find a garment in the size and colour they required in ready-made knitwear. This is a service that home knitters are increasingly filling. Mrs Anne Farmer, who organises the Cambridge Knitters and designs for them as well, advertises their services in fashion magazines and the national Sunday newspapers and this brings in enough orders to keep the group fully occupied.

There is no doubt that knitting as part of a co-operative group today gives women an opportunity to meet together for company as they did centuries ago. Now, however, they usually work at their own speed, although they normally have to finish a specific order within four to six weeks, and are not forced to work into the night through sheer necessity. Many demonstrate their art and sell their wares at craft fairs.

In Wales the shared knitting evenings of long ago were certainly part of the social scene. Often the stories told to the accompaniment of a harpist were ghost stories, which livened their occupation, probably much as many women knit today while watching films of horror or adventure on the television. Today, the social aspect of knitting groups is often extended to benefit the community as well as individuals.

A knitwear co-operative of particular interest is Antur Aelhaearn in the small Welsh-speaking village of Llanaelhaearn in the Llŷn peninsula of Gwynedd, where great and increasingly successful efforts have been made to solve the problems facing many of the villages of the British Isles today. At Llanaelhaearn the decline in local opportunities for work following the closure of a nearby granite quarry and the increasing mechanisation of farming, together with the general decline in local amenities now found in rural areas, drove the villagers to found this co-operative in 1974. Registered under the Industrial and Provident Societies Act 1965 as a Limited Friendly Society, 160 of the villagers have become shareholders and have a right to vote in the activities of Antur Aelhaearn.

The knitwear industry run by them was the first step in the effort to create work in this rural area. They employ 6 girls hand-framing and hand-finishing ladies' suits in 100 per cent Shetland wool, and 20-40 girls are seasonally required to hand-knit jumpers, cardigans and other garments in Welsh Black Sheep wool and Jacob Sheep wool in their own homes, mainly for the export market.

Their garments are sold in their own retail shop, which also sells the work of about a dozen other local craftsmen and women, including work by local disabled people. The shop is part of the work-centre built by the co-operative, which now houses their knitters, their offices and a pottery. The enterprise has grown to accommodate a production manager and an agent employed to sell their products.

That this type of co-operative might help other rural areas was shown by the interest taken in a week-long conference held in the village on 'The Problems of a Rural Revival' when people came from all over the United Kingdom. The enterprise generated by this co-operative has extended to other activities in the village which has seen improved facilities for the school, housing, roads, and the general social development of village life.

From all accounts it seems that much of the cottage industry of hand-knitting during the seventeenth and eighteenth centuries was carried on outdoors. In many areas it was so poorly paid that it was only a subsidiary occupation to farming and to make any money from it at all, it was necessary for every member of the family to knit at every spare moment. In the dales of the North of England waggoners knitted as they drove their teams to market. Eventually they were forced to knit only when indoors to avoid the curious stares of the increasing number of visitors to this area. In the Kendal area both men and women knitted stockings as they drove their peat carts into town. Around the coasts women knitted jerseys for sailors on beaches and on quays. In Wales, particularly in Merioneth where they were famous for their knitted stockings, they knitted at every possible moment, whether they were travelling by cart, on horseback or on foot (see Plate 9). In the eighteenth century great markets were held at Bala every Saturday morning, when it was reported that from £200 to £500 worth of woollen stockings were sold each week.

The yarn they knitted had first to be spun by the women, the fleece usually sorted in the evenings by their farmer husbands and carded by their children. The wool came either from their own sheep, or was purchased from other farmers or at the local market. When making stockings the finer wool was used for the legs, and the coarser wool, known as footing, was used for the feet. Darning stockings has never been a popular domestic occupation. In fact, some housewives in the North smeared the heels of the stockings with pitch and then dipped them at once into the ashes of their peat fires to form a hard but flexible heel.

The spun wool was wound into skeins. In the Highlands of Scotland this was done on a simple winding implement known as a Crois Iarna (Fig 6), a wooden bar about 2ft

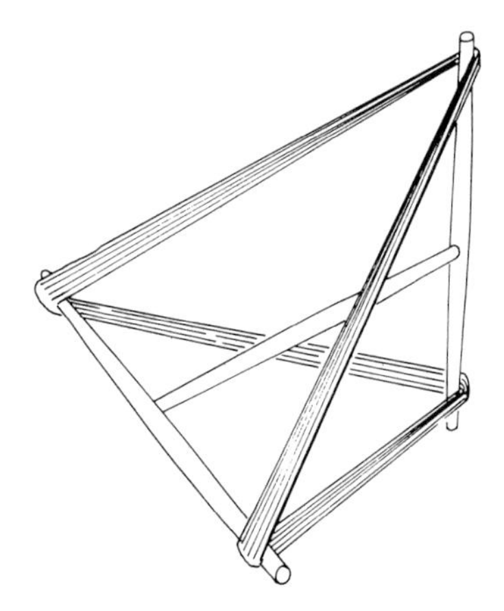

Fig 6 Crois Iarna: a Scottish wool winder

(600mm) in length, with small cross-pieces at each end pointing in opposite ways, sometimes with knobs to keep the wool in place. The wool was wound across and down from corner to corner, then up and across and eventually pulled off as a completed skein. Sometimes there was a joint so that the yarn could be slipped off with more ease. Many variations are found in these home-made winders.

Wool was also wound on a type of rimless wheel on a stand, known as a jack reel (Fig 7), and later a wool winder (Fig 8) that could be screwed on to a table was used by home knitters.

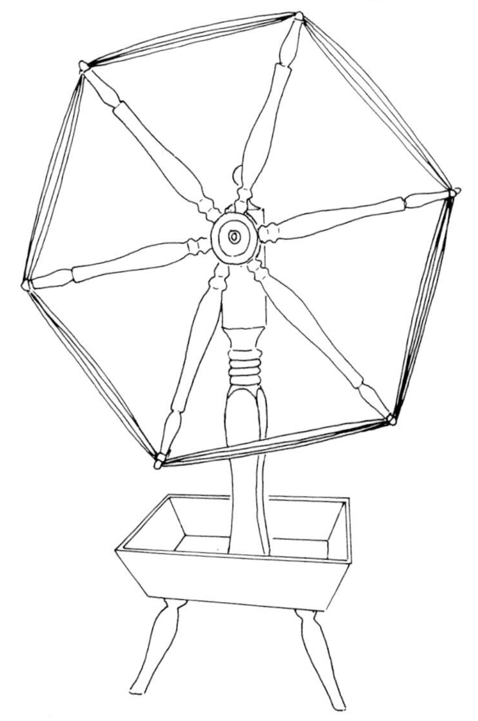

Fig 7 Jack reel on to which wool was wound

All over the countryside and around the coasts of Britain in the districts for which hand-knitting was renowned, men and women knitted by the light of rushlights and candles, or even by the light of a peat fire, often congregating in one cottage to share both light and warmth, sometimes singing songs which

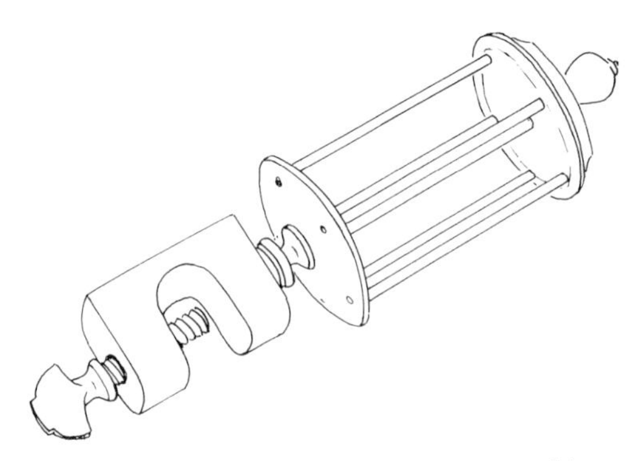

Fig 8 Wool winder for screwing to a table

came to be associated with knitting. These were first learned by the children in the knitting schools, the songs helping them to count the rounds and the number of increases and decreases in their work. William Howitt, writing of the knitters of Yorkshire at the beginning of the last century, said they knitted, rocking together as they did so, making a single uniform knitting motion. The old men sat round the fire with cloths pinned on their shins to prevent them being scorched while absorbed in their knitting and in the stories that were being told to pass the time. When sitting by the fire had been overdone, they would go outside and sit on a bench in a row to cool off, still knitting and wearing their shin cloths.

Husbands were often occupied in making knitting-needle sheaths, also known as knitting sticks or knitting bodkins, which were in general use at one time to hold one needle in position, usually the right-handed one, so that one hand was free to manipulate the yarn. These were sometimes elaborately carved, often as love tokens, but often just a wad of straw or a bunch of tightly bound quills was pushed into the knitter's belt

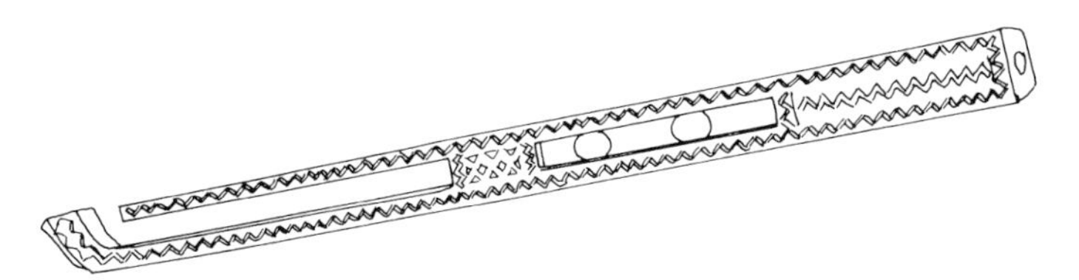

Fig 9 Eighteenth-century knitting sheath

Plate 9 Edward Llwyd in 1880, probably one of the last of the old men of Bala who knitted stockings *(Welsh Folk Museum)*

or apron to serve as a sheath. The most usual sheaths were about 9in (230mm) long with a hole at one end into which the needle fitted. Sometimes they had a slot that fitted over the wearer's belt, or a hook on which the completed knitting could be held to keep it off the floor. Many of these late eighteenth-century sheaths had caged balls carved into their tops and were curved to fit the figure (Fig 9). In the first half of the nineteenth century the 'goose-winged' sheath developed, with the top of the stick turned (Fig 10). They were 4-11in (100-280mm) long and were made out of oak, beech or

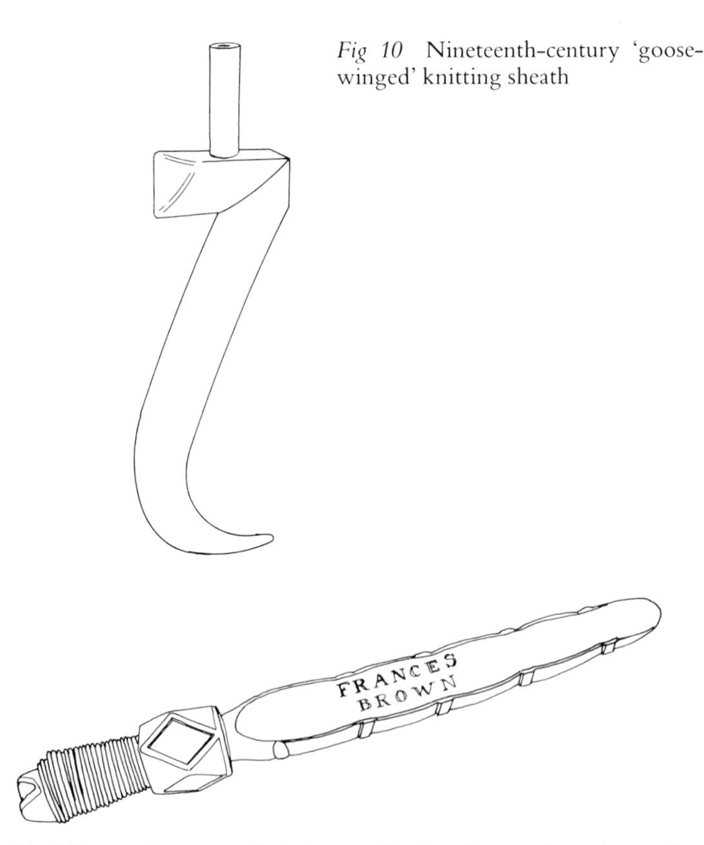

Fig 10 Nineteenth-century 'goose-winged' knitting sheath

Fig 11 Nineteenth-century knitting-needle sheath carved as a love token for Frances Brown

mahogany. The sheath inscribed 'Frances Brown' illustrated in Fig 11 is 8in (203mm) long and has brass-wire binding at the top. It was made in 1860 for the owner, Frances Brown of Devon, by her sweetheart when she was 14. It was held under the arm, as were the sheaths used in the north-east coasts to take the weight of the heavy knitting of the fishermen's jerseys. In these areas they were often carved by the seamen themselves, perhaps from wood from an old boat, and are found in a variety of interesting designs. Small rolls of sailcloth and leather are also known to have been used as knitting sheaths.

On Fair Isle, lying between Orkney and Shetland, knitting

belts are worn. This is a belt worn around the waist with an oval-shaped pouch which rests on the right hip. The pouch is filled with horse hair and has a hole big enough to hold and support a knitting-needle. The right needle is thus held stationary, leaving the right hand free to work with the coloured yarns and enabling the knitter to reach a higher speed and accuracy.

In the second half of the nineteenth century knitting-needle sheaths, which originated in country districts, were in use in towns, made in ivory and metal as well as wood. Many were heart-shaped. Quilted quills were also used, pinned to the dress.

As early as the Middle Ages knitting had become a cottage industry, under the control of craft guilds in the towns, where master knitters watched over the quality and quantity of the garments produced. In the remoter areas of the countryside and in the coastal fishing villages and islands, however, the craft escaped such control and organisation. In these somewhat isolated communities patterns were passed on from mother to daughter and became traditional for that particular district, especially in the fishing and coastal areas where the later knitting machines never penetrated. Here hand-knitting continued and the traditional patterns are still knitted in those areas today, although their popularity has now spread and their patterns are used all over the country.

Originally, the patterns were so closely associated with a particular village, port or even one particular family that it was possible to identify exactly where the wearer came from—sadly a useful means of identification in the case of a fisherman washed overboard whose body eventually came ashore away from his home. A community would have a particular combination of moss stitch, diamonds, cables, rope-ladders, flags and shells knitted into patterns that were passed on from generation to generation, often combining in one garment many of the symbols significant in the daily life of the seaman, from his tools to the weather.

In the Northern Isles of Scotland the patterns have endured the longest and still bear the names associated with them—Fair

Isle, Shetland and Orkney. Originally, these patterns were based on influences brought to the islands by foreign sailors and woven only by the crofter-fishermen's families. In Fair Isle some designs are said to have been copied from clothes worn by Spanish sailors when their ship the *El Gran Griffon* from the Spanish Armada was wrecked there in 1588. It was traditional in Fair Isle for a boy on attaining adolescence to wear a sweater knitted by his grandmother. This was called a Robe of glory and incorporated symbols depicting his journey through life. The groundwork of a true Fair Isle pattern is always knitted in white, fawn, grey or brown wool, with a wide band of a brightly multi-coloured pattern, alternating with a narrower band of one or two colours. These patterns cover the jersey, and no two of them are identical.

In the Shetland and Orkney Isles the patterns have a strong Scandinavian influence dating back to the ninth and tenth centuries when Vikings from Norway settled in the islands. Again, the jerseys have an all-over pattern with bands of the same width, but in truly traditional designs the patterns are different, one band having a dark pattern on a light ground, followed by a light pattern on a dark ground. The ribs of the jerseys are uniquely worked, the plain stitches being in one colour and the purl stitches in another. The hand-spun wool is fine and soft as it comes from those Shetland sheep which feed on the hill pastures and not in the richer valleys, where the sheep give a coarser wool. It is dyed with natural plant dyes which give softer and more subdued colours than those found in Fair Isle knitting.

The now so popular Aran patterns came originally from the Aran Isles which lie off the west coast of Ireland. Knitted in plain cream wool, the traditional designs which cover the jerseys were based on families and their connection one with another. Patterns were added with the birth of each child or grandchild and many trace a family history back for several centuries.

Thickly knitted jerseys were the chief garment worn by the seamen and fishermen of Britain, fitting snugly around their necks and allowing unrestricted movement during an active life; at the same time the thickness of the pattern helped to keep out the elements, much as did the heavily embroidered patterns on the countryman's smock.

The most usual form of the fisherman's sweater found all around our coasts is known as the guernsey or gansey. This is traditionally knitted in the round in thick dark-blue wool on four to ten needles. The needles were fine and the wool thick to give a weatherproof finish. No sewing was involved, the sleeves, neck and cuffs being knitted on to the main body of the garment, so that these could be, and were, replaced when worn. Some were plain, others patterned. Some wives knitted for those who had no family to provide for them, giving them a small addition to the family income. Many living near large ports sold the jerseys they knitted there, where there was a ready market for them, and in this case there was a thriving cottage industry in hand-knitting. One jersey took about two weeks' hard knitting to complete. They also made woollen hats, mittens and stockings (see Plate 10).

Elizabeth I was a practical person who used straightforward means to encourage home industry. When there was a complaint from the knitters that people had stopped wearing woollen caps, an act was passed in 1571 requiring everyone, with few exceptions, to wear one on Sundays and holy days. How strictly this act was enforced is open to doubt, and it was repealed in 1598.

In sixteenth-century London 8,000 workers were engaged in the knitting industry, other important areas for the production of knitted goods being Leicester and Derby.

Before that time any stockings worn in England had been made from cloth, cut to shape with a back seam. In fact, needle and cloth had been in use for all clothing until the making of knitted stockings produced the first garments where the knitted product was superior to the one made of cloth. The first knitted stockings worn in England were in silk and came from Spain in the reign of Henry VIII, but it was not long before they were copied in England and a pair of black silk stockings was presented to Elizabeth I in 1561, after which, it is said, she never wore cloth ones again. The ability to knit

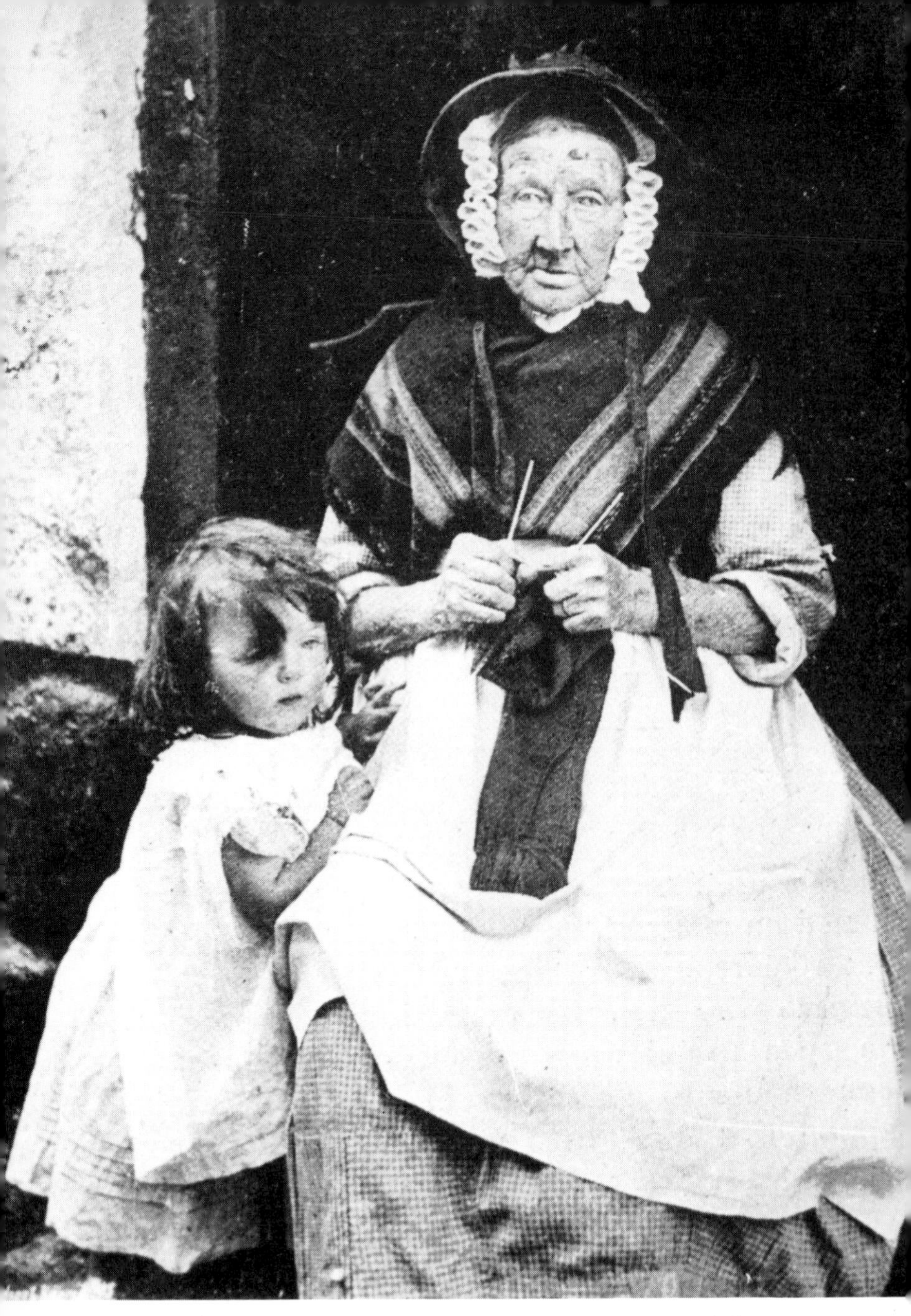

Plate 10 'Aunt Blanche', a Cornish fisherwoman, outside her cottage at Newlyn, Penzance, knitting stockings in 1902 *(Museum of English Rural Life)*

stockings soon spread and by the end of the sixteenth century 1,000 workers in the North Riding of Yorkshire were engaged in producing them. Other busy areas were Surrey, Somerset and Norfolk.

Stockings were, of course, only one item of knitting carried on in all the wool-producing areas of the country—caps, waistcoats, petticoats and gloves were also made. In Scotland the chief centre of the knitting industry was around Aberdeen, from whence knitted goods were exported to Holland and Germany. Cheap labour was abundant in Scotland and women and children employed in knitting earned little more than a few pence a day. The yearly export from Aberdeen in 1805 was estimated at £100,000.

In the Shetland and Orkney Isles the knitters remained independent and self-employed longer than anywhere else. They grew their own wool and marketed their own finished articles. When the making of shawls became an important part of the industry in about 1840, the industry came under the organisation of middle-men who supplied the wool and collected the finished shawls for sale. Even with the development of the shawl industry in the Paisley area of Scotland in the nineteenth century when weaving was no longer done at home, the weavers still owned their own looms and were paid by piecework. They produced fine soft wool shawls with delicate designs until the late nineteenth century, when the wearing of shawls was no longer so fashionable. The area remained important for the production of fine knitwear until modern times, as did the Border Counties of Scotland, where some of the best-known names of Scottish knitwear manufacture are found.

The hand-knitting of stockings was ultimately ousted by the sixteenth-century invention of the stocking frame by a country clergyman called William Lee at Calverton, near Nottingham. Although this machine laid the foundation of the modern hosiery and knitwear industry and was little changed in 200 years, it took some time to be generally accepted. Its inventor died in poverty and distress in 1610. The machine knitted eight stitches to the inch (25mm) and when it was first demonstrated to Elizabeth I she expressed disappointment that the work produced was so coarse. Although a state patent policy had begun in 1561, she refused to grant a patent for William Lee's machine on the grounds that it would deprive so many of her subjects of their employment. Its manufacture was still prohibited under James I, although he was keen on the production of hand-knitted silk stockings and did all he could to promote them. Many of the mulberry trees seen today in old gardens were planted during his reign to feed silkworms as he hoped to establish a silk industry in England.

Stockings were knitted in many colours both in Wales and Northamptonshire, a flourishing area for their production. They were produced in white, red, blue, black and grey. Northamptonshire was said to be the least wooded but the most woaded county in the country as it had an ancient industry in cultivating woad for dyers. At the beginning of the nineteenth century there were still woad or 'wad' grounds there and huts where the woaders lived during the summer while the crop was growing. They cut the leaves of the plant (*isatis tinctoria*) and ground them into a paste which was made into flat cakes or balls which had to be dried in the wind. A crop of about 12 acres would employ two or three families for the season. The cakes were mixed with limewater to bring out the colour, which depended for its richness and the permanence of the dye on the number of fermentations. This part of the work relied to a great deal on the skill of the woader. The work was dirty and the offensive smell of the dye penetrated the worker's clothes and hair. Woad was grown extensively in the Cotswolds, too, and its sale and storage controlled by the Dyer's Guild at Bristol.

Another popular dye was produced from dyer's rocket or weld (*Reseda luteola*), a type of wild mignonette which gave a fast, strong, yellow dye, which, when mixed with woad, produced Saxon green or Kendal green as it was known in another area famous for hand-knitting. It was made from the whole plant and, when alum was added, many shades of yellow were obtained. It was no longer used when commercial dyes were introduced as such large quantities of the plant were necessary to produce the dye commercially, but it is still used by home-spinners and dyers today.

The knitting-machine's introduction during the seventeenth century was slow, even after its manufacture was allowed. One of the reasons was that many people considered hand-knitted stockings to be warmer and more durable than those made by the frame. There was continual opposition from the hand-knitters and the first frames were set up in cellars and secret places, where they were busy night and day. By this time the knitting frame had been improved so that 20 stitches to the inch (25.4mm) could be produced. There was one needle on the frame for each loop; each had a spring hook which opened to receive the thread, which was laid across the needle by the 'sinker', then closed so that the fabric could be pushed forward over the needle hooks, which were very much like the hooks used in home carpet-making. The machine was a large one in a wooden frame, at which the operator sat on a fixed seat, much as did the weaver at his loom, working the pedals which moved the needles. It is surprising that such a machine with its wrought-iron parts was produced at this early date, but it was costly to build and required skilled men to work it. In spite of this, it was installed in many cottages, chiefly in what had been hand-knitting areas. It was not until 1771 that knitting machines made much impression in Scotland as hand-knitting was so extensive. The first centre of frame-knitting was at Hawick in the Cheviot Hills, but soon there were many areas manufacturing good quality knitwear, particularly in the South, areas still famous for high quality today.

Hand-knitting, which required no expensive equipment and which was mainly an occupation for women and children, continued to be widespread in many areas until the end of the eighteenth century, and in some isolated districts well into the nineteenth. At the end of the eighteenth century there were still 1,000 women and children engaged in stocking knitting around Wimborne in Dorset and a similar number around Christchurch. Other areas still at work at hand-knitting, apart from Wales and Scotland, were Somerset, Doncaster and

Nantwich. The hand-knitting of gloves by outworkers was still quite extensive in the Ringwood area of Dorset well into this century and every week 3,000 pairs of gloves for the armed forces in World War II were produced in this area.

In the Lake District the hand-knitting industry was an old-established one and extended through the villages of Westmorland and Cumberland into the Yorkshire Dales. The chief centre and market was at Kendal, where in 1801 the average weekly supply sent there was 2,400 pairs of stockings. In 1768 the industry around Kendal employed about 5,000 workers, including wool combers, spinners and knitters, making it the chief manufacture in the area at that time. From Kendal and the Yorkshire Dales hand-knitted goods were sent weekly by waggon to London.

In the North the industry continued along organised lines until the 1870s, with the knitting schools still flourishing and wives and children fully employed in knitting stockings, vests, pants and jackets for sailors in the Greenland fishing fleets, and gloves, stockings, waistcoats, caps, petticoats and frocks for home markets. Few single women could earn their living at knitting. A fast knitter working for 10–12 hours a day in 1843 could earn 6d (2½p) a day or at the most 2s–2s 6d (10p–12½p) a week. Their life was a hard one and they existed mostly on a diet of oatcakes and milk.

Eventually, knitting machines took over and although many parishes did their utmost to keep hand-knitting going by supplying materials to knitters in order to prevent them becoming a drain on parish funds, their efforts were in vain. In some parishes in Rutland at the end of the eighteenth century it was ordered 'that parents were not to obtain relief on account of any child above six years who could not knit'.

It is true that the giving of poor relief in the early nineteenth century seems to have had some effect on the decline of hand-knitting. Where it was more readily given in the South of England, the production of hand-knitted goods almost ceased. Where parishes in the North and West of the country were not so generous in providing poor relief, the knitting continued for a greater length of time. The decline continued relentlessly,

Plate 11 Spinners at Winterslow, Wiltshire, in 1901 outside a cottage that was the centre for the manufacture of Winterslow woollens, a home-based industry set up to provide work for inhabitants of some newly built cottages in the village *(Museum of English Rural Life)*

however, because even if they themselves continued to knit for such small remuneration, parents eventually refused to send their children to knitting schools and to put them into such unprofitable work. Efforts to revive hand-knitting in villages were made at the beginning of the present century (see Plate 11).

The home-workers at their machines in the framework knitting industry were no happier. The trade originally flourished in London and Nottingham. The Framework Knitters Company was given its original charter by Cromwell and a new charter by Charles II on his restoration. London made mainly fine silk wares from imported silk, while Nottingham specialised in worsted hosiery, helped by the fact that the local sheep from Sherwood Forest produced a fine silky fleece which was very good for making good quality woollen stockings.

By the eighteenth century the workers were in a distressed condition. The machines, which were worked by hand, were owned by their employers who charged them rent for their hire. The employer supplied materials and marketed the goods they produced. Whether times were good or bad the frameworkers had to pay the rent for the machines, a source of bitter resentment. The number of frames increased from year to year and the workers found it increasingly difficult to make a living. They petitioned Parliament several times for help, without success, and riots, with the smashing of frames, arose in the second decade of the nineteenth century. The industry, in fact, was severely overmanned: children of frame-knitters themselves became knitters, too many apprentices were taken on, and while demand became stationary, production soared.

With the introduction of steam power in the mid-nineteenth century to work the knitting machines, the industry changed. Production became centralised in factories that were near to the area of coal production, although this did not happen to any great extent until the latter part of the nineteenth century. By then, only in the remoter area of Britain were the hand-knitters still at work.

Today, many knitters are using modern knitting machines with enthusiasm and are producing work of their own designs, often from their own home-spun and dyed yarns. To meet the increasing demand for yarns suitable for machine-knitting, many large manufacturers are selling their yarns made up into cones ready for use on a machine. The hand-knitters, however, are also in extensive production. From Cornwall in the South-west to the islands of Orkney in the extreme North, the hills and dales, as well as the towns, are alive with the hum of spinning-wheels and the clickety-click of knitting-needles, and many women, both for pleasure and profit, are still 'actively and incessantly employed in knitting'.

4

SMOCKS, GLOVES AND BUTTONS

The smock was everyday wear for countrymen in the eighteenth and nineteenth centuries and, now that smocking is fashionable for dresses, particularly children's, it is a cottage industry once more. The smock was at first made at home for members of the family and then later, still made at home, as an occupation for gain. It was also known as a smock-frock or by the medieval name of 'slop'. For centuries the term smock had been applied only to a woman's undergarment, which in turn became known as a 'shift'. A 'frock' was an outer garment worn by men and the term smock-frock seems to have combined the male and female element in the garment. This is still the case today, in the revived cottage industry which makes smocks as fashionable garments for women and children, but a few plainer ones for men.

Only in the present century was the smock gradually superseded by overalls and dungarees as working garments; but the smock was far above these in the esteem of its wearers, for in its most ambitious form it was proudly worn on special occasions, weddings, funerals and for 'Sunday best'—a status one could hardly envisage for the working clothes of today that replace it.

Starting life in the eighteenth century as a type of long full shirt, undecorated, to be worn over clothes for protection while working, the smock developed in the nineteenth century to a form where the fullness was gathered together over the chest, back and sleeves by means of ornamental stitching. This gathering helped to give the garment some shape and at the same time allowed the wearer great freedom of movement while at work. The thickness which the embroidered gathers supplied gave added protection against the weather where it was most needed; the fullness enabled the worker to keep dry beneath the voluminous folds. It was first and foremost for practical wear, but ornamented to such an extent that it can well be regarded as a British folk garment.

The complexity of embroidery on smocks reached its height in the middle of the nineteenth century. It is shown in two embroidered smocks made by sisters Hannah and Esther Stimpson, two cottagers of Radley in Berkshire. The smocks were exhibited and won an honourable mention at the Great Exhibition of 1851 by the firm for which they worked, Harris and Tomkins of Abingdon, an important smock-making centre at the time. This firm employed many women as outworkers.

Hannah embroidered on her smock the royal crown and doves bearing olive branches on the sides, interworked with the mottoes 'Vivat Regina' and 'Peace with all the world'. The wristbands displayed the royal crown, enclosed in a scroll, with the motto 'Long live our gracious Queen'. The chest and sleeves were embroidered with the crown, rose, shamrock, thistle and sprigs of flowers.

Esther's smock represented industry, with 'Fame' crowning her with a wreath on the side panels, and wheatsheaf and flowers above. There were agricultural implements on the collars with 'God Speed the Plough' and 'Success to agriculture'. The shoulder straps showed a hive of bees, the wristbands oak boughs and acorns.

These were garments for agricultural labourers designed for the firm by Thomas Watson. Many of the cottage workers worked to designs supplied by their employers. The garments themselves were made in simple fashion from a selection of rectangular and square pieces of material, which were returned to the factory to be made up into a smock when the cottage embroiderer had finished her work. Such designs as those made by Esther and Hannah Stimpson were not unusual.

The complexity of the designs and the skill of the workers to carry them out knew no bounds. This was the more remarkable as the linen on which they worked was exceptionally thick. They worked with linen thread, waxed for them along with their needles by their children to make the work a little easier. The linen was usually of natural colour with thread to match; finer linen, often white, was used for the smocks which were made especially for wear at church, national festivals, weddings and funerals. When called from the fields to attend a funeral in the middle of a day's work on the land, a worker could easily change from his working smock into the one for official occasions. Often a set of white smocks would be kept at the church ready for the pallbearers. Such a set of six identical smocks was kept in readiness in the village church of Piddlington in Oxfordshire, along with black hats and black gloves. The first funeral at Piddlington at which these particular smocks were not worn was in 1950, on the death of the woman who had made the last set of smocks for the church.

It was usual for most workers to have a working smock and a best smock. The latter was usually made by a member of the wearer's family and often handed down from generation to generation—especially so with children's smocks. Smocked dresses for children have always been made, and women today still remember with affection their favourite smocked dresses worn as children. They were out of vogue and rarely seen for some years, but Mrs Peggy Tuck of Templecombe in Somerset found that the birth of her first grand-daughter in 1974 coincided with a revival of smocking on dresses for little girls. She had learned the rudiments of traditional English smocking at school and later had plenty of practice perfecting the technique, smocking dresses for her own three daughters as well as for nieces and daughters of friends. The dresses Mrs Tuck made for her grand-daughter created great interest and soon led to an invitation to demonstrate the craft and sell dresses at the New Forest Agricultural Show in 1975. She has exhibited there in the Rural Crafts section every year since, and in 1978 won the show's gold medal for the best rural craft. From attending this show she learned about the many local specialist craft shows, booming with the increasing public interest in handmade goods. By the birth of her second grand-daughter in 1976 she was so busy smocking for shows that she had little time to make dresses for her grand-daughter and taught the craft to her own daughter, Mrs Patricia Lacey.

Now both mother and daughter smock and the rest of the family lend a hand, selling the dresses at their favourite agricultural and specialist craft shows, such as the Living Crafts Show held each spring at Hatfield House, Hertfordshire. By deliberately keeping it as a family concern they aim to maintain the high standards they have set themselves, as well as the individuality of their dresses.

On the traditional dresses for babies, Mrs Tuck and her daughter smock a narrow strip under a yoke and, using the smocking in a practical as well as decorative way, smock the wrists of long sleeves to give soft elastication. For toddlers and girls up to 8 or 9 years, the smocking extends under the yoke to the waist, again sometimes with smocked sleeves; for a more modern look, some dresses are smocked from the shoulder to under the arm. They are finding an increasing demand for suits for little boys for which they make a smocked shirt. For special wear they make long party dresses for girls—up to 90in (228cm) of material smocked right round the bodice. Cream satin christening robes are smocked from shoulders to below the armholes and at the sleeve wrists, and come with a matching fully smocked hat for the baby.

Women customers visiting the shows and seeing the children's smocks frequently ask for smocked adult clothes. Now Mrs Tuck makes kaftans with a deep band of smocking finishing wide elegant sleeves and the traditional complementary decoration for smocking—pin tucking or feather stitching—on the yoke.

Many women in the last century started making smocks only for their own families. Others, working on their own account, supplied them just for their own particular village. Smocks were made all over England and Wales, but in Oxfordshire, Suffolk and Nottinghamshire especially, there were centres for making smocks on a commercial basis, employing numbers of outworkers in cottages in the surrounding villages. They could make about two smocks a week, for which they received about 2s (10p) a garment. each smock used about 8yd (7.3m) of material 36in (91cm) wide. The entire width was used for the front and the back. Some were reversible, known as round-frocks; some had a buttoned front neck opening; others were completely open at the front, like a coat, probably giving rise to some smocks being known as smock-frocks—the full coat of the eighteenth century being knowns as a frock-coat.

Simple traditional stitches were used in the embroidery, including various forms of feather stitching, chain stitching and French knots. The actual gathering and smocking was done in stem stitch in rope, basket, wave and chevron patterns. The elaboration was in the designs of the embroidery. Some designs seem to belong to a particular area, perhaps where one woman had a favourite pattern which she repeated many times, but often a design is found in several parts of the country, probably copied as travel became easier and ideas and people moved around more. It may have happened that some groups of workers, such as cow-men, shepherds, farm labourers, waggoners or horticultural workers, had specific designs embroidered on their smocks to identify themselves, but various emblems of the countryside are found mixed together on so many smocks that it seems unlikely that this occurred in general. Floral designs were particularly popular. Plain smocks were also extensively worn by tradesmen, such as butchers, fishmongers, brewery workers and tailors, and in many occupations other than farming. Men working in dusty conditions, such as stonemasons, required a smock without too many gathers that would collect dust. In Surrey and Sussex it was customary to leave smocks almost undecorated and with only a small amount of gathering round the neck opening, whereas smocks from Wales and Herefordshire usually have heavily embroidered shoulder pieces.

While natural-coloured linen was usual, smocks were found in other colours in various parts of the country, such as blue in the Midlands, brown in the South-east and East Anglia, and green in Essex, Hertfordshire, Bedfordshire, Cambridgeshire and Northamptonshire. Blue smocks were made at Newark in Nottinghamshire where there were ten manufacturers employing outworkers from 1826 to 1872. The pattern was printed on the linen by locally made metal blocks and then sent out by cart to the cottagers for embroidering. In some places the material was delivered on a Monday just to one woman in the village. She marked out the patterns to be embroidered before distributing the work, which was collected on a Friday. Smocks were usually sold at markets and fairs but were never

Plate 12 Smock made in French cotton by Jean Plisner and Dobrila Jenkins. The yoke panels are decorated with heart motifs, a popular design both past and present *(Peter Plisner)*

cheap articles of clothing for a labourer to buy, which is the reason they were handed down from one generation to another and were always well darned.

Two housewives in Cambridge, Jean Plisner and Dobrila Jenkins, both with families and both teaching in adult education, have been successfully making smocks for about six years and selling them at the larger craft fairs. Their skill in embroidery and smocking, first learned in their teens, now enables them to make beautiful smocks for women in cotton, wool and silk. They still use traditional designs, but slightly alter the basic pattern of the yoke to fit female figures (see Plate 12).

Women first began to take an interest in smocking for themselves and their children at the end of the nineteenth century, at the time when the smock was losing favour as a working garment for men. Just as the Victorians carved everything made of wood, so they embroidered everything that could be embroidered. It was not long, therefore, before they discovered smocking as an occupation for the long evenings. At first, fashionable ladies sent their fabrics for embroidery to the country cottage workers, but soon magazines and instruction books with patterns (the latter published by Weldons) showed them how to do the work themselves. Smocking appeared on nightgowns, dressing-gowns, blouses and even on tennis dresses and bathing costumes, as well as on girls' dresses and smocks for little boys.

Smocks became unsuitable working garments when mechanisation was introduced on the farm. This, together with the increase in the manufacture of cheap working clothes, contributed to the decline of the cottage industry. Overalls (still known as cow-gowns in some parts of the Midlands), dungarees, corduroy trousers and unbleached drill jackets, known as 'slop jackets', were increasingly worn. The latter were also made by outworkers for some time. Smocks continued to be worn, however, in some remote areas of the countryside into the early part of the twentieth century.

Today, they are worn as protective garments for a different type of worker, many of them engaged in cottage industries, such as spinners, weavers and potters. The traditional Dorset smocks of the nineteenth century are made today by Beverley Marshall of Beaminster in Dorset. She spent many months researching, measuring and documenting agricultural smocks in the museums of southern England and Wales, so her designs based on the nineteenth-century smock-frock are authentic, but are adaptable to the material and decorations of a customer's requirements. As in the past, the smocking is done by a team of craftswomen in their own homes and made up by an expert machinist.

Like many of the industries connected with the increasing prosperity and the greater interest in fashion that took place from the sixteenth century onwards, the glovemaking centres of the country had expanded considerably by the end of the eighteenth century and were flourishing at the beginning of the nineteenth.

Once mainly the prerogative of the rich and important, kings, clergy and aristocrats, by the Middle Ages gloves were also worn by lower classes—even labourers in the fields wore thick protective gloves. The glovers of London became separated from the leather-dressers, who originally made all gloves, as early as 1349, by the granting of a separate charter. By Tudor times members of the aristocracy were wearing elegant, embroidered gloves, often scented, which they imported from Europe, in spite of a ban on imported gloves (a ban which lasted for 300 years). Gloves were also worn for hawking and hunting—one of the reasons, perhaps, for West Oxfordshire becoming one of the most important areas for glovemaking from an early date. Such sporting gloves were required by the king and his court who frequently stayed at the Royal Manor of Woodstock and hunted in the nearby Wychwood Forest. In this mainly forest area, where work on the land was in short supply but animal skins plentiful, the local population soon made the production of leather goods—jackets, breeches, linings and gloves—their main occupation, particularly as the court provided a ready market. Only in the mid-twentieth century did the gloving industry decline in this area, although now it is again in production in Woodstock.

By the end of the sixteenth century it was possible to obtain gloves made in England from doe, sheep, horse, chicken and goat skins, as well as in satin, silk, velvet and worsted. They were favourite items to be given as presents on all occasions, and throughout seventeenth, eighteenth and nineteenth centuries it was customary to give all mourners at funerals a pair of gloves.

The industry was organised on cottage industry lines for several hundred years by master glovers who distributed the work to be done at home. Often one woman would act as the carrier, taking the bundles of finished gloves to the employer and bringing back the raw materials to distribute to the glovers, who sewed them by hand. In the early days the sewers had to provide their own needles and thread and in many districts were compelled to buy the latter from their employer, often at higher prices than elsewhere.

By the seventeenth century there were complaints that too many apprentices had been taken on, indicating that the industry was already well established. A further expansion of trade took place in the eighteenth century when women as well as men were employed as apprentices. From the eighteenth century onwards, however, the master glovers were mostly men, apart from a few women who were carrying on a family business after the death of a husband. Glove making was done by women in their own homes.

The main areas of the glove trade in the eighteenth century were in villages around Worcester, Woodstock, Yeovil, Hereford, Ludlow and Leominster. These were mainly agricultural districts whose farmers and land-owners complained that glovemaking was increasing the wages of servants and spoiling them for domestic service and employment on the land. The farmworkers' wives did not wish to work in the fields at the seasonal work expected of them because, apart from the financial aspect, they did not wish to roughen their hands which made glovemaking more difficult.

At Woodstock about 40 or 50 people were employed in gloving in 1767, but by 1809 the numbers had increased to 50 or 60 men and 1,400 to 1,500 women and girls. Large numbers were also employed in Worcester and Somerset. At this time it was usual for workers to be engaged on different processes of production. The tanning, staining and cutting out of the skins was done by men in the factory, while women and girls were exclusively concerned with the hand-sewing in their homes. Often the women worked on only one stage, such as 'sewing the sides', 'tambouring the backs', 'sewing the backs' or 'welting the bottom'. As the work was done on a piecework basis, payment depended on speed and efficiency, so this assembly-line type of production did help the worker to make more money. A sewer was rarely capable of completing a glove single-handed, although the workers in small firms or family businesses were probably able to carry out more than one process.

In some areas a gloving donkey was used to hold the material while the seams were sewn (Fig 12). The glove was held in this vice-like contraption while stitching was done and

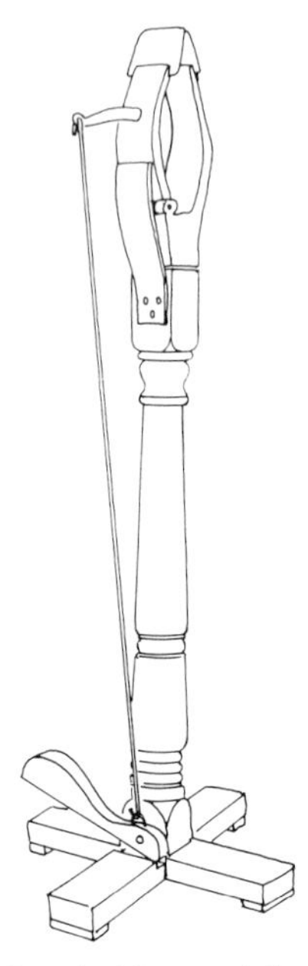

Fig 12 Glove donkey used to hold material while the seams were sewn. This one measures about 3ft (914mm)

then released by depression of the foot-pedal. Smaller ones of brass which could be clamped on a table were also used, chiefly in the making of kid gloves, for which the pay was better. However, the workers complained that these shone in their eyes. Glovemaking was, in fact, an unhealthy occupation for, apart from the eye-strain caused by the close work, the workers suffered from stooping shoulders as a result of bending over in one position for long hours.

Glovemaking, as so many of the cottage industries, suffered periods of economic depression, one of which occurred when the centuries-old prohibition on the import of foreign gloves was removed in 1826. French gloves, which were better and cheaper, were imported; at the same time the production of cotton, woollen and silk gloves in Nottingham and Leicester was stepped up as fashions changed and the demand for these types grew and was met by the increasing use of machinery. The leather glovemakers further south suffered greatly, as the marked rise in the poor rates in the gloving districts at that time indicate. Little as the wives and families of labourers earned at their glovemaking, it often made the difference between survival and starvation. Large numbers of glovemakers were dismissed during this period and applied to their parishes for relief. When the Poor Law Commissioners investigated the workhouses at Yeovil in Somerset in 1834 they found that most of the occupants had formerly been glovemakers. The distress in Yeovil, where the poor rates doubled at this time, was so great that soldiers were stationed in and around the town to keep order. In gloving districts further north the industry came to an end and never revived. When their husbands were suffering from depressions in agriculture, however, women were able to support their families by glovemaking. The labourers in Worcestershire and Somerset were mainly supported by the women and children employed in the glove trade and, as William Cobbett said, were preserved from the 'horrid misery' existing in other parts of the country in the early nineteenth century.

With the reorganisation of the industry and the improvement in the quality of English gloves in about 1840, the industry revived, especially in Somerset and Oxfordshire. There were again large manufacturers in Charlbury, Chipping Norton and Woodstock where hundred of outworkers were employed in hand-sewing gloves. Many of these firms were in business until the early decades of the twentieth century. They were helped by the advent of the railways which enabled them to take delivery more easily of imported hides, barrels of egg yolk from the Far East, used in dressing the leather, and Singer Sewing machines, which had been invented in the United States of America in 1850. The treadle-operated Singer machines were small enough for home use, one reason for the glove industry remaining a cottage industry for so long. Some of the machines were hired by the workers, while others were hire-purchased from the employers over the years. At first, machines were used chiefly for making kid gloves. The machines were eventually converted to electric power. Many of the machines in use today are eighty or ninety years old, having been carefully cherished over the years.

Many glovers believed that machines were more troublesome to use than to sew the gloves by hand. Nevertheless, all glovemaking was hard work and the hours long if the average 4s (20p) or 5s (25p) a week were to be earned. A single women would often work from 6am, or daylight in winter, until 10pm, with about two hours break for meals.

New factories were started up at Charlbury and Woodstock to which the skilled glovemakers in the district had attracted firms. Cottages were still being built for the workers as late as 1926. The gloving industry at Charlbury ceased in 1968.

Girls were taught gloving in their own homes or in the home of an agent or 'overlooker', at about 12 years of age. They were paid nothing for the first few months and only a small wage for the remaining twelve months during which they were learners. At 14 or 15 years they were allowed to work in their own homes, although many children started work at an earlier age than this. Although children worked at gloving from such an early age, however, it seemingly had no great ill-effects, as many of them continued glovemaking until their seventies and eighties.

Apart from leather gloves, suede gloves were made as well as those in 'chamois' leather sheepskin which was oil tanned. At the beginning of this century these skins were laid out to bleach on fields and hedges around Woodstock. Military gloves were in great demand from Woodstock and when a large army contract was received there would be celebration in the villages and on occasion the church bells would sound out the good news.

The backs of the gloves were decorated or 'pointed' by means of a multi-needle machine, a complicated and expensive piece of equipment and the most liable to break down. A simple design of the usual three rows of stitching was often done freehand, but the more difficult patterns had the design marked out on the glove or a template was used. The machines had a small pillar or post attached to facilitate sewing round the top of the fingers.

At one time there were about sixteen factories around Woodstock producing hand-sewn gloves; now there is just one—Woodstock Leathercraft Ltd—operating from a 350-year-old building in Harrisons Lane. Here Mr H. A. Napier and his workers produce sheepskin gloves, slippers and coats. The leather is prepared at the factory and the gloves are cut out there; they are then delivered to about thirty outworkers in villages around the area who sew up the gloves in their own homes. Many of these home workers at Woodstock are themselves the daughters of past glove-stitchers, from whom they learned their craft.

Buttons have been in use since the first fitted clothing was introduced in the Middle East in the 6th century AD, but in England few buttons have been found or identified in illustrations before the fourteenth century and then only on the clothes of royalty and the aristocracy. There is some evidence that the aristocrats who were buried in the burial mounds around Stonehenge in about 1600–1700BC along with their cherished possessions employed highly skilled craftsmen to make decorative objects of gold. Included in a woman's grave, among other objects of gold and amber, was a large conical shale button with a gold casing. It is thought that considerable use was made of gold at that time in the form of decorated thin sheets of gold for attachment to wood, leather or shale buttons. Like most of the earliest buttons, these were no doubt worn more as decorative items or badges of office than as a means of fastening garments. By Tudor times, however, buttons on clothing were in more frequent use with gold, silver and precious stones used in their making. Those lower down the social scale fastened their clothes with leather buttons or metal discs.

The use of buttons increased considerably during the seventeenth century, particularly on the garments worn by men, such as the frock-coat which had large buttoned cuffs. The buttons on the sleeves of the men's coats today are the only reminder of this now vanished style. Buttoned waistcoats were also introduced at this time and buttons for waistcoats were first made in Dorset in the seventeenth century.

The button industry in Dorset was started in 1622 in a cottage at Shaftesbury by Abraham Case, the son of a Cotswold farmer, who had travelled in Europe as a soldier and had seen the fine buttons being worn there. Until this time sheep farming had been the main occupation in Dorset and the sheep now provided the horn from which the first buttons were made. A delicate threadwork pattern was worked on linen to cover the sheep's horn discs. These buttons were known as 'high tops'. Lady Dorothy Neville said in her reminiscences that the high tops 'were principally used for hunting waistcoats, and were so excellently made that twenty-five years of use in no way impaired their efficiency'. This is not surprising as many buttonworkers were former lacemakers who took up this work when the lace industry declined.

By 1656 Case moved with his sons to larger premises and took on extra employees to meet the demand for his buttons. When Case died in 1658 the family firm was producing thirty-one different types of button. At first the business was continued by his sons and grandsons, and by 1730, 700 women and children were working for the firm making buttons in their own cottages.

The firm was reorganised after this date so that all the work was done by outside workers, the company preparing and issuing the raw materials and receiving back and packing the finished product. An office was opened in London to deal with the sale and marketing of the buttons and another in Liverpool to deal with exports to Canada and the United States of America—particularly New York, Boston and Quebec—and Australia and Europe.

There were depots around Dorset attended by the company's agents on certain days each week when the cottage workers would bring in their finished work and collect raw materials. Workers would walk as many as 12 miles (19km) from their homes to the depots on a Friday, where the atmosphere was often that of a fair. Until 1800 they were often paid in goods and sometimes received tokens instead of cash to exchange for bread, cheese and beer at one of the local inns. Children were employed at the main depots to unload the wire, which was brought in waggon-loads from Birmingham, and make it into the rings on which the buttons were made. (The rings were made of a rustless alloy, the secret of which is no longer known.) Some strung the rings into gross bundles and others prepared the skeins of thread. When trained for this work they received 1s (5p) a week for a long day's work. Women making the buttons in their homes received between 1s 6d (7½p) and 4s (20p) a gross for the best quality buttons. These were mounted on cards by women working at the depots. Blue cards were used for standard quality buttons and yellow for the lowest quality; only buttons on pink and blue cards were for export. Buttonmaking was also an occupation for the inmates of the Dorset workhouses whose governors had negotiated special rates for the work.

The cards of buttons were often transported to London in waggonettes which contained sliding drawers full of buttons classified according to shapes, sizes and quality, so that they could be handed out easily at warehouses and shops.

The buttons were made with needle and thread by tightly covering the wire rings with buttonhole stitching; the stitches were then turned inwards so that the outside of the ring was

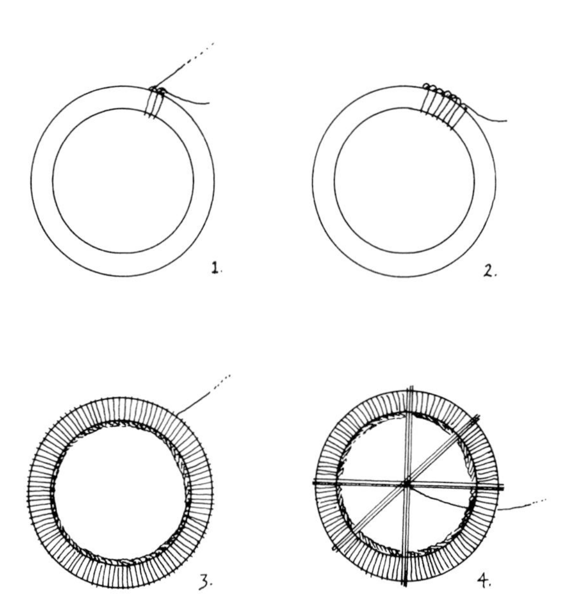

Fig 13 The stages in the making of a Dorset cross-wheel button

smooth. This work was often done by children of 6 or 7 years. The inside of the ring was filled with a variety of designs by their mothers, which had such names as 'Cross-wheel', 'Blandford cartwheel' and 'honeycomb' (Fig 13). Buttons which became dirty while being made were boiled in a linen bag.

This cottage industry was at its height in the nineteenth century when 4,000 people were employed in making buttons in Dorset; the annual turnover reached £14,000. Prizes were offered by the employers for the highest quality and output by the buttonmakers and individual families competed to make the best buttons or to be the best mounters.

In Cheshire and Staffordshire buttons were also made on a cottage industry basis by numerous women and children. The area around Leek in Staffordshire was one of the main centres for the silk button trade, employing hundreds in the town and surrounding villages. Gold and silver buttonmakers worked chiefly in London, the employer providing the gold and silver thread and paying for the completed work.

While a few expert buttonmakers were said to be able to

make a gross of wire buttons a day, the average was six or seven dozen a day. A married woman's earnings were about 6s (30p) or 7s (35p) a week, while a single woman who could do a full day's work probably made about 10s (50p) or 12s (60p). In some areas dealers established schools for the teaching of 'buttony'. One dealer in Shaftesbury in 1812 was employing as many as 1,200 women and children. When a dealer was also a grocer or a draper, he distributed the materials to be made up and paid most of the workers' wages in goods, often cotton goods and clothing, whether the workers wished to be so paid or not. Although illegal, this practice became more widespread as the handmade button industry declined. The use of pearl buttons lessened the demand for the wire-covered ones and the rates for the work decreased as times grew harder. The small amounts earned were still needed by the family of an agricultural labourer, so children in Dorset were allowed to make buttons between lessons at school to supplement the family income. Even though children could earn only a few pence a week at their work parents would refuse to send them to school if they could not make buttons.

Factories around Birmingham were soon employing workers to mass produce metal and pasteboard buttons at far less cost than the cottage industry buttons. At the same time the horn and shell button businesses were also starting up in the Midlands. The comparative peace and quiet of the Dorset workers continued undisturbed until 1851, when at the Great Exhibition Ashton's Patent Machine for making linen-covered buttons was exhibited. The machine sold well and the buttons it made were at a quarter of the cost of those made by hand. Within two or three years the Dorset industry of handmade buttons, only recently so prosperous, came to an abrupt end.

The buttonmakers and their employers alike were soon in a state of dire poverty. The loss of this cottage industry meant disaster to the villages of Dorset. The gentry of the county came to the aid of the workers and provided funds to enable whole village populations to emigrate and start a new life in Canada and Australia; 350 alone left Shaftesbury. The landowners of Dorset also provided employment for the former employers who had so recently been prosperous to save them from ruin.

One of the depots for the collection of buttons was at the Olde Button Shop at Lytchett Minster, which still sells buttons today. When the business came to an end in 1904 the Lytchett Mission, a charitable organisation for the poor, with the help of Lady Florence Lees of Poole, purchased all the remaining stock and equipment and endeavoured to run the business with its outworkers from the shop, but this endeavour failed in 1915. Women's Institutes in Dorset have managed to keep the art of buttonmaking alive to some extent, but few people sell their buttons today and the knowledge of making all the varieties of buttons that once existed has long been lost.

Diana Illingworth makes buttons—mostly the cross-wheel type—in the village of Milton Abbas in Dorset. These are for sale around the county in various shops, including the National Trust in Dorchester. There is still a future for buttons which have been made to match the garments produced by today's busy hand-knitters.

Some of them being made again by private Dorset buttonmakers are used by Jean Pegg, the Bournemouth lacemaker, on reproductions of Victorian blouses and underwear which she produces in conjunction with her friend Eileen Clark under the name 'Papillon'. This is a recently formed cottage industry handmaking the garments in pure cotton, voile and silk from authentic, original patterns. To go with the garments, they produce buttons, silk flowers, embroidery and boxes, and employ outworkers to help deal with the increasing number of orders they receive from local and London shops.

5

PRINTED TEXTILES

The printed fabrics that are used so widely in our homes today were introduced in the seventeenth century and soon became popular, especially in country homes. All of them were produced by craftsmen working in a small way and it is gratifying that, in spite of the great technical developments that more or less killed this cottage industry in the nineteenth century, it flourishes again today, albeit to a limited extent, with a number of modern craftsmen producing fine textiles with beautiful designs in their own workshops and studios.

In the eighteenth century chintzes and printed cottons became the most desirable furnishing materials and the village upholsterer, for instance, scorned the silk, brocades and damasks found in town homes and preferred to cover his furniture with patterns of roses, pansies and convolvulus, the designs which also brought bright colours to the curtains of cottage windows. Printing cotton textiles was already a flourishing industry in the North of England at this time in spite of the great opposition from the silk weavers. Ill-feeling between them and the textile printers lasted for many years and it eventually led to riots and street demonstrations.

The wearing of chintz became so popular that the weavers circulated the 'Spitalfields Ballad' decrying the 'Calico Madams' who wore chintz dresses.

The cotton industry was well established in Lancashire by the mid-seventeenth century, using the processes by which woollen and linen cloth had been made from the thirteenth century onwards. By the middle of the eighteenth century the industry was well enough established to include printing as well as weaving.

In the seventeenth century fast-dyed and brilliantly coloured cottons had been imported into Europe from India and the Dutch East Indies, where the art of fabric printing was far in advance of anything produced in Europe. There was such a demand for these by ladies of fashion that attempts were made to produce them in Europe. The first attempts were somewhat crude and it was not until the end of the seventeenth century that production became satisfactory by using carved wooden blocks to print the patterns and dyes made colour-fast with mordants (as was the custom in India). Many textile printers working today in their own homes use hand-block printing. They first of all draw their own designs and then make tracings of these. The tracings are retraced under pressure on to the printing block (usually made of heavy-quality lino mounted on wood). The areas of the design that are not to be printed are cut away with lino-cutting tools and craft knives. The prepared dyes are put on to dye pads which are squares of wood covered with felt or blanket, one pad for every colour to be used. The fabric is printed by pressing each block first on the dye pad and then on the cloth. After drying, the fabric has to be heat-treated by steam or hot iron to make the dye fast.

By 1700 the textile printing industry was flourishing in the South-east of England, greatly helped by the Dutch and French Huguenot refugees. Many were skilled textile printers, for the art of cotton-printing was by then well established on the Continent. One of them founded the first calico-printing factory in England at Richmond, Surrey, in about 1690. The business was soon successful and gave employment to many workers. Other centres were established at Bow and Old Ford and the industry became a source of prosperity.

Many of the foreign textile printers who settled in England, mostly in the London area, established small one-man businesses dyeing and printing calico. Sometimes they printed the customer's own fabric, and many of them travelled around the country, as did many weavers, working in out-houses of farms and inns until they had coped with all the orders in that area. Then they moved on to the next place with their families and apprentices. Many developed family businesses.

Each printer had his trade card, one of which from the seventeenth century (and now in the British Museum), reads 'Jacob Stampe living at Ye Sighn of the Callico Printer in Hounsditch Prints all sorts of Callicoes Lineings Silks Stuffs, New or Ould, at Reasonable Rates'. The card shows a printer standing at a table upon which is stretched a length of cloth, some of it hanging down to the floor. He holds a wooden block in his hand which he is applying to the cloth. There is a mallet in his other hand which is about to strike the wooden block to stamp the colour firmly into the material. His boy apprentice stands behind him by a tub of dye, preparing the blocks for his master to use.

The new patterned cloth produced in this way was so popular that it drove the silk and wool weavers to get a ban on all imported Indian printed calicoes and in 1720 a further ban on the use of all cotton printed in England. Women were even to be fined for wearing printed chintz dresses. The industry survived until the ban was lifted in 1774 by printing only for export or in printing on fabrics such as fustian—a material which had a cotton weft and a linen warp or on silk and cotton mixtures.

When Sir Richard Arkwright invented the improved spinning frame, resulting in the first all-cotton English calico being produced from his water-powered spinning mill in large quantities in 1771, a new industry was born and the producing and printing of cotton proceeded apace from that time. The designs of this period were rather heavy, but soon improved. Cotton printing had achieved fine quality by the late Chippendale period when Chinese designs for furniture and dressmaking fabrics had a great vogue.

In the second half of the eighteenth century machinery took over most of the textile printing from the small craftsmen, and the mechanical processes, which used engraved metal plates, turned the printing of cloth into a national industry. From the small workshops of the South-east it became centred in the industrial North, particularly in Lancashire, where the gigantic cotton industry took over the textile printing industry. The machinery enabled larger repeat patterns to be produced with greater detail of design than could ever be made with wooden blocks.

A Scotsman, Thomas Bell, patented the first successful rotary printing machine in 1783, which also speeded up the transfer of textile printing to the industrial North. After 1820, a small amount of hand-block printing, particularly of the small items such as handkerchiefs, was carried on in London.

The fabric to be dyed was usually bleached out of doors to give a white background against which the bright colours would stand out. The printers used many of the plant dyes used by the cloth-dyers, such as madder for brown, black, red and purple; woad for blue; weld for yellow, and mixtures of these. Various methods were used to obtain patterned and coloured cloth. The colour designs were sometimes printed directly on to the cloth as previously described. Sometimes the cloth was dyed with an even colour and then a bleaching agent applied by a block to remove the colour from the background so creating a pattern in reverse to the former-mentioned printing method. At other times a mordant (or dye-fixer) was printed on the cloth in varying strengths and the cloth then dipped in the dye, producing a variety of shades of colour. Another method was called resist-dyeing: often a starch-paste or a hot wax, was drawn on the cloth to resist the dye when the cloth was dipped.

This latter method is similar to that used by the many textile printers working as batik artists today. This craft, which originated in Java, is now very popular. Wax is applied with a brush or by hand to those parts of the design that are not to be coloured when the material is dipped in the dye. This can be repeated several times to vary the colour in different parts of the material. If the wax is cracked at various stages in the process the dye will penetrate the cracks giving the design a characteristic lined effect.

A Sussex artist, Mary Potter, who works in Lewes with her husband, uses the English countryside as her main source of inspiration for her batik designs which are used as wall hangings, pictures and silk scarves, sometimes made for special commissions. She also does silk-screen printing and welcomes

Plate 13 Mary Potter at work in her textile studio in Sussex

visitors to see her at work—provided that they make a preliminary telephone call to her purpose-built studio. A display of her batik pictures, silk-screen prints, cards, hand-printed scarves and traditional prints of Sussex themes and scenes are all for sale there (see Plate 13).

Screen-printing is a popular method of printing fabric today and is practised by the many textile printers working in their own homes or small studios. A stencil is hand-cut to the desired shape out of a special stencil film and positioned on the fabric. A silk-covered screen is then placed over the fabric and dye is forced through the screen, so creating the pattern the artist wishes for.

Claire Chambers studied printed textiles at Southampton College of Art and started her own workshop in 1978 at the Old Granary, a craft centre, at Bishop's Waltham, Hampshire. She screen-prints by hand lengths of household textiles and dress materials with mainly floral designs. The hand-cut stencils used with the silk screen give the finished fabric the appearance of having been printed by wood blocks. The simple patterns are usually executed in two colours, chosen either by Claire or her clients, using Polyprint or Sericol dyes, mixed as required. The process is a laborious one as the screen has to be placed on the fabric repeatedly to print the pattern with the dyes on cotton, viyella, voiles or velvets. All the patterns are washable and the dyes are made colour-fast by the application of a hot iron. Claire Chambers herself makes up many of the materials she prints into an assortment of cushion, kitchen sets and tea-cosies for sale at the Granary and at various shops and craft fairs around the country. She recently despatched a big consignment of her tea-cosies to the United States of America.

A similar silk-screen printing enterprise is carried on succesfully by Pin Linni Prints at a workshop at Camelford in Cornwall, where the designing and printing is done by Lynne Sandbach. The fabric is made up into ladies' and children's dresses in the firm's workshop and also by five outworkers in their homes in the village. They also make up the printed fabric into items for the kitchen and a variety of holders for hanging on walls to keep small articles, such as shoes, socks and gloves, tidy. The printing is done on 100 per cent cotton fabric and also on velvet, wool and some polyester. The goods are sold at their shop, at agricultural shows and through their mail-order catalogue.

6

BEEHIVES, BONNETS AND BASKETS

The first seeds of civilisation that were sown in the Near East 10,000 years ago were those of wheat and barley plants. This happened when men first stopped wandering from place to place, hunting and gathering their food, and discovered how to grow crops and domesticate animals and, once settled, to build permanent homes in communities that later grew into villages and cities. The seed from the wheat they grew provided their bread, but it cannot have taken long for them to discover that the straw remaining after harvesting could be woven into useful containers of various sorts. Probably the wild grasses from which the crops were developed had already been used by primitive peoples in this way for centuries, but settled communities had more time to develop such crafts. We know they had a well-developed technique of basketry by 4,500BC in Egypt where it already had a variety of uses, such as linings for grain storage pits and baskets which were possibly used for sowing corn. Some of these baskets have been preserved for centuries in the dry sand; they were made by the coiled technique, whereby a bundle of grass was coiled into a spiral and the layers then sewn together with a strand of fibre, a method today known as straw rope or lip-work (see Figs 14 and 15). Chairs in this same shape are still made today by basketmakers, as well as cradles which have probably changed little in shape since biblical times.

The beehive chair gets its name from the straw beehives made for centuries in lip-work, when beekeeping was more common than today and honey the only sweetening agent

Fig 14 Large garden chair made by David Buck of Norfolk

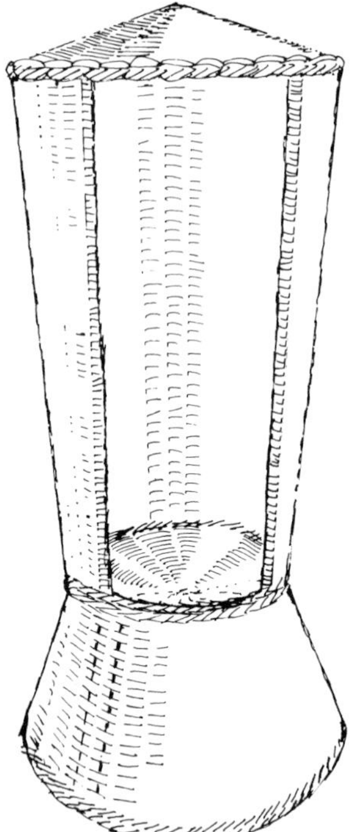

Fig 15 Eighteenth-century basketwork beehive chair and cradle made at Newbury using the method known as rope or lip-work

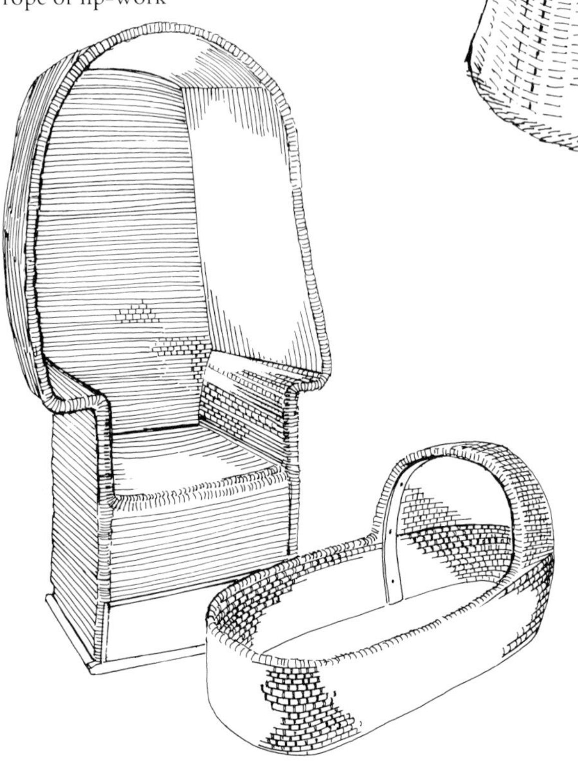

available. Until recently they were used instead of wooden ones and thought by many to keep the bees warmer in winter than modern beehives. In the North of England the straw skeps were kept in recesses in south-facing walls, known as bee boles, to protect the bees from northerly winds. They were made of either rye or wheat straw. A ring or section of cow-horn was used to standardise the diameter of the coils. Each coil was bound to the next by long lengths of briar, bramble or holly. Later, cane or string was used for binding. The briar was gathered in the summer and hung up ready for use in the long winter evenings. The thorns were removed by pulling a piece of leather threaded with wire and bent in two along the length of the briar, which was then split and the pith scraped off with a knife.

Craftworkers in the past always used local materials. On the windy west coast of Scotland they made baskets of the bent grass that grew there and coiled it in the same way as straw lip-work. The baskets, which had straight sides and were known as 'coisans', were used for holding dry goods, such as grain or meal. Bags for similar purposes were also woven out of this grass which was very strong. In areas of the Highlands where wood was in short supply basketwork was used for many purposes. Plates and baskets were woven to contain and serve food on, including meat, bread and oatcakes ('chicken in a basket' as served in inns today is not such a modern idea). Cupboards for the storage of food had wickerwork sides on wooden frames. In some Highland districts coffins were also made of wickerwork. A chair that is still made in the Orkney Isles today has a basketry seat and back of lip-work set in a wooden frame.

Similar straight-sided baskets to the coisans are made today in a cottage at Rousay, Orkney, by Keith Colsell (see Plate 14). At first he made his baskets from coils of oat-straw as was usual for lip-work, but after successfully making a basket from the local rush about two years ago at a time when no oat-straw was available, producing a basket of unusually beautiful appearance, he has used it ever since. Rush grows profusely on the islands and cleaning it merely requires removing the

Plate 14 Keith Colsell, basketmaker, at Rousay, Orkney

flower-head (pulling several rushes at a time between finger and thumb). This is a far less time-consuming process than cleaning straw, when each loose blade must be detached from the node on the stalk and the seed-head then cut off—although the result is straw with a beautiful golden shine.

Keith starts cutting the rushes with a sickle in early August, carries them home on his back in a pack and then dries them in an airy shed. They are then stored in the roof of the byre. Unlike most rushwork where the rushes are worked in a damp condition, these rushes are used dry. Any shrinkage caused by damp rushes drying out would tend to weaken the baskets, which should be as rigid as possible.

He uses a few simple tools—scissors, a packing needle about 5in (127mm) in length, and various rings, usually from plumbing fittings—but he has recently acquired a traditional cow-horn for measuring the diameter of the coils. He makes a wide variety of baskets by the coiling method, ranging from small 6in (152mm) diameter bowls and lidded work-baskets of about 10in (254mm) diameter to large linen and peat or log baskets. They are bound with 2-ply sisal twine. The local bent grass growing on the shore, which was twined by hand into great lengths ready for use, was formerly used as binding material.

One of the earliest uses of rushes was as floor coverings. Either they were strewn on the earth and stone floor of Saxon and medieval homes to form a warm covering or later woven into rush matting. This floor covering could be kept clean in spite of mud and spilled food for, as a visitor from the Netherlands observed in 1560, 'their chambers and parlour strewed over with sweet herbs refreshed me'. With sweet herbs added to the rushes and regularly changed, the floors were probably no worse than many a country home in later times. Carpets at this time were used only as coverings for cupboards and tables and never put on floors. Sometimes rushes were woven into mattresses for beds. In Dorchester Museum a bed dated 1700 can be seen with a rush mattress which was made in nearby Purbeck by craftsmen working the local sedge.

Until the end of the last century rushes gave the only form of light in many country homes. They were peeled and dipped in fat several times to give them a good coating and then burnt in a rush-light holder.

Rushes grow not only by the sea-shore but on any marshy land or by streams, lakes and ponds. The most common rush is the flowering rush (*Juncus effusus*) which grows about 3-4ft (91-120cm) high. It is easy to pick and can be dried in the sun or a dry, airy barn or shed. The rushes are cut near the roots, kept as straight as possible and tied into bundles called bolts.

A larger variety of rush which grows 8-10ft (2.4-3.6m) in height (*Scirpus lacustris*) is the one most commonly used, but needs to be harvested by experts who stand up to their waist in the water to cut them below water-level. These rushes must be kept damp while they are being worked and are used by craftsmen today to make baskets, plant-holders, tablemats and floormats.

For chair seats salt-water rushes from Holland are mostly

used as they are stronger than those grown in fresh water, but not so easy to work with as the English rushes. The latter are harvested some time between the hay and the corn harvests, but after the longest day of the year. They must be carefully but quickly dried because if affected by damp during the drying period they become mouldy and blotchy. Again, they must be carefully stored—strong sunlight will bleach them—to maintain the colours which are so attractive in woven rushes. They are usually woven into a simple pattern of checks, the colour of the rushes being sufficiently pleasing in themselves without necessitating complicated patterns. Where special shapes are needed for, say, bags or hats they are more easily woven over a mould of the required shape; the rushes are often plaited first and the plaits then sewn together. A large-eyed packing-needle or rug-needle is needed for this, but on the whole the rushworker needs few tools.

At the beginning of the century rushes that came from the rivers and marshes of the Oxfordshire border were taken in vans to Buckinghamshire to be distributed to the workers who made the rush seats for chairs. This was considered a dirty job because the rushes had to be kept damp and smelled unpleasant and it was said in High Wycombe that 'you could smell a matter a mile off'. Rush seats were common in churches. A cleaner form of seating was made of woven cane.

Both rush and cane seating is still a cottage industry today, caners being much in demand for the repair of antique chairs. Few chair-making firms employed caners in their factories; in the High Wycombe area most of the work was done by women, and children from the age of 7, in their own homes. Before World War I they would make the cane seats as they sat at their cottage doors. Caning superseded the lacemaking that had formerly occupied them in the Buckinghamshire area.

One process in the making of chair seats that was eventually mechanised and which must have brought great relief to the workers was the boring of the holes around the seat frame to take the cane. About sixty or seventy holes were needed and making these by hand was a laborious task. A boring machine in use in 1890 was capable of boring 35,000 holes a day. The

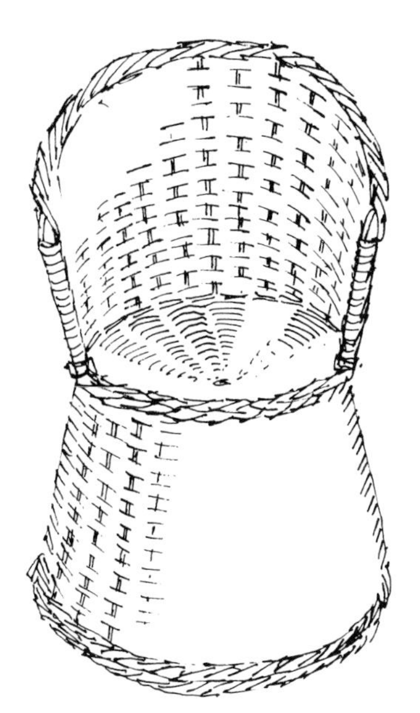

Fig 16 Child's chair made by David Buck in the ancient style of basket-work

canes were usually prepared by men who removed the pith when the canes were split and produced the even strips necessary to weave a pattern. This work was also done in cottages, the round cane being collected from an agent in High Wycombe and returned when split into the required sizes. The workers often received groceries, rather than money, in return for their work.

Basket chairs are also known as wicker chairs, wanded chairs, even 'twiggen' chairs when made from twigs, and are still found in styles not unlike those made in Roman Britain (see also Fig 16).

The tomb paintings of ancient Egypt depict people wearing simple hats made of straw, grasses or rushes. Figures of an even earlier date are shown wearing headgear of coarse woven or plaited fibres. Records from many other ancient peoples show that the straw-hat industry had a very early start in history.

The earliest hats were made by fastening a bunch of straws together at one end, bending them out to cover the head and holding them in position around the head by a narrow band. Plaiting the straws and sewing them into the shape of a hat in spiral rows was a much later development. From early English manuscripts it is apparent that straw hats were worn mainly by workers in the fields, but by the later Middle Ages there are more frequent references to straw hats. In 1667 Samuel Pepys wrote that on a visit to Hatfield the women in his party derived amusement from trying on some of the straw hats then much worn in country districts 'which did become them mightily, but especially my wife'.

While a straw-plaiting industry flourished in Europe in the sixteenth century and was probably then introduced into England by Flemish refugees, the earliest fashionable straw hats worn in this country were imported from Italy. After seeing them, country hatmakers were soon able to copy the Italian straw plaiting, as they had without doubt been making cruder versions for themselves for centuries.

By the end of the seventeenth century a straw-hat industry was firmly established in England in the south-east Midlands. In fact, by 1689 the straw hatmakers of Bedfordshire, Buckinghamshire and Hertfordshire were already petitioning against a bill which advocated the wearing of woollen caps. this, they said, would ruin nearly a thousand families in towns and villages around Luton and Dunstable. Within another thirty years they were petitioning against imports of straw hats from Europe.

The work of making the straw plaits for the industry and also in the making up of the plaits into completed bonnets and hats, was done in village cottages, mainly by women and children.

The making of straw rather than woollen hats, at the expense of the wool-spinners and knitters, continued to grow throughout the eighteenth century. Arthur Young on his tour through Dunstable said that the industry has reached 'great perfection of neatness' and included also the manufacture of boxes, baskets and toys. The boxes were in marquetry work in which coloured straws were pasted in patterns on a wood or cardboard box. The same method was used to cover tablemats.

Dunstable, which gave its name to Dunstable Bonnets, was situated on the main Watling Street where a plait market was held. Another important plait market was held at Luton, which also became famous in the hat industry. At these markets the stalls were piled high with golden plait which had been collected by dealers from the surrounding villages. Women who had no dealer stood on the pavements with their plait for sale in loops over their arms.

Before the growth of the straw-hat industry in the nineteenth century the cottagers in the corn-growing belts of East Anglia and the Midlands had always plaited knots of straw to wear in their button-holes; they made picture frames of straw as well as baskets, beehives, chairs and mattresses, and they wove cockerels, crowns and various ornaments to put the finishing touches to the thatch on their straw ricks. At holiday-time, they plaited straw into the manes of their farm horses when they drove them to the fair. So they were well skilled in manufacturing articles of straw long before their skills were needed by the straw-plaiting and hatmaking industries spreading across the East Midlands in the nineteenth century. At the turn of the century straw bonnets, hats and boaters were the most common form of summer headgear for all.

In fine weather women and children sat outside their cottages or wandered about country lanes busy plaiting, a comparatively light and easy task compared with many cottage industries. Sometimes they bought the straw for a few pence, ready cut into lengths and made into bundles, or, if they were lucky, many a cottager grew his own small patch of wheat to supply his wife's needs. It was said that you could not beat garden-grown wheat for plaiting.

Women who bought their own material were free to sell their work as they wished, even if this meant walking many miles to market. When the trade increased and more agents and dealers moved into the market, they distributed the straw to the women as outworkers who then had no bargaining power over the amount they received from the dealers. Often they were obliged to take the amount they earned in goods from the village shop, whose owner was also the local plait agent.

The straw had first to be bleached, which was done by damping the cut lengths and placing them around the inside of an old tin or barrel, lowering a lump of lighted brimstone or sulphur in a cup into the middle, and then covering the container with a piece of sacking or cloth. Later, chemicals were employed instead of the brimstone or sulphur and a hydrogen peroxide process, still in use today, was invented.

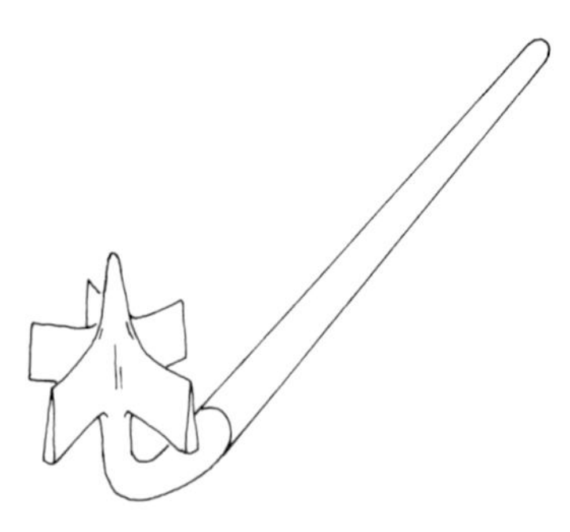

Fig 17 Straw splitter or 'engine' used to prepare straw for plaiting

After bleaching, the straws had to be split, at first done with a knife until the 'engine' or straw splitter was invented (Fig 17). This consisted of a sharp prong with blades radiating around it like spokes of a wheel. The number of steel or bone blades, from four to ten, depended upon the grade of straw and the fineness of the work for which it was needed. The prong was inserted into the pipe of the straw and then pressed between finger and thumb till the split straw fell away in narrow ribbons. This enabled the plaiters to make a greater variety of fancy plaits and greatly increased the demand. A plait dealer in 1810 said that the invention of the straw splitter increased the returns from straw plaiting by £3,000-£4,000 and that no employment for so many thousands had been discovered since the introduction of spinning by hand. At the same time the quality of the straw grown for plaiting was improved, helping the industry to compete with the fine straws formerly imported from Italy.

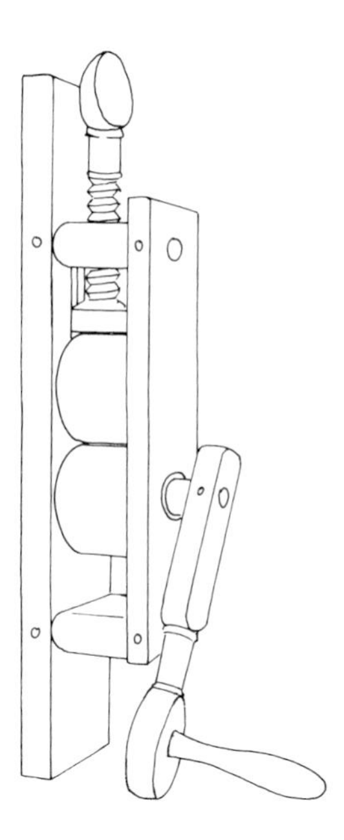

Fig 18 Splint mill used to flatten straw

Before the straws could be used for plaiting they were flattened, either with a rolling-pin or with a 'mill' (Fig 18), a job usually done by children. The mill consisted of a beechwood frame with two rollers, usually of boxwood, about 3in (76mm) in diameter, which revolved as the splints were passed through them, which could be fixed against a wall, the edge of a table, or screwed to the cottage door. The finished plaits were eventually put through a similar mill to flatten them again, but this had grooved rollers to take plaits of various width.

Most women could only plait in their spare time, but even so, they often earned more at their plaiting than their men did working on the land. Children could either learn the craft from members of their families or attend a straw-plaiting school held in the mornings, often in the small room of a cottage in the village, for which they paid 2d (1p) a week. There were sometimes as many as forty to sixty children in a room 10ft sq (3m sq) heated in winter by a pot full of charcoal as there was no room for a fire. The children could soon plait as many as 10yd (9m) of plain patterns in a morning. Most boys learned plaiting before eventually taking up farming and as adults they would plait as a second occupation when bad weather or a bad harvest forced them off the land. Some wove a four-straw plait called 'scollop' with whole straws and made it into field baskets which were narrow and deep, with handles fitting loosely into an overlapping lid. They wore these on their hips or hanging from a braid over their heads and shoulders as they worked in the fields.

All the patterns had names. The most popular was the Double Whipcord, made from seven straws double. There was Satin made with 9 straws, Short Cake with 11, and Diamond with 13. Brilliant, which fetched the best price and required the best straw, was made with up to 24 straws; it acquired its name from the way the light shone on the various facets of the straws in the more elaborate weave.

The moisture needed to make the work easier was usually applied to the straws before plaiting by drawing them over the tongue. As the straws were only 9-10in (228-254mm) long it was necessary to add new straws at regular intervals. This was done by leaving a small part of the heads and tails of the straws projecting from the plait, to be cut off later.

Although farmers profited from the sale of straw they viewed this cottage industry with displeasure, saying 'it made the poor saucy and averse to husbandry and caused a dearth of indoor servants and field labour'. In spite of the farmers' protests, however, the straw-plaiting industry flourished.

When hand-spinning came to an end in Wiltshire at the beginning of the nineteenth century women were reduced to picking stones and repairing roads, for which the parish paid them 1s 6d (7½p) to 3s (15p) a week. Parish councils were therefore prepared to employ instructors from London to teach women and children to plait to prevent them becoming a drain on the parish. After they had learned to plait, nearly a hundred women and children were earning from 3s (15p) to 10s (50p) weekly, selling their plait to a dealer in Bath.

Plaiting spread to many villages in this way, particularly in

Essex, Bedfordshire, Hertfordshire and Buckinghamshire, where the most suitable straw for plaiting was produced, but plaiters were also busy in East Anglia, Wiltshire, Hampshire and Dorset.

The industry survived longest in Essex and the south-east Midlands, the largest and longest established centre, whose products were also superior to those of other districts. In the 1870s, however, cheap plait from China was imported and the industry began to decline everywhere. At the same time machine-sewing for hats and bonnets was introduced and the home plaiters were unable to produce the increased supplies needed to satisfy the vast amounts consumed by the machines. After 1891 Japanese supplies of plait were also imported and the cottage industry collapsed. The British Straw Plait Association made an effort to revive it in 1896 without success. By the beginning of World War I there were still about sixty people making plait in the villages around Luton and some of them continued until the 1930s.

The Straw Hat Manufacturers' Association had been formed in Luton in 1852 to deal with the difficulties of short measures being given in plait. The plaiters who had no dealer usually sold to independent makers of bonnets, large numbers of whom worked in their own homes or in sewing-rooms in nearby towns or villages.

The dealers bought plait in large quantities for the hat manufacturers who employed several hundred women to sew the plait by hand into hats and bonnets in their workrooms, principally in Luton and Dunstable (Fig 19). Many factories employed as many workers at home as in the factory. The work was slow and tedious, tiny stitches being used to make the work as invisible as possible. Large sculleries were built on to houses for use in the process of stiffening and blocking the hats.

Originally, all the processes in hatmaking were done by hand. Towards the end of the nineteenth century sewing-machines were adopted for sewing the plaits and machine-blocking used to shape the hats and bonnets. The making of the wooden blocks on which the hats were modelled was an

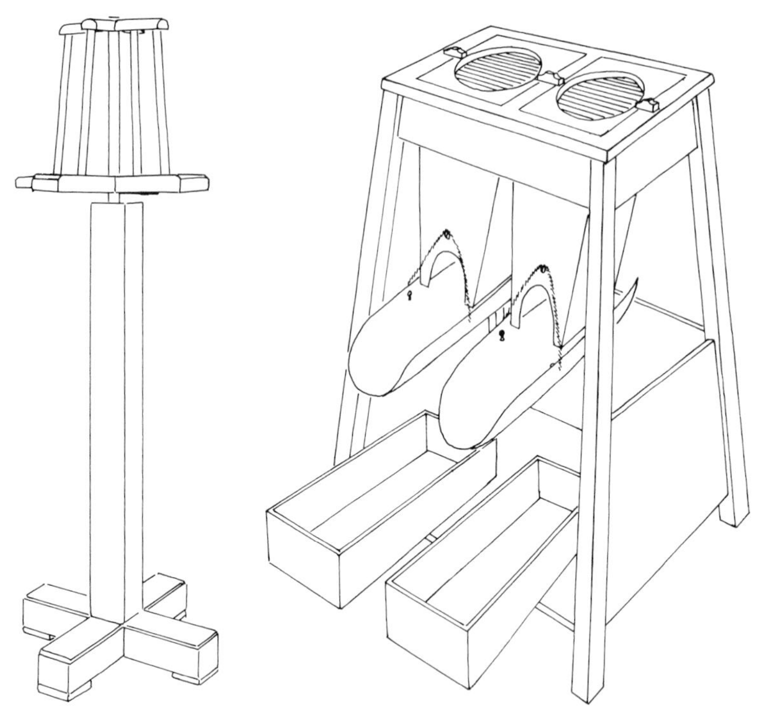

Fig 19 Nineteenth-century hatmakers wound the finished plait round a straw-plait winder while sewing the hats. These winders are still used today in the factories where straw and braid hats are made

Fig 20 Straw sorter made of wood

important and highly specialised subsidiary craft connected with the hat industry. They were usually made from alder or lime, wood that was able to stand the heat and moisture during continual use. Ribbons and decorative accessories for the hats gave work to many subsidiary firms. They also made straw sorters of wood (Fig 20). Wire sieves of various meshes could be fitted into the top of them, the straws were loosely jolted over the mesh and those of the required size fell into boxes below.

Hatmaking as a cottage industry continued until after 1920, with home workers still using treadle sewing-machines long after electric motors were in general use in factories. Many of these small factory businesses were successful. It was always

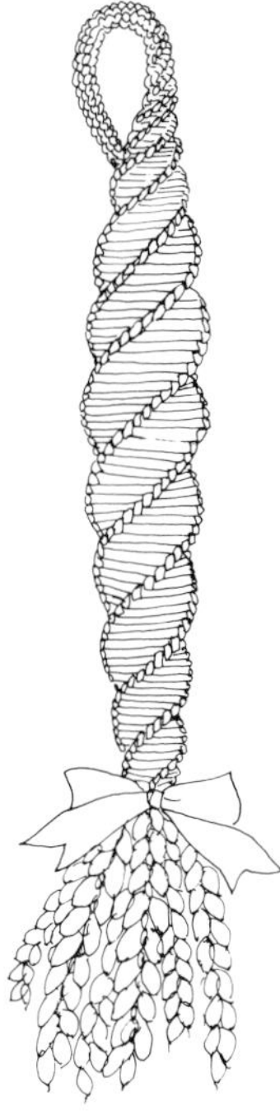

Fig 21 Corn dolly

possible to start such a manufacturing unit since little capital was involved and the machinery needed was not expensive.

During slack times the plaiters occupied themselves making straw flowers, toys and dolls. One aspect of straw weaving that has probably never completely gone out of fashion and is now having a revival as an absorbing leisure craft is the making of corn dollies, used for decoration in church at harvest festivals (Fig 21). Their origin is lost pre-history when the harvest was a matter of life and death to all, and everything was done to placate the Earth Goddess thought to rule over it. Until comparatively recent times it was the custom in certain parts of the country to leave some wheat standing in the fields uncut as it was believed that bad luck would fall on anyone who cut the last stalks.

Until the last century it was customary in Devon to plait a column of straw from the last row of wheat to form a thick pole-like dolly called the Nek. The dolly was placed in the middle of a circle of reapers, held with the ears of wheat uppermost, and each reaper in turn would bow to the centre and bend the ears of wheat to the ground to ensure that the spirit of the corn remained in the earth and would bring forth a successful crop the next year. The custom's roots lie in a primitive harvest ritual from Asia Minor, the birthplace of the grain harvest, called crying the Nek, which involved a human sacrifice in the middle of the last sheaves of corn.

When Christianity was well established in this country a religious significance was attached to corn dollies. In some districts it was believed that the devil was inside the dolly made from the last of the straw, so it was tossed away. For the most part, corn dollies are now associated with thanksgiving at harvest-time.

Each part of the country had its own form of corn dolly and its own name for it. It is known as the Neck in Devon and Cornwall, the Mares in the Midlands, the Hag and the Flag in Wales and the Harvest Queen and Kirn Maiden in Scotland and the North of England.

When farmworkers attended a local hiring fair in the autumn, where they offered themselves for new employment, it was customary for them to wear a small emblem made of barley straw to indicate their calling—whether they were cowmen, waggoners or labourers. These traditional and regional designs are being made today by home workers for sale, particularly at craft fairs.

Today, basketmaking is demonstrated at country fairs with the basketmakers' wares on sale as they were centuries ago. At one time there would have been a basketmaker in every village and it is difficult for us in this age of synthetic materials to realise the extent to which baskets were once used and the great variety that was made. Every trade had its own type of basket container: they were used for transporting everything, including coal, potatoes, fish, fruit, straw hats and woollen goods, and for collecting and trapping food. Eel traps and lobster pots were made in basketware (see Plate 15). At one time it was possible to identify a trade from the type of basket used, and the wares of a street-crier or tradesman in the same way.

Plate 15 Eddie Williams preparing withies to make a lobster pot at Aberdaron, Caernavonshire, in 1966. This is a traditional shape in use in the Llŷn peninsular, although lobster pots were made in various shapes around the coasts of Britain *(Welsh Folk Museum)*

Many items of basketry were found in the home: clothes-baskets; coal scuttles; chairs; cradles; bird cages for pet birds, and fowl cages to hold a fowl until it was needed for the pot. There were also baskets for storing and carrying plate and china, and cutlery trays.

On the farm, corn was sown from basket seedlips, there were riddles for separating chaff from grain, and a variety of sieves. Baskets were used as measures, made to specific sizes for vegetables in bushel and half-bushel measures. These usually had a handle at each side for lifting—one point in favour of baskets was that they were light to carry. Where sacks were used they were often filled with basket funnels. The traditional Welsh basket known as a gwyntell, a round, bowl-shaped basket, was used for potato picking and fodder carrying (see Plate 16). The rim was made of hazel or blackthorn, the 1in (25mm) wide laths were of hazel or willow, and the

Plate 16 David Lewis making the traditional Welsh basket known as a gwyntell, used for potato picking and fodder carrying *(Welsh Folk Museum)*

willow rods were closely woven in and out of them to make a basket that would hold the finest grain.

Osier beds for the growing of willows are mentioned in Bedfordshire in the twelfth century and this was one of many important areas for basketmaking and the growing of willows until the present century, although there were osier beds in any suitable low-lying area of Britain. The willows used today are grown chiefly in the low-lying areas around Sedgemoor in Somerset, always an important area. At Burrowbridge near Bridgwater, a family firm, W. Gadsby & Son, established in 1864, is still making baskets, from willows which they grow in nearby fields, for every purpose and in every shape and style imaginable. They also make basket furniture, including settees, tables and chairs, some in the traditional beehive-chair shape. Few basketmakers now use their own home-grown willows (many obtain them from this Somerset area), with the exception of those family firms who have the labour force to tend the willows. The young willows must be kept free from weeds for three years before the crop can be harvested. When a new plantation is required—which can take about 16,000 to 24,000 cuttings to an acre—14in (355mm) cuttings are planted in early spring. Each district has its own special varieties of willow, but the one most commonly grown commercially is the *Salix trianda* or Black Maul. It gives willow rods of about 6ft (1.8m) in length, but will grow to 10ft (3m) if longer rods are needed—for, say, the balloon baskets for hot-air ballooning, now increasingly in demand.

The willows are harvested from October onwards and are then dealt with according to the colour of the basket to be made. If it is to be white, then the willows must be peeled. They are stood in water until the spring when they begin to sprout roots and the sap rises; by about the second week of April they are ready to peel. At one time peeling, usually women's work, was done by pulling the willow through a break—two pieces of metal in the form of a narrow V-shape (see Plate 17). Now they are mechanically stripped by passing through a revolving drum.

If the bark is left on the baskets will be brown; if the characteristic red-brown colour is required the willows are boiled in a tank and the peeled—the tannin in the bark stains the rods which are known as buffs. When the basket industry was more widespread they were boiled in one of the many boiler houses with square brick chimneys that can be seen, now empty and no longer working, in the Somerset willow district. Willow peelers were paid by tokens for a certain number of prepared willows and exchanged the tokens for money at the end of the day.

The basketmaker sits on a low wooden platform called a plank, with his legs either side of a sloping platform or lapboard raised only a few inches off the ground which supports his basket in front of him. His tools consist of a beating

Plate 17 Willow stripping through a break—two pieces of metal in the form of a V-shape—at W. Gadsby & Son, Bridgwater, Somerset, in 1957 *(Museum of English Rural Life)*

iron to knock down the weave as it progresses, a bodkin, shears or secateurs, and a knife for trimming. He also requires blocks for shaping square baskets, hoops to drop over the upright stakes to keep them in position while the willows are woven in and out, a board to work on and a weight to put inside the basket to keep it in position in the early stages of its construction. Apart from self-employed basketmakers most basket firms today still use outworkers who make the baskets in their own homes; those that employ basketmakers in their factories do so on a piecework basis.

Traditional shapes continued to be made for uses that no longer existed—an oblong shape with a handle across the middle for carrying butter to market; an oval or round shape for carrying eggs; potato and grain baskets for use on the farm were rounded and deep with two small handles at the top at each side. Now, however, baskets are made by craftsmen for today's needs and include log baskets for wood-burning stoves, dog, cat and pigeon baskets, bicycle baskets, angling and picnic baskets, as well as industrial baskets of all kinds.

Rush and cane have always been used by basketmakers. Baskets made of thin splinters or laths of woven oak, known as spelk baskets, swills or spales, are still made in the Lake District. The industry was centred in the woods around Furness Fells for over 200 years, where straight oak poles about 6in (152mm) in diameter were split into pieces and boiled in water for several hours. When pliable they were split again. The swillmaker, sitting astride a 'horse', like the one used by most woodworkers, then shaved and thinned them again. A machine is now used to cut the laths to 1/16in (1.5mm) thickness and another to plane them smooth, processes formerly done by hand, thus saving much time in their preparation. The oval rims of the swills are made from hazel or ash withies, boiled to make them pliant when they are nailed into shape. The basket is then woven by hand from the oak laths. When well made they were said to be capable of holding water, but were actually used anywhere where a hard-wearing basket was needed—in farming, for carrying coal or refuse and on board ship. Thousands of these swills were exported every year from the Lake District, all sizes being made from 16in (40cm) to 36in (91cm) in length. Swillmakers are diminishing in number and there are few young people willing to learn the craft and take their place.

The Sussex trug basket gets its name from the Old English word 'trog' meaning boatlike. It has changed little since the day Thomas Smith the founder of the Herstmonceux firm of that name, walked 60 miles (96km) to London to deliver personally some of the first baskets to Queen Victoria. The handles and rims of the trug basket are made of sweet chestnut or ash, but instead of being woven the body of the basket is made of five to seven strips of shaped willow slats. The trugmaker prefers to select suitably shaped wood from locally grown willows. When cut the wood must be well seasoned to prevent shrinking or warping later.

Trugs have been made for 150 years in Sussex by firms at

East Hoathley and Herstmonceux. The willow strips are cut mechanically and then shaped and thinned with a draw-knife by the basketmaker who sits astride a wooden horse in the same way as the swillmaker. The craftsman thins the strips so they can bend, but must watch the grain of the wood so that he does not cut through it. The pieces are then steamed in an oven to make them pliant, after which they are nailed into position. Nailing starts at the bottom, the pieces slightly overlapping each other until the rim is reached, when the protruding ends are trimmed. The trug stands up on two pieces of willow nailed underneath. As many as twenty-three different styles of trug are made in all sizes, and, apart from their popularity with gardeners, they have a variety of uses on the farm and in the

Plate 18 Quarter-cran herring basket, from the Stanley Bird factory, was a recognised measure in the herring trade, each basket being officially stamped before use *(Museum of English Rural Life)*

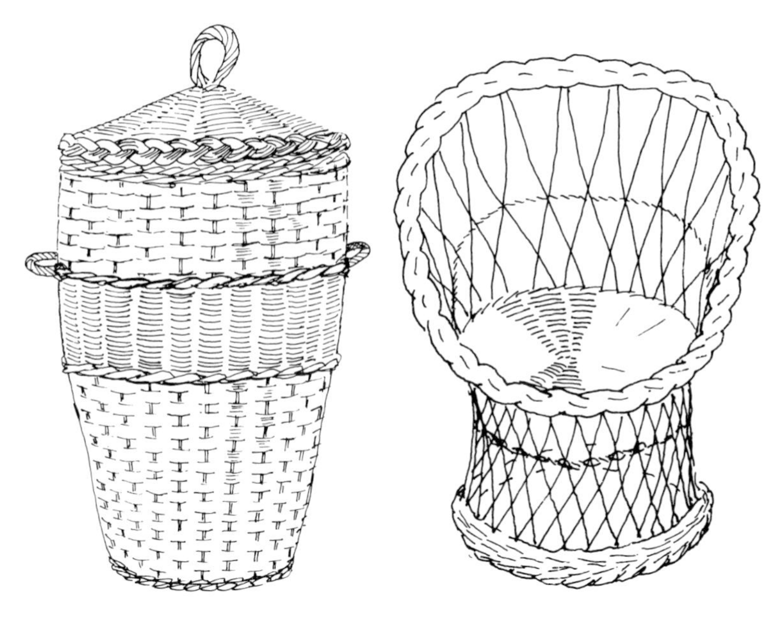

Fig 22 Linen basket

Fig 23 Garden chair

Fig 24 Two-bushel skep

Fig 25 Oval arm basket

home. Originally, trugmakers hawked their wares around the countryside, but today the trugs are sold at the firm's premises as well as in shops throughout the country.

At one time the making of fishing baskets formed a large part of the basketmaking industry. It is no coincidence that David Buck lives at Gorleston near Great Yarmouth, Norfolk, an area once famous for its fishing and basketmaking, and he recently won a prize for war pensioners for his fishing-tackle basket.

David Buck started basketmaking at the age of 15 when the fishing industry was still flourishing in Great Yarmouth and large quantities of quarter-crans and swills were being made (see Plate 18). Before going into the Army in 1953 he served a four-year apprenticeship with Stanley Bird of Great Yarmouth, then one of the largest basketmakers in the area whose company is still in business. He learned to make round, oval and square baskets in white, buff and brown willows, also the art of cane turning and framemaking for basket chairs. He learned how to cut, peel and sort the willows which he obtains from Somerset.

David Buck now makes baskets for many different uses, including cat carriers and dog baskets for any size of dog: he recently made one for an Afghan hound with arthritis of the legs. He makes cradles with carrying handles, linen baskets (Fig 22), picnic baskets, garden chairs (including the shape shown in Fig 23 which was sprayed with white enamel paint), and cutlery trays. He makes any type of basket or canework to order, and recently made a bed-head with a canopy above which was made to screw to the wall.

While traditional basket shapes are still made, including the two bushel skep (Fig 24) and the oval arm basket (Fig 25) in which the farmers' wives used to carry their eggs to market, many of these are now used for different purposes; the oval basket, for instance, is useful to flower arrangers for collecting cut flowers, and more fishing-tackle baskets are needed by fishermen for sport than traditional fishing baskets by the professionals. Undoubtedly, the basketmaker always has a ready market for his wares.

7

ROPES AND NETS

The county of Dorset seems to encourage cottage industries old and new. Bridport has long been famous for its rope- and netmaking industry which utilised the hemp and flax growing extensively in the area until about a hundred years ago, and a cottage industry still flourishes there today (see Plate 19). Bridport, one of four Saxon boroughs of Dorset, with its own mint for making coins, was already an important commercial centre over a thousand years ago. As early as 1213 King John ordered the cordage-makers there to work night and day to make ropes for the Navy. This work still goes on today at the firm of Bridport-Gundry Ltd, the largest firm of rope- and netmakers in Europe, which supplies nets and lines to the fishing fleets of the world.

When the Spanish Armada threatened the English coast Elizabeth I ordered that all the Bridport hemp grown within 5 miles (8km) of the town was to be reserved for the making of nets and ropes for the Royal Navy.

Ropemaking was an important craft in medieval times, controlled by one of the earliest craft guilds. Apprentices were indentured at the age of 7 and learned their trade in the long alleys behind the streets of Bridport and on the pavements of its roads, built especially wide for the ropewalks, up to 80ft (24m) in length, where the fibre was stretched and twisted. Such 'ropewalks', 'rope lanes' and 'rope yards' are still found so named in many towns today, evidence of the occupation formerly carried on in them.

Nets and ropes for uses other than the fishing industry have always been made and still are today. There are early records at Bridport of orders for horse-hay nets, rabbit nets and nets to

Plate 19 Mrs Olive Legg making nets at Loders *(Bridport Museum)*

keep thatch on houses—evidence of the many agricultural and horticultural uses still needed today, extending to the large nets for the growing number of vineyards now being planted in England. Nets are made for all manner of sporting activities, too. The rope so often in use in medieval times for the hangman's noose, known as the 'Bridport Dagger' in Elizabethan times, is no longer required; the hemp used in its making was known as gallows grass or neck weed.

While ropemaking in its early days was done by hand it was largely done outdoors by the men and boys. The women and children of all ages were principally involved in making nets or 'braiding' in their own homes.

Samuel Gundry, whose name continues in the Bridport Gundry firm today, was a netmaker who started up his business in 1665. Soon others followed his example, expanding outside their immediate families to become small merchants with enough money to buy the raw materials and distribute them to outside twine- and netmakers and collect the finished work for sale to their customers.

By the eighteenth century the first complicated netmaking machinery to cope with the amount of nets and ropes needed by the ships of the ever-expanding British Empire was devised at Bridport. A good twine- or netmaker would buy one of these machines when he could afford it, then be able to pay others to help him, and later to buy more machines. In this way the first factories were set up. Eventually, the most successful names among the net- and ropemakers of Bridport—Gundry, Hounsell, Rendall and Coombs, Edwards, Tucker, Gale and James—many of whom had specialised in particular branches of the trade, gradually amalgamated after World War II and today exist in the firm of Bridport-Gundry Ltd with branches, depots and warehouses all over the country, as well as two distributing organisations in Canada.

In the last hundred years home-grown hemp and flax has given way to imported hemp and cotton, home-grown flax being more often grown for its seed and used for making linseed oil and cattle food. Today, artificial fibres have largely superseded many of the natural fibres because of their greater durability.

Although most of today's netting is made by machine, nets have always been required for which no machine exists to make them. These have always been made by hand in the homes of the networks in and around Bridport in twenty or so Dorset villages. Only simple tools are required: a thin gauge is used equal in width to the size of the mesh required and a netting-needle. Many netmakers use their fingers as a guide to the size of mesh to be worked instead of a piece of wood. Bridport-Gundry still has a hundred or so skilled outworkers and up to a hundred more who can be called on to deal with any special order. Loders is one of the villages where netmakers lived (see Plate 20). The children would take their turn at braiding when they came home from school and in many villages almost everyone, male or female, learned to braid at an early age.

Plate 20 Netmakers at Loders, Dorset, working outside *(Bridport Museum)*

In North Yorkshire ropemaking methods have remained unchanged for the past 200 years. W. R. Outhwaite & Son are a firm of ropemakers at Hawes. When Mr W. R. Outhwaite took over the business in 1905 it was situated at the Gatehouse outside Hawes, but it is now carried on at Town Foot in Hawes. Since 1975, when his son retired, the business has been owned by Dr Peter Annison. The traditional ropemaking methods used there today have changed little over the years. The installation of an electric motor in 1952 to power the twisting machine has not changed the process, simply speeded it up. Today, most of the ropes made at Outhwaite's use natural fibres, with a limited amount of nylon for clothes-lines and polypropylene for rope ladders and animal ties. Most of the company's products are used for agricultural purposes.

The tougher fibres are sisal and the softer ones cotton and

hemp. Mercerised cotton is used to make coloured pony halters, leading reins and stair ropes. High quality Egyptian cotton is used for rope which must be especially soft for halters for young animals and calving ropes. (Cow-horn is still used for parting the strands when ropes are made into halters and cow bands.) Halters for cattle and horses are sold principally in the spring and summer and cowbands for tethering cows have the greatest sale in winter-time. Tapered plough lines, plaited cow ties, leading reins, waggon ropes, bacon twine, rabbit snares, tow ropes and dog leads, are all in demand. Outhwaite's welcomes visitors to their rural workshop where many of the craft items made from their rope and twine are on sale.

The growing local interest in making items with decorative knots, particularly the art of macramé by which small hangings for pot plants are made, has helped to keep their rope business in production. On the other hand, Albert Kirby of Hayling Island, Hampshire, a self-taught craftsman and designer in ropework, is making a name for himself constructing large rope hangings, all more than 4ft (1.2m) in length and made of rope over ¼in (6mm) thick. These creations are specially commissioned and designed by Albert himself to fit into the particular decor of homes, hotels, hospitals and offices all over the United Kingdom—in fact, anywhere where a large hanging can be seen at its best. His work has been exported to France, Denmark and Belgium.

He prefers to use natural fibres, especially sisal rope, that can be knotted tightly so that the knots do not slip. About 3,000 different knots can be used and every hanging is unique; a pattern is never repeated unless identical pieces are requested for one situation. He also makes ornate hand-rails for staircases; boat fenders; rope ladders, and garden hammocks, including an ornate double hammock 14ft long and 5ft wide (see Plate 21). One of his ambitions is to make a ropework creation for a church where the length of the hanging would have no limit.

The tools Albert Kirby uses are a fid (a wooden pin used as a splicing tool), a marlin spike, a serving mallet, needles and a sailmaker's palm. He prefers the old tools he has acquired in

Plate 21 Hanging table made by Albert Kirby of Hayling Island, Hampshire. He used about 481yd (440m) of rope, all of which had to be knotted

preference to modern versions. His tools were used in the past for making the rigging of ships, and he himself would like to expand into the maritime side of ropework. The year 1982 was designated Maritime Year and at the exhibition held by the British Tourist Authority to launch it at the Guildhall in London, Albert Kirby was asked to set up a display of his ropework—British maritime craftsmanship at its best.

8

COUNTRY POTTERS

Pottery-making is one of the oldest industries and has been a vital aid to archaeologists and historians in the identification of peoples, places and dates of the distant past. Pottery can tell its own history and something of the people who made it. Every age has revealed some of its characteristics in the pottery it produced for, while most of the techniques of pottery-making have changed little since prehistoric times, the way in which the potters have expressed themselves in the decoration and shapes has changed with the desires of their customers.

Pottery-making today is one of the most widespread crafts practised by both amateurs and professionals, individuals and small potteries, producing pottery ranging from the purely functional to works of high repute by artist-potters in their studios. The popularity of the craft probably stems from the special ability of the clay—more so than any other material used by craftsmen—to lend itself to all types of creative expression at the hands of the potter. Today, when so much work is void of self-expression, pottery-making is very satisfying.

Archaeologists now have the scientific means to trace the origins of the material from which a piece of pottery was made. It is not even necessary to have a complete pot to date and identify the pottery of a particular region; a broken sherd is often enough for an archaeologist to see a distinctive decoration or shape and identify the people who made it. Identification of a pot's origins is not always straightforward for while centuries ago no potter would go far afield to find the material to make his pots—clay being a heavy material to transport—the pots themselves often travelled extensively.

The importance of the identification of pottery can be seen by the naming of the Bronze Age people who came to England from Europe in about 1800BC, bringing with them their knowledge of metalworking. They are known as the Beaker-people owing to the drinking vessels of beaker shape which they made and which were also found in the countries from which they came. From these beakers it was possible to trace their migration from Europe to the places in which they settled in Britain. As no potters in the past wasted time in making vessels that were not a necessity, we can assume that the Beaker-people were heavy drinkers, and as they also arrived in this country complete with bronze daggers and battle axes we can also imagine how they worked up their thirst. Now potters are busy making beakers for today's coffee-drinkers who prefer them to the cups and saucers which were made for the growing number of tea-drinkers of the eighteenth century. Clay has always been an adaptable medium in which potters could satisfy the needs of their customers.

When man first discovered that clay, formed into shapes when wet and baked hard in the Middle East sun, could be used as containers, he made pots primarily for the use of his own family. It is obvious from the styles and decoration of prehistoric pottery, however, that before long one man or group made the pottery for the whole village or district—the local potter was born.

The earliest known pottery, dating from about 6000BC, comes from Catal Hüyük in Turkey. Before this, clay had been used to build homes and ovens for baking bread (such ovens were still in use in Britain in the present century) and as a lining for storage baskets. Perhaps it was discovered that a satisfactory container could be made without the basketwork when such a basket was accidentally burned, leaving the clay lining baked hard. Many early pots resemble the shapes and decorations of containers which had formerly been made in basketry and leather, more suitable for use by nomadic tribes; pottery, however, is the material used by a settled community.

A considerable period of trial and error must have elapsed before usable pots could be baked to the stage where many of

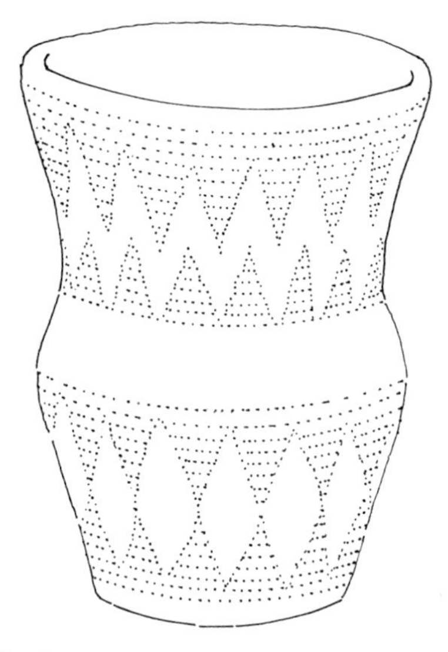

Fig 26 Bronze Age beaker, c 1600 BC

them have lasted until the present day. The earlier potters built up their pots in spiral coils, strips or rings, scraped them smooth and perhaps decorated them with incised patterns made with a variety of objects from a comb to the potter's nail or thumb. The very large pots used for storage were built up in this way. The Bronze Age beaker illustrated in Fig 26, found in Somerset, is 7in (177mm,) high and dated about 1600BC and has a characteristic geometric ornament made with a toothed comb. These potters were skilled in firing in some form of kiln with a forced draught, a technique they also needed for smelting the metals they used. They also moulded clay over a stone or other object to give it shape. Both these methods are used by potters today. A thin layer of liquid clay or 'slip' was sometimes applied to give a smoother effect. This is still used today and consists of clay mixed to a smooth cream with water. The potters learned over the centuries that the clay changed colour when fired, according to the temperature of the kiln in which it was baked, the type of clay used, the other minerals added to the clay when it was mixed and the atmosphere produced in the kiln; if this was oxidizing it produced a red pot, or if it was rich in carbon monoxide, which was a reducing atmosphere, black pottery was produced.

All the early pottery—in fact, most of the pottery made by country potters for centuries—is known as earthenware. This is fired in a kiln between 700°C and 1200°C and is porous until a glaze is applied and the pottery given a second firing. The first firing brings the pot to a state known as the biscuit stage—it is hard enough to be handled and decorated. Then it can be painted or glazed. The glaze comprises a variety of finely powdered minerals which are fused when the second firing takes place, giving a glass-like finish. While less fuel is needed for firing earthenware, the potter is also able to use a greater range of bright colours derived from oxides which cannot be used at the temperatures needed to make the harder non-porous stoneware. Metal oxides are added to glazes to colour them. Earthenware covered with a glaze containing tin oxide was known by several names—majolica, faience and delft. This was the type of pottery most widely made until the seventeenth century.

An important discovery in the history of pottery-making was the use of the potter's wheel, a revolving disc on to which the clay is 'thrown' and then shaped by the potter's hands as it revolves. The earliest surviving example of a potter's wheel in the Middle East is dated 3250BC. The making of wheel-thrown pottery spread from there all over Europe, reaching Britain with the arrival of the Celts in the last centuries BC.

The earliest pottery found in Britain comes from Windmill Hill near Avebury, Wiltshire, and is dated about 2500BC. This hill is thought to have been a place of tribal assembly, perhaps for religious purposes and also for the buying and selling of goods and animals—a fair or marketplace in fact.

The methods and equipment used have changed little over thousands of years, except that kilns have become more efficient and can be heated by electricity, gas and oil, although some potters still prefer to use wood. All modern kilns give potters greater control over the temperature of the kiln than they had in the past. They can also power their wheel by electricity, although again, many potters prefer the treadle-operated wheel which they feel gives them more control over their work. They are no longer confined, however, to the use of clay from their own region, and the styles and decoration are more likely to be those of a particular potter and not a particular place. Now they experiment with designs from all over the world, and many mixtures of prepared clay powder and glazes are obtainable from pottery suppliers to cater for all their needs, whatever the type of pottery made and whatever the kiln used.

As early as the fourth century BC pottery-making was already in the hands of merchants who supplied the cooking vessels for an area, as well as better quality tableware. Production soon came to be centred in areas of good clay and where there was an ample supply of water, and wood for firing the kilns.

The Iron Age Celts were skilled craftsmen who produced beautifully decorated wheel-thrown pottery, particularly in the southern half of Britain, before the Romans arrived here. They made great pots for the storage of food, as well as funeral urns for the ashes of their dead. The native craftsmen continued this work after the Roman invasion, gradually introducing their wares to supply the more sophisticated requirements of the Roman home. The main centres of production were around Castor in Northamptonshire, in the New Forest area of Hampshire, Colchester in Essex, Warwickshire and Yorkshire. Pottery from these areas has been found distributed over a wide area of Britain, much of it stamped with the individual marks of the potters who made it about 1,800 years ago.

Castor ware was often decorated with a slip decoration on a dark lustrous surface (Fig 27). In this process clay was squeezed through a nozzle to form a pattern in relief, much as one would ice a cake. These patterns took native Celtic forms with animals, leaves and scrolls. Pottery is still decorated with slip in this way today; it is the most traditional method of pottery decoration in Britain, which reached the peak of craftsmanship in the seventeenth and eighteenth centuries. Many types of slip-trailers for applying the patterns have been

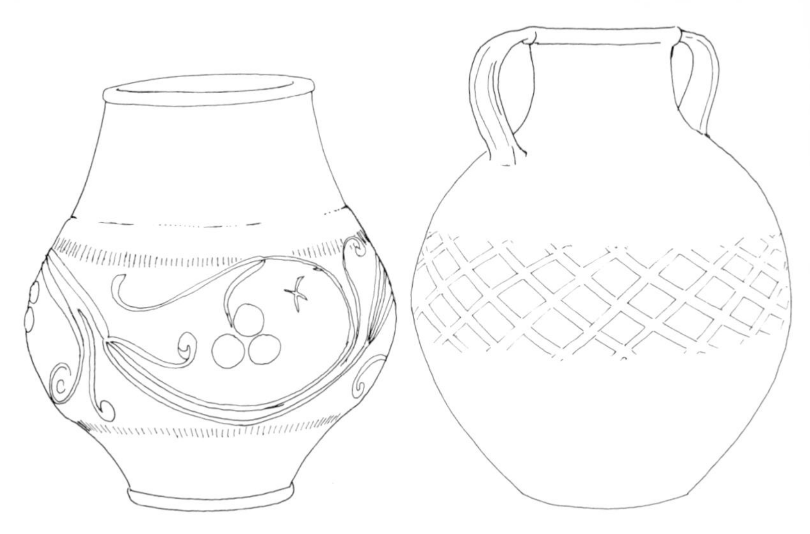

Fig 27 Castorware beaker of the second century AD

Fig 28 New Forest Roman storage jar. It was found buried with 7,717 coins at Rockbourne Roman villa, Fordingbridge

used: sometimes a type of baby's feeding-bottle with a reed at one end, the potter blowing gently into the other end to control the flow of liquid clay; sometimes a cake-icing set, a cow's horn or a tin pierced with a goose quill. Today, slip-trailers can be bought made of rubber or plastic.

At first the Romans imported a great deal of pottery, both coarse ware for cooking purposes and the highly decorated red Samian ware, which came from France, for tableware. By the second century AD the Romano-British potters were themselves dealing with the increased requirements, as the increase in the number of the remains found in kilns of that date reveal. They were making cheese presses, wine flagons, and dishes in all shapes and sizes, including matching sets of graded pie-dishes. By the fourth century they were producing copies of the red Samian ware which had formerly been imported. The New Forest potteries produced this type of pottery as well as cooking dishes and pots, beakers, bottles, and flasks with a dark metallic surface and white painted ornament (see also Fig

28). These potters built themselves simple kilns in the forest. The kilns of the Castor potters, on the other hand, were built to take 500 or 600 items at a time.

The New Forest potters worked in family groups and moved about the forest as they used up an area of firewood. There are still potters in this area today, and one family work at the Burley Pottery in traditional ways. They make hand-thrown pottery on a treadle-operated wheel, a type well known in medieval times, and fire the pottery in gas and electric kilns they have built themselves, but modern technology is used for maximum efficiency. Their stoneware pottery is baked at 1280°C to achieve the non-porous hardwearing pottery expected today. Their clay, a type that will bake at such high temperatures, comes from suppliers in Staffordshire.

Their workshop and showroom, found in the village of Burley, near Ringwood, Dorset, are combined (see Plate 22). Here they make a large variety of wares, some traditional for domestic use, some with modern designs for decorative purposes. They make pottery models of country cottages and pottery sculptures of ponies and their riders. The most popular of their pony sculptures is that of John Willie, the aged pony belonging to the owner of the saddlery next door to their pottery.

At another part of the forest at Verwood in Dorset there is evidence that the local clay was in use for at least 400 years from before 1600, and maybe much earlier. A community of potters was established on the edge of the nearby heathland at Alderholt by the early fourteenth century, where they would have found adequate supplies of wood, water from the many springs and streams in the area, and suitable clay from the deposits in a belt that ran from Fordingbridge to Wimborne, clay that had been used by the New Forest potters of Roman times. This clay is still used by potters in the area, mixed in a baker's dough mixer, a mechanical aid popular with potters today, with prepared clay powder obtained from commercial suppliers.

By the seventeenth and eighteenth centuries there were

thirty or more kilns in the Verwood area and a large proportion of the people, mainly in family groups, were employed in this local industry. Small potteries were operated in one family for several generations, often a wife continuing to run a pottery after the death of her husband.

The potters cut the clay from the ground in blocks and were supposed to refill the clay-pits afterwards so that animals or people did not fall into them. The clay was mixed with water in a shallow pit to make it soft, which took about three days. After this it was evenly trodden by foot or 'wedged' on a brick floor sprinkled with sand, and then rolled up. This process was repeated three times and eventually gave an even mixture of ten parts clay to one part sand. After a final mixing by hand, it was cut up into the required sizes for the various items to be made. The wedging process is still done today, usually by hand, and is the most energetic part of pottery-making. The clay, cut into large pieces, is kneaded, turned and banged, perhaps a hundred times, to remove air and lumps.

In many small potteries around the country the clay was broken up in a horse-driven pug-mill. The horse, fastened to a shaft, was led in circles by a boy to work a large coopered churn which had revolving knives inside to break up the clay. Later potteries had mills driven by electricity, but in the Verwood district the practice of wedging with the feet was continued into the twentieth century.

In the nineteenth century boys also helped to turn the wheels on to which the pots were thrown by working a pole attached to a crank.

Susan Blair has been making stoneware pottery with her husband Alex at the Stornoway Pottery at Borve on the Isle of Lewis since 1974 (see Plate 23). Their pottery is made from an iron-bearing grogged clay body producing an improved pot when fired in their electric kiln at 1280°C, which gives an oxidised atmosphere. The capacity of their kiln is 18 cu ft (0.51m^3). Most of the larger pots, such as cider jars, large bowls and plates, tall vases and lamp bases, are made by Alex. The tools hanging on the rails are turning and modelling tools, some made of plastic or boxwood, and some a loop of wire set

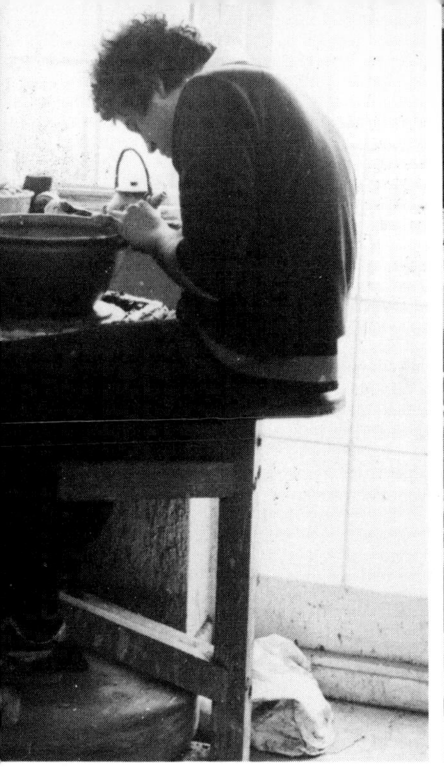

Plate 22 Simon Crowther of the Burley Pottery in the New Forest, where traditional ways are still followed

Plate 23 Susan Blair turns a pot on a modern electric wheel set in a shallow tray which catches any waste clay and water spillage. The extended adjustable pipe helps her to produce pots of equal height; callipers help to measure and produce pots of equal diameter *(Keith Barnes)*

in a handle, which are obtained from pottery suppliers. The wire hanging over the pipe with a handle at each end, like a cheese-cutter, is used to cut under the pot to remove it from the wheel.

Most of the pots produced in the Verwood area were undecorated, although some had simple incised lines or finger-impressed bands. The technique of rouletting, used since Roman times, was first introduced at Verwood in the eighteenth century. One method of producing the continuous pattern was to hold a type of pastry wheel made out of old clock parts mounted on a handle against the pot as it rotated on the wheel. Roulettes are usually made of wood or cast in plaster of paris from clay models in the shape of a small roller, which is run round the pot.

Some of the nineteenth-century pottery at Verwood is inscribed by the potters, but these were probably pieces made especially for their families and not for general distribution. Most of the work of country potters went unnamed.

The method of pressing the clay into or over a mould was used to produce the flattish pans and saucers. This method is used where a number of articles of the same shape or size are required, in which case all the decisions as to the shape are made beforehand when the moulds are being made and not when the clay is being handled.

After turning, all pots are left in a warm place until they become what is known as 'leather hard'. At this stage a foot can be turned at the base of a bowl or a handle added if required. The base of the pots can be trimmed with a knife. Before they are fired in the kiln all pots must be well dried as any water left in the clay might expand in the kiln and cause damage to the pot and those around it. At Verwood the drying on sanded boards was done out of doors in the summer-time and indoors in sheds, which were kept warm day and night by peat fires, in the winter-time.

From about the seventeenth century onwards, the potters collected scrap lead which was heated until it became a grey powder to make the lead glaze used on the pots. Most glazes used today are leadless because of the dangers of lead poisoning, but lead glaze was extensively used in medieval times, giving the domestic pottery of the Middle Ages its characteristic golden colour. The use of this lead powder was forbidden after World War I and commercially produced powdered galena or lead sulphide was used at Verwood instead. This produced a finished glaze which varied from apple green to yellow or orange. These variations were caused by the clay used, impurities in the lead and the temperature of the kiln. When copper was added to the lead a green glaze was produced; when iron was added the glaze was brown and the brown pots thus produced were known as Wiltshire Brown Ware, although made in this part of Dorset.

The brick kilns at Verwood, which were wood-fired, were loaded from above, the potter himself doing the important job of stacking the pots as they were handed to him. It was necessary to stack the glazed pottery particularly carefully so that the pots did not touch each other and spoil the glaze. Pots were only fired once at Verwood, the temperature of the kiln being a matter of experience and judgement, but it never exceeded 1000°C. About seven firings a year would have been normal. The kiln would be left to cool down for two days and it would then take two days to unload it. Some kilns held as many as 2,000 pots.

The Verwood potteries provided all the pottery needed in the seventeenth- and eighteenth-century homes of their locality, whether it was for kitchen, dairy or brewhouse, and it was tailored to their customers' requirements.

The pottery wares were packed in heather, bracken and straw and taken round by hawkers, potmen or cratemen who had bought it from the potters, to farms, estates, and eventually shops, within an area of about 40 miles (64km) around the potteries. In medieval times the pottery would have been taken around the countryside by packhorse, just as it had been in Roman times, and later larger quantities would have been distributed by horse and waggon.

The Verwood potteries survived into the early years of the twentieth century. It is doubtful whether any of the potters were rich, and those that appeared better off than others were probably combining their pottery-making with farming. Many of the cottages associated with a kiln and workshop had gardens and a small plot of land which would have supplied food for the family, particularly when times were hard. It is possible that some potteries operated only during warm weather since cold temperatures are harmful to pottery and so much of the work was done outside or in primitive buildings.

The last pottery in Verwood closed in 1952, beaten by increased competition from mass-produced methods. There has been a revival in pottery-making in the area, however, with the increasing number of people, including tourists, who appreciate the original designs of handmade products.

There have always been these ups and downs in the pottery trade. The earliest potteries at Verwood no doubt produced a much more restricted variety of pots than had been produced in Roman times. Most drinking vessels in the Middle Ages were made of wood and the medieval cooper supplied the village with its equipment for the dairy and kitchen. Pottery was restricted to simple jugs, pitchers, cooking pots and bowls, lamps, mortars for pounding or grinding food or medicines, and curfews for covering fires at night.

From Tudor times until the end of the seventeenth century some Surrey potters made a wider range of green glazed pottery, known as Tudor Greenwares, from the white clays of West Surrey. Their range included cups, jugs and chafing dishes for tableware. The latter were shallow bowls on pedestal bases, with knobs around the rim. When in use they were filled with hot charcoal and placed beneath a second bowl (that rested on the knobs) containing food that needed to be kept warm. This pottery had a French influence, but by the seventeenth century pottery was largely influenced by the Dutch who fled to this country to escape religious persecution. They were used to a larger variety of domestic pottery, much of it decorated slipware, which became the most popular pottery of the seventeenth and eighteenth centuries. The Dutch introduced delftware with its blue painted decorations to this country. Bristol and Liverpool both became important centres for the production of this type of pottery, although English delftware was not always blue. Metal oxides were painted on the glaze before firing to give a variety of colours: cobalt was used for blue, copper for green, manganese for a browny mauve and antimoniate of lead for yellow.

Pottery-making in factories began at this time, particularly in such areas where there were the advantages of a good range of clays, coal for the kilns and good trade routes for the distribution of their wares. Industry in the Midlands was developing rapidly so there was a growing market to supply.

Delftware chipped easily and was not suitable for the continual washing up that was necessary when tea drinking became popular in the eighteenth century. The potters then used new materials to make the porcelain, such as ground calcined flint, Cornish China Clay, and China-stone which had formerly been imported from China and from which the aristocracy first drank their tea. By the eighteenth century pottery factories were producing high-quality wares in such quantities that no single potter working on his own could compete.

Many eighteenth century potters, however, who gave their names to some of the most famous pottery, still well known today, started as individual potters in a small way. Josiah Wedgwood was one who, at 29, was making pottery on his own in a thatched cottage in Newcastle. When he died at the end of the eighteenth century he was worth £½ million and had founded one of the first model factories. His creamware became famous and put well-made pottery within the means of the ordinary housewife. It became known as 'Queen's Ware' after Queen Charlotte, wife of George III, accepted a gift of it. He then made a set of 986 pieces for Catherine of Russia, each piece decorated with a different view of Britain, for which he was paid £3,500. He also made Jasperware, stoneware fired to a high temperature and still made by Wedgwood today using the eighteenth-century designs.

Many small potteries, particularly those furthest from the Midlands in the South and West, did survive and even flourish in the eighteenth and nineteenth centuries, producing many of the domestic items formerly supplied by the village cooper. They also made many small items formerly made in wood, such as chicken feeders, beetle traps, tea caddies, candle holders and butter dishes, as life became more prosperous and the articles demanded by the housewife became more numerous. A large number of items were also made for farming and horticultural needs. Flowerpots, both plain and highly decorated, were produced as houseplants became popular. Frederick Mitchell's pottery at Rye in Sussex made some of the most interesting. Pressed from moulds decorated with flowers, leaves and birds, the clay was stained with coloured metallic oxides. This pottery continued in production until 1920.

Plate 24 Pottery kiln at Ewenny, near Bridgend, in 1893, It was demolished in 1920 *(Welsh Folk Museum)*

Kitchen and table wares were well made and all well designed. No local potter wanted to hear complaints from the customers in the village around him, which would soon have been forthcoming if his wares were not satisafactory.

Some of the more important of the small potteries around the country were at Barnstaple in Devon, Poole in Dorset, Hailsham in Sussex, and Weathriggs in Cumberland. Each produced the requirements for a local area as far as the local clay was suitable. Later, where coal for fuelling kilns was available locally, small potteries as well as factories grew up around the coal areas.

One such area was Ewenny, near Bridgend, where in the last century there were at least seven small potteries in production which sold their wares in the local markets. The Jenkins family have operated a pottery at Ewenny from the sixteenth century until today (see Plate 24). Potteries may have existed at Ewenny from an even earlier date as a fifteenth-century document refers to the area as 'pottersland'. This pottery was at the height of production in the late eighteenth and early nineteenth centuries, when glazed slipware, including pitchers, jugs, ornamental bowls, vases, puzzle-jugs and wassail bowls, were made. These were first emersed in a thin liquid slip and allowed to dry, and then emersed in the glaze to render the pottery non-porous. At Ewenny the glaze was prepared from manganese. Wassail bowls were highly decorated and were used in folk ceremonies throughout the year. Large quantities of these were produced in small potteries in the eighteenth and nineteenth centuries. One such lidded bowl from Ewenny was heavily decorated with incised zig-zags, floral and geometrical patterns and applied figures of animals and birds and had eighteen handles around the bowl. It was probably used in Twelfth Night or New Year ceremonies.

Today Alun Jenkins and his wife run the Ewenny Pottery, producing glazed earthenware, handthrown and decorated in the same way as that used by Alun's grandfather. The pottery is sold direct to tourists, the wares being mostly small kitchen items and souvenirs. The larger domestic and agricultural wares have disappeared, along with the old coal-fired kilns, which were dismantled and moved to the Welsh Folk Museum at St Fagans, Cardiff. The old pottery building was closed and a new workshop and showroom built nearby. Modern electric kilns are now in use and all raw materials are obtained from suppliers based at Stoke-on-Trent as the local clay originally used has been exhausted.

Wassail cups were also made in North Devon at Fremington where the pottery run by the Fishley family produced some of the best nineteenth-century earthenware country pottery. The grandfather George Fishley who died in 1865 was one of the few potters producing well-made original figures of people and animals. He and his sons and grandsons produced many fine pieces in solid clay with applied decoration. In Devon and Somerset as well as in Sussex it was common practice to wassail the orchards, drinking to the trees with festive songs to encourage a good apple crop. It was from these wassail cups that cider and ale with roasted apples, sugar, nutmeg and toast was drunk at these midwinter ceremonies. The two-handled cups from the Fremington potteries are about 9in (228mm) high, round in shape with a lid and a spout at the front from which the beverage could be sucked. Applied figures decorated the cup and often another figure sat on the lid, with a verse cut into the white slip which had been applied to the lid. Today the Litchdon Potteries at Fremington make clay flowerpots and garden and domestic ware from the local clay.

Harvest-time was another season when the country potter provided a multitude of earthenware vessels to contain the liquid which quenched the thirst of busy harvesters and to celebrate the harvest safely gathered in. These were well-designed harvest jugs, flasks or costrels, which had been in use since medieval times for such purposes (Fig 29). Costrels were also used by travellers for carrying refreshment as they could be fastened to the belt or carried over the shoulder.

The Verwood potteries produced yellow-glazed harvest bottles or costrels which were dipped into the glaze halfway up the pot (Fig 30). They were known as Dorset pills (from their round shape) or sometimes Dorset owls (from the owl-like appearance given by the two scalloped lugs, pierced so that they could be suspended by a cord). These were widely used in the vast agricultural areas of Dorset, Hampshire and Wiltshire

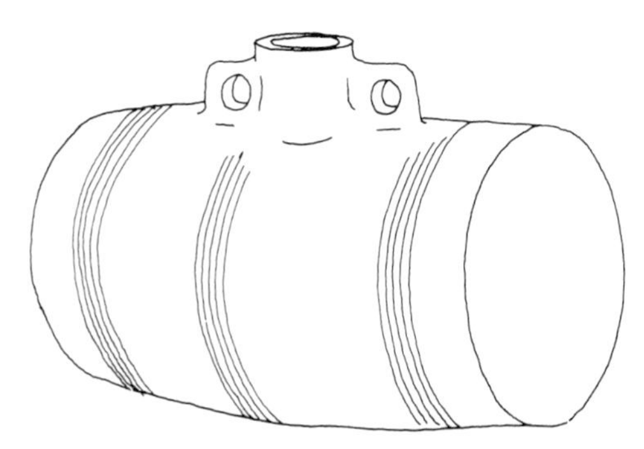

Fig 29 Medieval costrel found at Cardiff Castle. Measuring about 8in (203mm) it imitates a wooden barrel bound with willow twigs

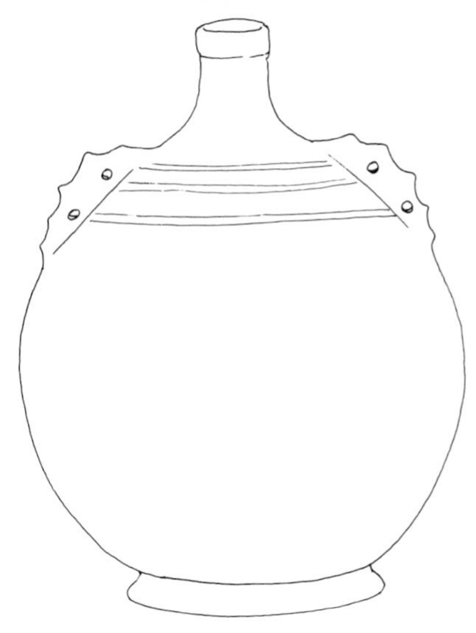

Fig 30 A costrel (also known as a Dorset owl or pill) made at one of the Verwood potteries. They were still being made as recently as the early 1950s

in the nineteenth century and were still being made by traditional methods, along with plain harvest jugs, until the early 1950s.

In Sussex harvest kegs or flasks were made at Brede and spirit flasks at Lower Dicker and Herstmonceaux; these were in the shape of a large pocket-watch, with pierced holes to take a suspension cord. Both of the circular convex sides were decorated, some with fine inlaid work and others with the names of potter and recipient, and rhymes extolling the virtues of the contents.

The harvest jugs made by potters in North Devon in the late seventeenth, eighteenth and nineteenth centuries are some of the most highly decorated. The red earthenware of Devon was covered with a white slip on which elaborate animal, plant and figure designs were etched, as well as inscriptions and rhymes. The custom of 'crying the neck' at harvest-time—the ceremony described in the history of corn dollies—was also the occasion for celebration at which these jugs were in great demand. The method of scratching away the white slip to leave the red background is known as *sgraffito*. Many modern potters use this technique today. Some of the eighteenth and nineteenth-century makers can be identified by their work as each potter favoured certain designs and rhymes.

Posset cups were another favourite drinking vessel made by country potters, popular from the seventeenth until the middle of the nineteenth centuries. These usually had two handles and could hold up to 8pt (4.5 litres) of a drink that was made from hot milk curdled with ale, wine or lemon, with added sugar, cinnamon, ginger or nutmeg. The cup was handed round a group of people as a nightcap drink, dispensing with the need to wash up many cups or mugs afterwards.

That the smaller potters did not lose their sense of humour during the ups and downs of their businesses is shown in the large numbers of elaborate puzzle cups and jugs produced from the sixteenth to the nineteenth centuries; there were vessels which made it difficult or impossible for the drinker to get the liquid out; trick jugs that guaranteed that the liquid spilled everywhere (particularly popular in the West Country); and mugs that had a moulded pottery frog at the bottom which came into view only as the last drops of the drink were reached. The main region for the production of the latter joke was Halifax.

The nineteenth century saw a period of rapid change. The huge brewing jars made by local potters in great numbers, particularly in the North of England, at the beginning of the nineteenth century were no longer needed by the last quarter, as by then over 95 per cent of Britain's beer was produced commercially. The large milk pans, churns and butter pots gradually fell into disuse when butter was produced commercially; milk churns were made of metal, and enamelware was factory produced for the home. The large vessels for salting meat and fish were not needed when food was no longer preserved at home. In coastal areas of the West Country, whenever there had been a glut of fish the local potters would race each other to the coast, their waggons loaded with preserving pots for the housewives to salt the fish for the winter.

Furthermore, the local potter could not always meet every demand for new wares, the type of kiln and fuel available to him and the type of local clay he used often limited the articles he could make. These are no longer problems for today's potters, who produce porcelain, earthenware and stoneware from all manner of clays, decorated with a variety of glazes unavailable to a small potter in the past.

During the nineteenth century machines gradually did more and more of the work of pottery-making in the factories and mass production enabled large amounts of decorated pottery to be turned out. As in the case of the factory-produced furniture and domestic decoration of the late Victorian period there was a reaction against the assembly-line products, led by William Morris. As a result individual potters started to make pottery by hand again, returning to the functional pottery of the earlier cottage potters of the seventeenth and eighteenth centuries.

Bernard Leach was one of the best known of these potters whose work and books have had a great influence on the generation of potters who started making pottery after World War II. Members of his family are well known for their work, both in functional pots for use in the home and as works of art. The pottery at St Ives in Cornwall, which Bernard Leach established in 1920, is still in operation. His son David worked at this pottery for some years and then set up the Lowerdown Pottery at Bovey Tracey in Devon where he makes stoneware and porcelain domestic ware. He is well known as a widely travelled teacher and lecturer and has exhibited his pottery both in Britain and abroad. His son John was born at Pottery Cottage in St Ives. After being apprenticed to both his father and grandfather, since 1964 he has lived and worked in an old thatched farmworker's cottage, with its outbuildings, at Muchelney, near Langport, Somerset (see Plate 25). With two assistant potters he produces a high standard of hand-thrown domestic stoneware in the Leach tradition (see Plate 26); he uses a wood-fired kiln, the flames from the burning wood passing directly over the pots, giving them a warm and distinctive finish. Off-cuts of larch and spruce from the local sawmills are used to fuel the fire and the pots are made from a 'body', mixed at the pottery, of clays from Dorset and

Plate 25 John Leach's pottery at Muchelney, Somerset *(H. Whittick)*

Plate 26 John Leach making a chicken-brick at his pottery. He concentrates on hand-thrown domestic stoneware *(D. Evans)*

Devon. The pots are glazed on the inside in a range of subdued earth colours.

Sixteen hours of continuous stoking are needed to bring the kilns up to 1300°C and then two days for them to cool down before the pots can be withdrawn. A wide range of casseroles, from small individual ones to large hotpots, are produced (see Plate 27); jugs in all sizes; large storage jars; small herb jars; bowls; plates; baking dishes; chicken-bricks; pestle and mortars, and not forgetting large jars for Somerset cider and the tankards from which to drink it—in fact, everything for the kitchen and table from large bread crocks to egg cups.

The wood for the kiln is stacked behind the cottage. There is also a small craftshop run by John's wife Elizabeth, but most of the pots are sent away to leading craftshops in Britain and overseas. John is a member of the Craftsmen Potters' Association and his pots are on sale at their London shop as well as at the Victoria and Albert Museum Craft Shop and several London stores.

The South-west of England is still an important area for the making of pottery by traditional methods; some of it is hand-made by artist-potters in their studios and much is made from the clays of Devon and Cornwall. At the Truro Pottery in Cornwall three generations of the Lake family made pottery there. The pottery, which has been in existence for at least 200 years, and probably much longer, is now enjoying a new lease of life under the ownership of Dennis Hills and his family, having been saved from redevelopment in 1980.

It still occupies its original site on Chapel Hill, overlooking the city and Truro Cathedral. Centuries ago the pottery used clay from under the nearby fields, which are built over. From the end of the seventeenth century, however, most of the clay was imported from St Agnes on the north coast of Cornwall (where it was used by the local tin-miners to stick candles on their hats and known as 'candle clay') or from North Devon where the same clay was used at the Fremington Pottery near Barnstaple. This was sent by ship from Appledore around the coast to Truro. The clay was first mixed in a horse-drawn pug-mill and then wedged by hand. The early wheels on which the

Plate 27 Hotpot from the Muchelney Pottery *(H. Whittick)*

pots were made were turned by young boys who became expert in varying the speed of rotation required by the potter.

At Truro the pots were placed in a drying room, the floor of which was covered with heaps of burning charcoal giving out a gentle heat. Resting on wooden racks, the pots dried out in about three days.

The oldest kiln still standing was built in the late eighteenth century but was much modified over the years. It was fired by furze and wood to a temperature of 950–1000°C. Considerable changes were made at the end of the nineteenth century after Mr Lake visited the Ewenny Pottery in Wales and saw the brick-domed kilns there. The kiln at Truro was in use until 1945, but a new coal-fired kiln was installed in 1943.

The furze originally used was cut by the potters on Potter's Down on the outskirts of Truro, or purchased from professional furze-cutters who brought it to the pottery in waggon-loads to be stacked in ricks. As it burned the furze imparted a different colour to the glaze of the pots according to the season of the year when it was cut. In the spring, when the sap was rising, the pots had a dark green to yellow glaze. In mid-summer the glaze was khaki coloured, while those fired with the dry furze cut and stored from August onwards were a rich red-brown colour. About 500 faggots of furze were used at a firing.

Later, coal-fired kilns were used and then replaced eventually by the gas and electric kilns used today. It took the potters four days to stack the kilns with their wares: the Cornish pitchers, made since Elizabethan times and still made at Truro Pottery today (Fig 31), were the first to go in, then the plantpots and bussas (the bussa was the tall pan for salting Cornish pilchards), and finally all the other wares. The Truro Pottery was one which raced with their waggons to the coast to sell their bussas when a glut of fish was reported. According to tradition, which claimed that their competitors' horses stopped at every public house on the way from force of habit, Truro Pottery's waggon always won.

The firing of the kiln stacked with such a variety of wares

Fig 31 Cornish pitcher of the type made since Elizabethan times

was a matter of considerable skill and experience and needed constant watching and checking. Firing proper started on a Friday morning and was usually completed by that night or Saturday morning. The kiln was left to cool over the weekend and unpacked the following Monday.

Besides the usual kitchen bowls and domestic items, country potters also made ridge tiles and chimney pots and the cloam ovens of the type made in clay, used extensively in the West of England and Wales for centuries, and made at Truro until 1937.

While there are potters at work in small potteries all over the country today, probably there is a greater concentration of them in the South-west than anywhere else. They still use local clay and traditional ways of working and are seen by the many visitors to the area. Adjoining Truro Pottery is the Old Kiln Museum where visitors can learn about the history of pottery in Cornwall and see the wares made in the past. There is also a showroom where coffee sets, wine carafes, goblets, casseroles, and so on, may be purchased.

Today, it is more usual for the customers to come to the pottery than for the pottery to make the extensive journeys to their customers that they made centuries ago.

9

COUNTRY FURNITURE-MAKERS

One of the first craftsmen to set up in business in his own cottage and use his skills both for the benefit of his neighbours and to provide his own livelihood was undoubtedly the village carpenter. In Anglo-Saxon times simple housing and furniture would have been made by the individuals who required them. The very earliest type of wooden container, whether chest or coffin, was home-made, gouged or dug out of a tree trunk, probably a hollow one. Chairs made in this fashion as late as the eighteenth and nineteenth centuries still exist today. These early craftsmen learned their skills through experience: small cottages were built using the cruck construction whereby the natural shape of the timbers formed the arch of the end walls; oak boards used to make chair and chests were riven not sawn, and the furniture was fastened together with oak pins or hand-forged nails, the side boards being extended to form feet. Soon those with a particular ability in carpentry were specialising in this work and by the early Middle Ages were already organised into guilds in towns, which set standards of work and training—for instance, the use of glue was forbidden by carpenters' guilds. Although these guilds did not extend their influence to most village carpenters, their existence shows how important the carpenter had become in that age of timber-framed houses and sturdy oak furniture.

While we tend to think of all early furniture as being of oak, and no doubt much of it was, the country carpenter would have used whatever wood was available locally. He would have used fruitwood, cherry, apple and pear, as well as elm, which was plentiful in Devon, and beech, which in Buckinghamshire was known as the Buckingham weed. Much of the fruitwood furniture has not survived, whereas that made of oak has lasted for centuries.

As well as being the most durable, oak was also the most difficult to work and one can only marvel at the effects achieved with the simple tools then available. Oak also needed to be well seasoned before use to ensure that the work would remain sound. Today, however difficult oak is to work with, furniture-makers still use it, although aided by modern tools and some machinery.

Oak is the favourite wood of the craftsman Maurice Leach, who has a country workshop at Langport, Somerset. His wood comes from oak trees about ninety years old which have been left to mature for three years. Some comes from Honiton and is air dried, as oak was for centuries, and some is kiln dried by modern methods in the Midlands. He also works in elm and ash, giving his own individual touches to many traditional styles which have been popular for several hundred years, such as dressers, gate-leg tables and rocking-chairs. He makes ladder-back chairs with rush seats, favourites with both chairmakers and buyers since they first appeared in the North of England in the seventeenth century and which were one type of country chair that eventually made the journey to town in the eighteenth century to be made in mahogany by fashionable cabinetmakers. He also makes Windsor chairs in the light, graceful styles that became so popular in eighteenth-century America, where the Windsor chair was another country style that made its way into fashionable drawing-rooms. In England this popular and comfortable chair was usually found in the kitchen and the country inn, where its sturdy and serviceable shape was appreciated.

Ash was another popular hardwood, needing only six months to a year to mature. Furniture is still being made from it today by the firm Treske, whose workshop is in a 150-year-old converted maltings in the country market town of Thirsk in North Yorkshire. The firm name is an early spelling of Thirsk. Here they specialise in furniture made from English ash grown in Yorkshire, sawn in nearby mills and dried out on the premises, although oak, mahogany, beech, elm and yew are also used.

Using internationally known names for their designs, their furniture is well suited to modern homes. Indeed, their range of designs makes it possible to furnish an entire house with Treske furniture. They make everything from a bread board to a delicate church organ. Much of their business is carried out for churches, where anything but the highest standard of traditional craftsmanship would be out of place.

Ash is lighter to handle than oak, but is porous and at Treske they have perfected a finish using cellular sealers and clear melamine, which gives a surface which is both smooth, shiny and heat resistant. The furniture is in solid wood—no veneers are used—and comes in white, tan, brown and olive.

While solid wood furniture is more expensive than chipboard or plywood, it is able to stand up to years of hard use, without dents and scratches showing that its beauty is only skin deep. With solid wood furniture these marks of time and wear only serve to give a feeling of continuity, serenity and timelessness as the furniture settles into the lives of its owners.

Treske furniture is supplied with traditional wooden hand-turned knobs on the drawers and cupboards or with a wide range of alternative handles for those who prefer them. As in the past, the blanket chests can fulfil functions other than as storage pieces, such as a seat at the foot of a bed or beneath a window, or as a coffee table. Their dressers are made in two halves, which may be brought separately (Fig 32). The earliest dressers were in this form, particularly in the North of England: the lower half was a three-drawer sideboard and the top half an open plate-rack with grooves for holding plates on edge; the back of the dresser was left open, but covered in if required. The shelves either stood free on top of the sideboard or were hung on or built into the walls above. A dresser was originally a sideboard on which one 'dressed' food before it was served. In the seventeenth century it acquired shelves above for the display of pewter and delftware, so that the dishes for serving the food were near at hand. In some parts of

Fig 32 Dresser made in traditional style by Treske, furniture-makers at Thirsk, North Yorkshire

the country a dresser is still known as a delft-rack.

The doors of the Treske dressers use a type of door popular since the seventeenth century with solid 'fielded' panels, that is, they have a flat centre portion bevelled at the edges so that the panel appears to be raised. They also use traditional methods to make elegant four-poster beds and more modern pieces, such as sturdy bunk beds, which will not creak under the roughest treatment that children can give them, and hi-fi units built to customers' individual requirements.

The firm has standard designs for seven different types of table, most of them available to seat from four to ten people, but the table tops can always be adjusted to suit the needs of the customer (Fig 33). Much of the furniture is made to suit the individual requirements of customers overseas, the church and

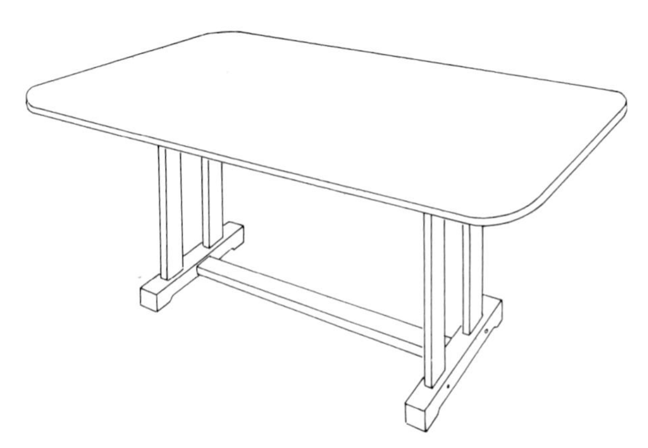

Fig 33 Six-seater family dining table made by Treske

large corporations, but a large amount is still sold to the local farmers and community, as was the case with country furniture-makers in the past. About seventeen people are employed at Treske and it is possible for the public to visit the workshops to see all the stages of furniture production in progress, including the work still done by hand. The furniture is on sale there seven days a week. The manager and his wife and their apprentices live and work on the premises, in the way that many small firms operated years ago. While their approach to the work is traditional, all the equipment, glues, finishes and training methods, however, are completely modern.

Country craftsmen throughout the centuries have always designed furniture for the particular purpose for which it was needed and in designs to please an individual customer. It was usually made in styles that had been well tried for generations and handed down from father to son, furniture that was made to stand the wear and tear of country life for people well known to the craftsmen. After a century of factory- and machine-made furniture in mass-produced styles for unknown buyers the public is today pleased to be able to obtain individually made furniture, often handmade to order, in English hardwoods, by furniture-makers working in their own small businesses.

The oak furniture of the earliest carpenters was not always a success. The method of joining it together with nails or oak pins did not allow the wood to expand and, especially if it was not well seasoned, it was inclined to warp and split. Wood is sensitive to changes in atmosphere and even well-made antique furniture can be ruined in centrally-heated rooms.

In the fifteenth century a new method of joining furniture was introduced into England from the Low Countries. A framework of horizontal rails and vertical stiles were joined by mortice and tenon joints, a section (the tenon) of the rail being fitted into a corresponding socket (the mortice) of the stile; both parts were further secured by squared oak pegs driven through round holes made through the joint. A grooved edge was made inside the frame so constructed, into which a panel with tapered edges was fitted. This allowed the panel to move freely in the frame allowing for weathering or ageing.

From this time on most furniture was constructed in this way by craftsmen known as joiners. There was a great increase in all types of furniture, especially when life became more settled and prosperous during Tudor times. The methods of construction used for what was known as joined or joint furniture are still used today.

In medieval times, furniture had achieved the double distinction of being both heavy and movable. The all-purpose chest, the most common article of medieval furniture still in existence, was strong enough to act as bed, seat and storage unit, but must have been heavy to move on the perpetual journeyings undertaken by the owners of castles and manor houses. Tables were simply boards resting on trestles so that they could be dismantled and moved at the end of a meal to the sides of the hall, originally to leave room for the household to sleep round the central fire. The trestle supports, usually of oak, were either independent or held in position by one or two stretcher rails; these passed through the ends of the trestles and were kept tightly in position on the outside by oak wedges which went through the holes in the ends of the stretcher. The wedges could be removed and the trestle supposedly taken apart when necessary, although several strong men would have been needed to remove the tops of many of these long tables. These boards were made of several thick planks, usually of elm—a tree which provided thick planks, of the necessary width. Many of these tables were actually built in the halls for which they were needed as they were too wide to go through a door. This design of table is still popular today, particularly in pine, but is made with a fixed top.

By the Elizabethan era a table with a fixed top, known as a table dormant, which stood permanently in the middle of the room, was common. This was a framed or joined table with the top fixed to the underframing and tenoned into four, six or eight legs. When merchants and yeoman farmers of this prosperous period were lavishing their increased wealth on furnishing their homes, this was one of the many articles of furniture that was decorated with elaborate carvings on the legs. Tables were still made with removable tops, often with one side plain and scrubbed as a working surface and one side polished for grander occasions.

All furniture was purpose built and much of the work of local carpenters and joiners was actually done in the homes of their customers. In small cottages and farmhouses every corner was utilised: seats were built into the sides of the large ingle-nook fireplace (although in poorer homes a log fixed at each side sufficed); any cavity in the wall near the fireplace was given a door and used as a dry cupboard for salt or storage of dry foods; larger spaces in walls had cupboard beds built into them—sometimes there was a cupboard bed one side of the fireplace and a settle the other.

The settle, basically a bench or chest with a back, became the most popular piece of furniture of inn and country kitchen at this time and was one of the first practical steps towards comfort in the home. With a settle each side of the fireplace and often with a curtain on a rail between, there was at least one warm spot at night in a country home. The need for the settle was well described by Thomas Hardy in *The Return of the Native*—it was

> the necessary supplement to a fire so open that nothing less than a strong breeze will carry up the smoke. It is, to the hearths of old-

> fashioned cavernous fireplaces, what the east belt of trees is to the exposed country estate, or the north wall to the garden. Outside the candles gutter, locks of hair wave, young women shiver and old men sneeze. Inside is Paradise. Not a symptom of draught disturbs the air; the sitters' backs are as warm as their faces, and songs and old tales are drawn from the occupants by the comfortable heat, like fruit from melon-plants in a frame.

Some settles were made to fulfil several fuctions. They were made with cupboards in their backs to store a side of bacon, with storage-room in their seats, or even with a pen under the seat to house a sitting duck or goose; some are known in old inventories as a 'long-settle bed' and many were fashioned to fit a particular corner or curve or used to partition rooms. One version, known today as a 'monk's bench' but more often found in a country inn than a monastery, has a back which can be folded over to make a table. This versatility is typical of so many country pieces. Even if a housewife had a trough to hold bread or flour, she required it to have a top that could also be used as a kitchen table or ironing board as well.

During Elizabethan times there was a vast increase in the types of furniture made, when all craftsmen in wood must have been working at full capacity. Many storage pieces were needed, such as court cupboards to house newly acquired plate. One of the first investments by a yeoman farmer was in a large carved bedstead. All this eventually resulted in an increase in different types of specialist woodworker: carpenters, who concentrated mainly on timber-built houses and cottages, outside work on farms and the simple chests and cupboards they had always made; arkwrights, who made the large, heavy arks for storage, often for bread and flour; hutchiers, who made hutches—small storage units on legs with doors, usually for food; cofferers, who made coffers—small, portable wooden chests covered with leather and who later made leather covered and fabric covered upholstered chairs and stools; and the joiners who did so much of the work. As well as joined and framed furniture they made most of the internal fittings of a house—doors, panelling and, later, staircases. Then there were the craftsmen who decorated the joiners' work, the carvers and turners. The latter had years of experience making elaborate chairs out of parts turned on a lathe, and spindle decorations for cupboards, chests and chests of drawers.

By the seventeenth century craftsmen in towns were in dispute as to which of them should carry out the various jobs; in country areas, however, one man usually fulfilled most of these occupations, changing his styles to suit his customers' requirements.

During the Jacobean period furniture became less heavy, more movable and less decorated. Much of it made from that period has survived until the present day. The country woodworker continued to make what was needed, including the lighter styles of chairs with more canework and more delicate carving, as well as quantities of boxes, plain and ornamented, to house the one book then found for the first time in so many cottages and country homes—the Bible.

The greatest divide between furniture made in the country and that made in the town came towards the end of the seventeenth century, when cabinetmakers in London began working in new imported woods such as walnut and mahogany and used veneers and new methods of construction which gave flush surfaces, enabling completely new styles of furniture to be produced. It was no longer possible to see at a glance exactly how a piece of furniture had been made. These new methods of construction date from the time of the restoration of Charles II who brought the ideas from France and the Low Countries where he had spent his years of exile.

By the eighteenth century the making of such furniture started on the drawing-board, designed by men who have given their names to styles that are now world-famous, names such as Sheraton, Hepplewhite and Chippendale. The latter was the grandson of the village carpenter at Otley in Yorkshire and the son of a joiner. Chippendale was not only a cabinetmaker and designer but also an upholsterer, general household furnisher and coffin-maker.

Cabinetmakers can be found today in small country villages making furniture of the highest quality. Peter Pike, whose work-

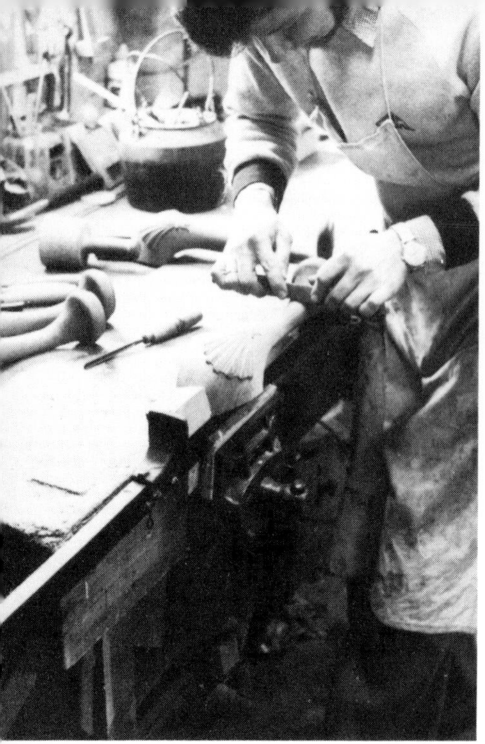

Plate 28 Peter Pike, cabinetmaker, shaping a cabriole leg with a shell design carved on the 'knee'. This was a shape popular with eighteenth-century cabinetmakers. It was not turned on the lathe but made from a solid piece of wood cut down to the required shape by the cabinetmaker on the bench *(Peter Pike)*

Plate 29 W. R. Evans at work with a pole-lathe at the Welsh Folk Museum, St Fagans, Cardiff, in 1950 *(Welsh Folk Museum)*

shop is in the old stables of his home at West Wellow, near Romsey, Hampshire, is a young man now working successfully on his own, after five years' apprenticeship to a cabinetmaker in Southampton (see Plate 28). He makes both original designs and reproductions and restores antique furniture—an important and much sought-after service today. He also undertakes ecclesiastical work and wood turning.

During the eighteenth century the designs of the great names in cabinetmaking reached many country furniture-makers, who adapted them to their own styles, using hardwoods and fruitwood instead of imported wood and adding such things as stretchers to chairs with straight legs, a necessity in country homes both for sturdiness and to keep feet off cold and muddy floors. For the most part, however, they continued to make furniture in the traditional styles and construction although they introduced some new items of furniture, not at first found in towns, but in keeping with seventeenth-century ideas of lighter and less ornate furniture. They made the gate-leg table that could be folded away to make extra room in a small home. It was produced in large quantities at the end of the seventeenth century and is still useful and popular today for small modern houses. It was made in a variety of designs, particularly in the turning of the legs. Improved lathes in the late seventeenth and early eighteenth centuries enabled the turner to make oblique cuts and turn spirals on his lathe, where formerly he could only cut shapes at right angles, and these new abilities were shown to great advantage in the legs of gate-leg tables.

The expert turning and woodwork done for centuries by country craftsmen enabled them at the end of the seventeenth century to produce a new style of chair—the Windsor—which became a symbol of country craftsmanship (Fig 34). It was originally known as a stick-back chair, having its parts—at first simple turned back supports, legs and arm supports—all socketed into a solid seat. It may have developed from the three-legged stool into a three-legged chair—one or two early specimens have been found. Three legs had long been found to be the safest on uneven floors and the chair had probably been made like this in the country for years. It appeared in large numbers with four legs only at the beginning of the eighteenth century—the country craftsmen's answer, perhaps, to the lighter type of chairs being made in large numbers in towns, where chairmaking had by then become a separate craft.

While Windsor chairs were made in various parts of the country, the largest area of production was around High Wycombe in Buckinghamshire, where the surrounding beechwoods provided both the material and the working areas for the men who made the chair legs. From this district large quantities of chairs made their way to London via Windsor Market, from which they probably take their name. They

Fig 34 Wheelback Windsor chair

were popular in the United States of America and were known by this name from as early as 1708.

That the chair was eventually produced in such large numbers by the end of the nineteenth century—4,700 chairs a day in the High Wycombe area were being made—is no doubt due to the fact that it has always lent itself to assembly-line production. It was usual for the various parts to be produced by different craftsmen, even in small workshops.

The legs, back spindles and stretcher rails were made by the turners, often working and living alongside their materials in the local woods where they were known as 'bodgers'. They were either self-employed or worked for a farmer as part of their seasonal employment. Living in a portable hut in the woods, the bodger would move from place to place as he worked through the stand of trees, bought by himself or by the farmer, which lasted about a year. After felling, the trunks were trimmed with an axe and then sawn into 18in (457mm) lengths, cleft by hand with a beetle and wedge into as many pieces as possible. These hand-split legs were thought to be stronger and less liable to warp than those later cut by machine. A country woodworker always had the advantage of selecting his trees and particular parts of them for the job he was doing. It was easier and cheaper for bodgers to take their equipment to the woods than for the wood to be transported to them in their workshops.

The bodger then reduced the pieces to the rough outline of a leg or stretcher with a few strokes of a small axe or metal froe; then, sitting astride a shave-horse, which held the piece of wood in a clamp, he shaped it as near as possible to the shape required, pulling the draw-knife held in both hands towards him. The piece was then turned on a pole-lathe, a V-shaped chisel forming the shapes required in about two minutes—a type that has been in use since the Iron Age. The wood was turned while still green and stacked to dry afterwards for several weeks before the next stage of the chair was completed. After the bodgers left, the remaining wood was either sawn into planks and chair seats, used for kindling, or left for the charcoal burners, who were also forest workers.

The pole-lathe was still in use in factories at the beginning of the twentieth century and was well adapted to work in the forests, some turners using the living tree for the pole which gave the lathe its power (see Plate 29). The pole was joined to the foot treadle by the cord which was wrapped once or twice around the piece of wood to be turned, held between two uprights of the lathe. The wood turned when the foot treadle was pressed, springing back when the foot was removed. The chisel could be applied only when the foot was pressed down and the material moved forward.

As well as beech, ash, willow, yew, oak, walnut and various fruitwoods were used to make Windsor chairs. Several woods in one chair were often used, the maker relying on staining, painting and polishing to 'match up' the parts where the various woods joined.

The bottomer shaped the solid seat, which was usually of

elm, with an adze; the sawn parts were provided by the benchman in the workshop and the bows at the back of the chair and any curved parts were steamed and bent into shape by the bender. The whole chair was assembled by the framer, who also stained and finished the chair, unless, as was often the case, it was to be sold in its natural state 'in the white'; many chairs were sold like this and kept clean by scouring with sand. In some small workshops a craftsman might combine several of these processes, but few were able to make a Windsor chair from start to finish. One of the last to do so was H. E. (Jack) Goodchild, who died in 1950. In his Naphill workshop he produced chairs of outstanding quality.

We know few of the names of any of the Windsor chairmakers. Sometimes a benchman put his initials and a pattern number on the back edge of the seat and these can sometimes be traced to records in chairmaking factories or in old directories.

Two eighteenth-century chairmakers from High Wycombe were Samuel Treacher and Thomas Widgington. The latter is believed to have established the first actual chairmaking factory in High Wycombe in about 1810.

About fifty Windsor chairs have been found made by a group working in the Rockley area of Nottingham between 1825 and 1865 where the wood of Sherwood Forest was used. They bear the impressed mark of 'F. Walker/Rockley'.

A type of low-back Windsor appeared in the early nineteenth century originating in the village of Mendlesham in Suffolk, made by the local wheelwright and chairmaker, Daniel Day. We know that Windsor chairs were also made in the North of England, East Anglia and Wales, as well as South-west England, but the names of the men who made them are largely unknown.

Occasionally, we find the name of a local carpenter in an inventory of possessions made at his death. These possessions were often few and seem to indicate that he had little time to spend on making furniture for his own home. However, one Essex carpenter, Laurance of Roxwell, who died in 1688, had a hall that was well furnished for the times, with two tables, two forms, a bench, four little stools, a dresser board (an early form of what later became a dresser or a sideboard), a cupboard, a hanging cupboard and three chairs, with beds and chests in his bedrooms. John Day, who died at Writtle in 1725, had one long table in his hall, six joint stools, two small tables, four old chairs and one cupboard, with an 'indifferent' bed, chest of drawers, cupboard and table in one bedroom as well as two 'sorry old chairs', and one 'sorry' bed, small table, three hutches and two trunks in another. In another room were two more beds 'with what belongs to them very mean', one cupboard and two hutches. Perhaps the descriptions 'indifferent', 'sorry', 'mean' used by those making the inventory were in surprise that a carpenter who had worked hard all his life had not done better. Even in the late nineteenth century country carpenters worked a 60 hour week, often walking 4 or 5 miles (6.4 or 8km) to distant farms, carrying all their tools with them each day or perhaps staying at the farm for several days to complete their task. Furniture-making for their own homes must have been low on their list of priorities.

Their tools, which were sharpened to their own requirements, were personal and cherished possessions and were never willingly lent to another. Peter Pike, although a young craftsman, still much prefers working with the old woodworking tools he has acquired rather than with modern renewals.

After the mid-seventeenth century old furniture inventories often list a chest-of-drawers among the contents of a house. These were a marvellous development of the medieval chest. As possessions became more plentiful, the problem of finding them at the bottom of a deep chest was solved first by putting what were called 'drawing boxes' into it. Later it became a 'chest with drawer', a hybrid piece of furniture known as a 'mule chest', with a chest at the top and a drawer at the bottom. This eventually became the chest-of-drawers, a popular storage item, and frequently they stayed downstairs as it was impossible to carry them up narrow cottage staircases.

The increasing mechanisation of the processes of furniture-making that took place during the nineteenth century resulted in much cheap factory furniture appearing in country homes. By the middle of the century William Morris led a movement against this Victorian mass production and a cry went up for a return to handmade furniture that was well designed and used traditional woods and methods.

In 1861 William Morris founded Morris & Co with the aim of making this type of furniture in oak and beech available in every home. His motto was 'Have nothing in your house that you do not know to be useful or believe to be beautiful'. This thought had probably unconsciously been at the back of the minds of many of the best traditional furniture-makers for centuries. The furniture produced by this firm was designed by the artist Ford Madox Brown and the architect Philip Webb among others, especially George Jack. Their work was later continued and Morris's ideas interpreted to better effect by the Cotswold School of designers. Morris's firm never really produced the furniture he had hoped for in the quantities he visualised to compete with machine-produced furniture, but his ideas had a great effect in checking declining standards of taste and were to influence some of the best twentieth-century designers.

The Cotswold School of designers and craftsmen— notably Ernest Gimson and the brothers Sidney and Ernest Barnsley— set up a workshop near Cirencester in 1893, producing well-designed and well-made furniture aimed at keeping alive the best traditions of craftsmanship. Sidney Barnsley's son Edward continued the work of his father and uncle and is today one of our country's leading cabinetmakers, producing superb furniture from both English and imported woods.

While Sidney Barnsley handmade all the furniture he designed himself, his son makes use of modern power tools which leave the craftsman free to use hand skills where they are most effective. Edward Barnsley stresses that there is no drudgery in planing up wood by hand, except perhaps in the case of some foreign timbers; the wooden planes of the early days were, in fact, a delight to use and it was a pleasure to hear the sound of their sharp blades. Craftsmen find present-day metal planes somewhat disappointing and heavy to use because of friction over the wood. Powered tools can, however, work eight or nine hours a day doing as much work in that time as could be done by hand in three weeks. For economic reasons most craftsmen furniture-makers now use powered tools, such as the band saw, the circular saw and especially the cutting morticer, which produces technical perfection that no man could match.

In 1923 Edward Barnsley took over the workshop at Froxfield, near Petersfield, Hampshire, where he had earlier served his apprenticeship with Geoffrey Lupton, who was then working on the designs of Ernest Gimson. Lupton was principally a builder and worked on the hall and timber-framed library at Bedales School, which Gimson had designed. Although the traditions of the Cotswold School that he grew up with obviously had a great effect on him, over the years Edward Barnsley developed his own unique style of furniture. Today, most of his time is spent designing the furniture that bears his name, the craftsmen in his workshop carrying out the designs and producing work of remarkable quality—a form of perfection—for both the individual customers who come to Froxfield, as well as for schools, colleges, churches and the boardrooms of larger businesses. His work is a reflection of his respect for the principle laid down in Owen Jones's book *The Grammar of Ornament:*

> As in architecture, so all works of the decorative arts must all possess fitness, proportion and harmony, the result of which is repose. True beauty results from that repose which the mind feels when the eye, the intellect and the affections are satisfied by the absence of any want.

His father and the Cotswold School were part of the arts and crafts revival movement of the period just before World War I, and Edward Barnsley has lived to see another craft revival movement come round again. He lives today in a cottage adjoining his workshop which makes furniture that can compete with and more often than not improve on that produced by the famous eighteenth-century cabinetmakers—furniture that will be among the most sought-after antiques of the future.

10

WOODCARVERS, TURNERS AND CHAIRMAKERS

When an apprentice started work with Robert Thompson, woodcarver and furniture-maker of Kilburn, Yorkshire, his first task was to learn to carve the mouse that is still found today carved on everything produced by the craftsmen in the firm he founded, Robert Thompson's Craftsmen Ltd. There was no time limit to the apprenticeship—it lasted until the young craftsmen could carve the mouse to Thompson's total satisfaction.

Robert Thompson carved his first mouse in the 1920s on a beam of a church roof on which he was working; another carver with him, Charlie Barker, commented that they were as poor as church mice. On the spur of the moment Robert was inspired to carve a mouse on his work. This mouse became his trade mark and appeared on all his work, whether on domestic oak furniture or on work in cathedrals, churches or even village inns.

The firm is now under the direction of his grandsons, Robert Thompson-Cartwright and John Cartwright. They served their apprenticeship with their grandfather, and after his death in 1955 continued to run the business from his workshops and timber-framed Elizabethan cottage, known as 'The House of the Mouse', hidden away in the Hambleton Hills. Here with a group of craftsmen they continue to uphold the high standards he set and to carry out his motto 'Industry in Quiet Places' (see Plate 30).

The mouse symbol has become famous probably because it illustrates Thompson's motto and the difficult task of carving

Plate 30 Woodcarver at Robert Thompson's Craftsmen Ltd, Yorkshire

English oak—as Robert Thompson said, it was like a mouse working quietly scraping and chewing away the hardest wood with its chisel-like teeth.

Apart from travels to cathedrals, churches large and small, public buildings and stately homes to see for himself where his work was to stand, Robert Thompson lived all his life of nearly eighty years at Kilburn. Although the son of the village joiner, carpenter and wheelwright, he did not at first join his father in business, but served a five-year apprenticeship with a firm of engineers 60 miles (96km) from his home. This was an unhappy time for Robert and at the age of 20 he asked to return home and join his father in the carpenter's shop. This he did and worked in the village for about twenty years doing a variety of jobs from household repair to making gates and coffins, and mending carts and fences.

During his early apprenticeship, Robert Thompson had to pass through Ripon on the way to and from his work. He frequently stopped at the cathedral to see the work of the fifteenth-century Ripon School of carvers who, under the direction of William Bromflet, carved the wonderful oak choir stalls, misericords and bench-ends. Robert later admitted that these carvings had greatly influenced him. During his leisure time he made a detailed study of the work of the medieval carvers, the oak they worked on and the tools they used. While working as a village carpenter he practised carving.

In 1919 Robert received his first ecclesiastical commission from Father Paul Nevill, a future headmaster of the nearby Ampleforth College, to make an oak cross large enough to carry a statue of Christ, the beginning of the extensive work that he was to undertake both at the college and at the Benedictine Abbey at Ampleforth right up to the end of his life. His greatest achievement and also his favourite work was in the college library, where his earliest work there is found, a large table weighing 1¼ tons. Then followed the carrels, the alcoves for private study, the chairs, the bookcases, and finally the library door, completed just before his last illness in 1955—work that had spanned over thirty-five years. His first work at Ampleforth was also the beginning of the task that was to occupy him for the rest of his life. As a maker of ecclesiastical and domestic furniture that can be found all over Britain and in many other countries, he achieved his early ambition of reviving the spirit and craftsmanship of the medieval carvers.

The English oak used by the firm today can be seen stacked on every available piece of land around his cottage, sawn lengthwise and propped apart with short staves to allow the air to circulate and the wood to season for about five years. Nearly all the finished work is ammonia-fumed and wax polished, a process which brings out the silver grain of the oak because the remaining wood is darkened by the fumes. The oak furniture that Robert Thompson made for his own home was scrubbed every week with soap and water to give the dull chalky whiteness he liked to see. He was told that to achieve this effect commercially would involve using chemical agents, which he would not do. (It is often forgotten that the oak used so extensively in the Middle Ages did not give rooms the dark appearance that we associate with antique oak furniture today; the darkening took place over the years only through age and usage.)

The furniture from Thompsons is distinguished by its smooth undulating surface which catches the light, an effect produced by an adze, a tool like a hoe which has been used for centuries for this purpose. With the adze, shavings of about the size of a beech leaf and 1/64in (0.4mm) thick are scooped from the wood.

The firm continues to produce work to Robert Thompson's high standards, whether for churches, cathedrals or the home. They have many visitors who want to see where 'the mouse man', who became a legend in his own lifetime, lived and worked. They can ask for an individually designed item for a church or school, or order anything ranging from a large table, sideboard, bookcase, grandfather clock, wardrobe or chest down to a chair or a stool, or even buy something as small as an ashtray or napkin ring. And everything, large or small has a mouse carved on it.

Robert Thompson's work can be seen to great effect at York Minster, Westminster Abbey and at Ripon. While most of the carver's work in medieval times was carried out in churches and cathedrals, the carvers also did most of the decorating of chests, cupboards and chairs. Many areas of the country that had fine ecclesiastical carving also had carving of superior quality on the furniture in their homes. This is apparent in Yorkshire, Somerset, Norfolk and Suffolk. When many years later carved furniture was no longer considered fashionable in the home, it was often donated to the churches that had originally inspired the designs.

After Henry VIII's break with the Church of Rome, many carvers who had formerly worked for the Church were free to work for the newly rich class of yeoman farmers and merchants. Their prosperity and social status demanded highly decorated furniture and, as a result, furniture for the next hundred years was decorated with a mixture of Gothic designs

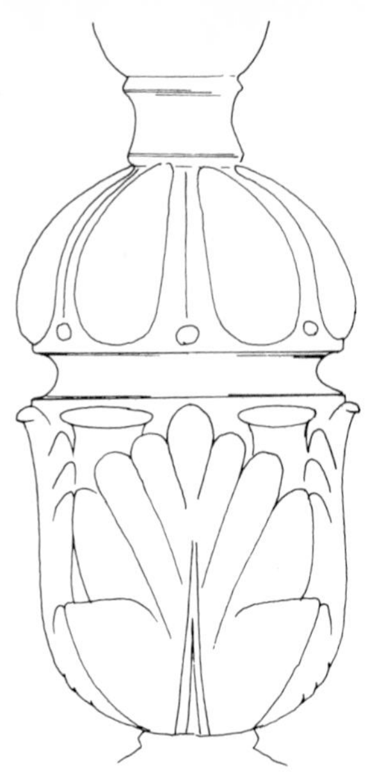

Fig 35 'Cup and cover' design found on table legs of the Elizabethan era

and continental influences, which reached a climax of exuberance in the reign of Elizabeth I. Table legs in particular were heavily carved, often with acanthus leaves or the popular 'cup and cover' designs, on their large and bulbous shapes (Fig 35). Beds, among the first items to be purchased for the Elizabethan home, were highly decorated. Some of this carving was done by joiners and some by specialist carvers, who were usually members of the joiners' guilds.

The Puritan influence of the Commonwealth period brought a severe restriction in the carver's work. This elaboration was frowned upon by the Puritans, although there was already a tendency for plainer furniture during the Jacobean period. By then the turners had taken over the decoration of furniture, the Puritans approving of the turners' craft which produced simpler designs. They produced a variety of turned spindles, pendants and bosses, which were then split in half and glued into place as decoration. These were often stained black to look like ebony and appeared on the fronts of the chests, chests-of-drawers and cupboards. They produced graceful balasters and columns in a variety of turned patterns which formed the stretchers and legs of chairs and also of the gate-leg tables which became so popular from the seventeenth century onwards. After the restoration of Charles II, the turners produced a still greater variety of spirals and twists by the aid of a special device added to their lathes which enabled them to cut barley-sugar shaped twists obliquely, instead of only being able to cut shapes at right angles to the lathe.

The turners did all their early work with a pole-lathe, shown in Plate 29, which continued in use until this century. It can be seen in action at the Welsh Folk Museum at St Fagans where the turner produces bowls on a pole-lathe as well as on a modern electrical lathe. The pole-lathe was a tiring machine to work for the turner had to stand on one leg, while lifting the other leg up and down with some force. It had the advantage, however, that as the tools cut on the down stroke only, the up stroke cut away the shavings, which often clog a tool used in the continuous motion of a modern lathe. Wheel-lathes turned by hand and lathes operated by a treadle also existed before power was available to make the turner's work easier. Many turners made their own tools. Today, they are purchased from specialist tool manufacturers from a selection of about twelve different types of scrapers, gouges or chisels. At one time there was a choice of over seventy different types.

In medieval times turners made some of the earliest chairs, no doubt a development of the stools with turned legs produced in large quantities throughout the ages. These chairs had a wide variety of turned parts for arms, backs, legs and stretchers, which became more and more elaborate by the sixteenth century. They were not unnaturally known as 'turned-all-over' chairs and sometimes as 'thrown' chairs, the turner's craft of shaping a piece of wood as it revolved being similar to the potter throwing his clay on his wheel to shape it. Many were made in ash, although most turners used whatever suitable wood was near at hand. The more ornate examples come from the Severn Valley, Wales, Cheshire, Lancashire and the West Country. Many were three-cornered and most of them build for effect and not for comfort. It was in Lancashire that

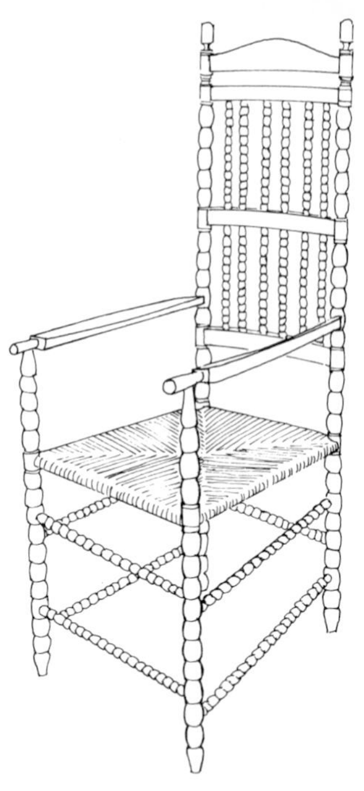

Fig 36 Spindle-back, bobbin-turned chair by Ernest Gimson

the later spindle-back chair developed in the eighteenth century, a style revived in this century by Ernest Gimson and the Cotswold School (Fig 36). Their version has rush seats and bobbin-turned spindles, legs and stretchers, and is still popular in a simpler form today, along with similar chairs with ladder-backs.

The problem of finding a craftsman to reseat these antique rush-bottomed chairs when the old seats wear out is not such a difficult one today now that more are engaged in this work. Tony and Kate Handley are two such people. They work under the name of Country Chairmen in one of the buildings on the Home Farm of the Lockinge Estate in Oxfordshire, which now houses a variety of cottage industries. They undertake the rush seating of chairs in fine and standard grades of rushes, which they harvest near the Thames in July and also sell to those who want to tackle the work themselves. They also recane chairs and have an open-ended job of recaning all the seats in Salisbury Cathedral. About a thousand chairs a year pass through their workshop. They also undertake antique furniture restoration and repairs to furniture, often having to restore parts of the chairs they are reseating before they can put in the new seat.

Cane seats and backs of chairs became popular after 1660 when a lighter type of chair was required. The carvers regained their popularity, but their work was more restrained and delicate. The walnut trees that had been planted in Elizabeth I's time came to maturity in the reign of Charles II. Working in walnut instead of oak, the carver's job of producing the lighter type of carved chair with cane seat and back associated with this period became easier.

Furniture-making, woodcarving and turning are inter-related skills in the woodworker's craft and although some workers specialise in one type of work, many, especially those making furniture, need to combine all three. One young craftsman, Nigel Griffiths, who worked for seven years in the old watermill on the Lockinge Estate, has recently moved to

Plate 31 Nigel Griffiths, a furniture-maker specialising in carving, who works at The Old Cheese Factory, Grange Mill, near Matlock

Derbyshire to The Old Cheese factory, Grange Mill, near Matlock, where he hopes to have more room for his work (see Plate 31). He requires all the skills of the furniture-maker, turner and carver, as well as designer, to make the large pieces of furniture that come from his workshop. He specialises in carving.

Nigel Griffiths moved to the old mill to set up in business on his own after working for some years with his father Rupert, at his firm, Monastic Woodcraft Ltd. His father has been a maker of traditional handmade oak furniture for over forty years. His workshop and showrooms are at the Saracen's Head Coaching House at Brailsford, about 7 miles (11km) from Derby. Members of the Griffiths family appear to settle in surroundings well suited to the ancient crafts they practise! Rupert Griffiths's main workshop is in what were once old farm buildings, the showroom occupying the old stables of the coaching house.

Both father and son buy well-seasoned, quarter-sawn oak for their work, but keep it in dry conditions for a further six months before using it. Oak that is sawn crossways through the trunk in layers, producing planks that diminish in width the further they are cut from the centre, gives wood that is economical, but plain and uninteresting. When the trunk is quartered lengthwise and the quarters sawn towards the centre this shows up the silvery or figured grain of the oak—not such an economical way of cutting up an oak tree, but the way to produce wood to make beautiful furniture that is also stronger, more durable and less likely to warp.

The name Monastic Woodcraft originated from the fact that the firm's earliest work was for churches, and producing oak furniture for churches has remained a regular part of their output. They also produce staircases, gates, bow windows and doors, as well as cocktail bars and reception desks.

Most of Nigel Griffiths's work is specially commissioned. He specialises in large refectory tables, sideboards, dressers and bedheads. The pieces are carved in traditional patterns or with panels of his own or his customers' designs. He makes both ladder-back and spindle-back chairs, with either

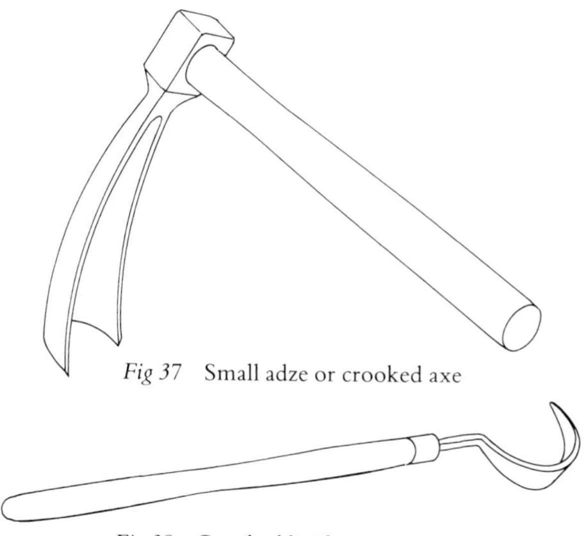

Fig 37 Small adze or crooked axe

Fig 38 Crooked knife or 'twa cam'

wooden panelled or rush seats. The latter are made either by his former neighbours at the mill, the Country Chairmen, or by the workshops for the blind in Oxford. While both father and son use mainly traditional hand methods they do not spurn the use of such aids as high-speed drills or modern glues, waxes and polishes.

Other workers in wood used both turning and carving skills to make a variety of small domestic wares that were at one time of vital importance in every home. Many of these wares we now know to have been made since pre-historic times.

The shaping of a piece of wood by turning it at speed on a lathe, while applying various tools to cut away the part not required, was a craft known in ancient Egypt and already developed to a remarkable degree by the craftsmen in Britain over 2,000 years ago. When the Iron Age village of Glastonbury in Somerset was excavated, a selection of wooden bowls, tubs, spoons and ladles were found, hardly different from those still produced today by rural craftsmen. The ladles have the same hooked handles for hanging on the side of bowl, bucket or shelf as those made in Wales today. These can be skilfully made in about 15 minutes by an expert, with quick

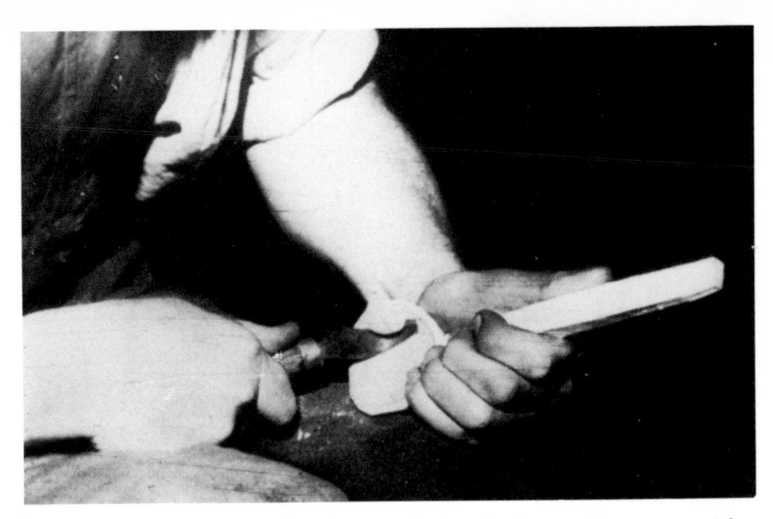

Plate 32 W. R. Evans hollowing out the bowl of a wooden spoon with a crooked knife *(Welsh Folk Museum)*

Plate 33 (Opposite) Bowl turners George William Lailey and Mr Keene who practised their craft at Bucklebury Common, Berkshire. Mr Keene is sitting on a shaping horse *(Museum of English Rural Life)*

movements and few tools, relying only on his experienced eye to produce an article designed for a particular purpose. They are carved from a solid log of the required length, roughly shaped with an axe, then placed in a vice for the bowl of the spoon to be hollowed out with a small adze, which has a cutting edge shaped like a gouge (Fig 37 and Plate 32). Then, held on the turner's knee, it is finished with a crooked knife with a small curved blade, known in Wales as a 'twca cam' (Fig 38). The craftsman usually makes this tool himself from an old file or chisel. The outside of the bowl of the spoon is finished by an ordinary spokeshave, the hooked handle being carved with a knife.

The bowls of 2,000 years ago were probably turned on a pole-lathe, similar to the ones used by the bodgers of the Buckinghamshire beechwoods to turn the legs and stretchers of a Windsor chair and by the many early turners who found it easier to take their lathe to the forest rather than bringing the wood to their workshops. The bowl turners worked in the

woods alongside the makers of rakes, broom and tool handles, and the weavers of wattle hurdles.

So skilled were many bowl turners that they could turn a number of bowls from a single block of wood, one bowl fitting inside another with little wood wasted. Such a turner was George William Lailey whose family had been turners for over 200 years (see Plate 33). He practised his craft at Bucklebury Common, Berkshire, for nearly eighty years, until he died in 1958. He lived and worked at Turner's Green where, fifty years ago seven or more families of turners worked. Elm trees grew profusely on the common and it was from this wood, which did not easily crack or split, that the turners made their bowls. It was the tough properties of this wood that enabled one bowl to be turned inside another. The blocks of elm from which the bowls were made had to be stored for at least five years before they could be used. The bowl turner would sit on a shaping horse, which had a shaped block at the end on which the upturned bowls could be rested, and finish the bottom of the bowl with a spokeshave (Fig 39). The inside of the bowl was finished with a gouge (Fig 40). Most woodworkers used some kind of 'horse' on which they could sit astride to shape a piece of wood, moving the centre rungs with their feet to hold the wood firmly while they worked (Figs 41 and 42).

Sycamore used for many of the domestic utensils, grew profusely in the west of Wales where turnery was so plentiful at one time. It is a quick-growing wood, without smell or taste, so that it does not taint the food it was designed to hold. It was thus particularly suitable for the many containers used in dairies before enamel and metal was introduced. The wood could be turned while still green and it did not crack or warp when immersed in water. In the days when all butter and cheese sold in markets was produced on the farm, an enormous quantity of spoons, ladles, bowls, plates and milking stools, butter-beaters, cream-skimmers, cheese vats and butter prints were needed, so that the wood turner was a vital craftsman in country districts who supplied all domestic needs from his workshop. Those that were not sold in his village,

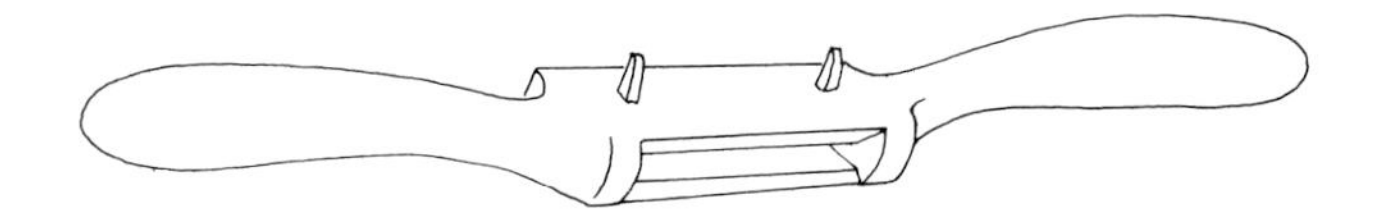

Fig 39 Spokeshave to finish the bottom of a bowl

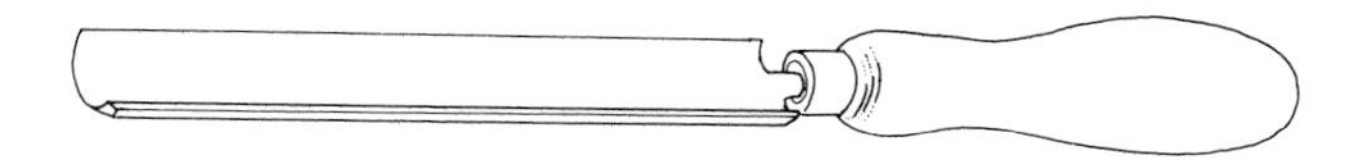

Fig 40 Gouge to finish the inside of a bowl

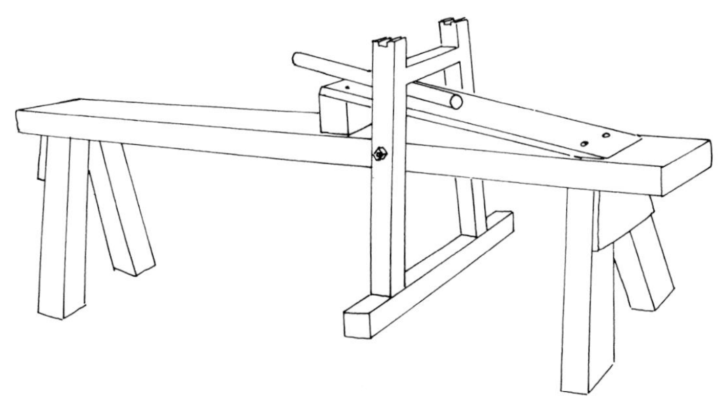

Fig 41 Shaving horse on which the turner would sit astride to shape a piece of wood

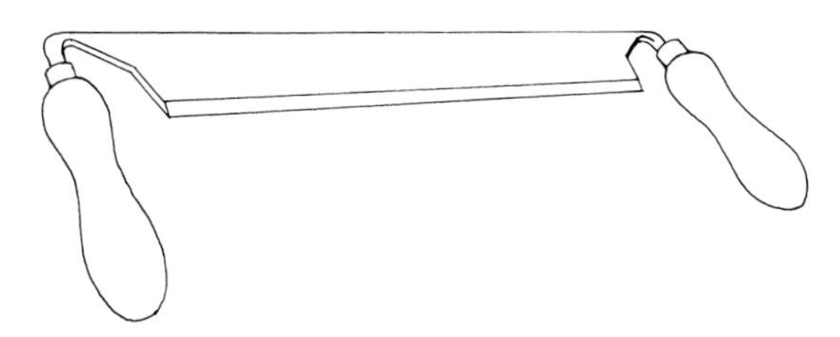

Fig 42 Drawknife used in wood turning

were taken, sometimes 20 or 30 miles (32 or 48km) on horseback or by pony and trap to the nearest market or fair.

Decorating wooden spoons with carving was not a part of the busy turner's work, but from the seventeenth to nineteenth centuries it became the fashion to carve wooden spoons in many farmhouses during the long winter evenings. They were usually for presentation to a loved one as a token of affection and were never intended for use (see Plate 34). It was not unknown for them to be presented to a girl's parents to show the skill of her betrothed. for the carving became very elaborate, involving chain links and hollow handles in which small wooden balls ran free, all carved from a single piece of wood. In Victorian times, fret-saw types of carvings in which the handle became a carved rectangular panel were made, reflecting the style of fretwork undertaken by many amateur carvers at that time. People are still fascinated by these carved love-spoons which today may be bought in Wales.

The Victorian period brought a renewal of prosperity to woodcarvers, for the newly rich from the industrial areas required ornate furniture to display their wealth. The influences on designs at this time did not come from Europe as in the fifteenth century, but from medieval Gothic styles. Much of this influence was derived from the romantic novels of Sir Walter Scott, so popular at the time. The very elaborate furniture then in vogue, known as 'Abbotsford', took its name from the name of Sir Walter's Scottish home.

Unfortunately, the Victorian carvers, both amateur and professional, were somewhat carried away by their love of carving, extending it to many plain antique chests, so that it is difficult today to date them exactly.

When the dairy utensils produced by turners were no longer required in such quantities by farms, many family businesses disappeared, but some turners continued to work as artist-craftsmen, producing individual items more for their pleasing appearance than for practical use. They used a greater variety of woods than before, producing decorative bowls in rosewood, fruitwood, yew, mulberry and walnut.

Other turners were occupied making the many wooden

Plate 34 A selection of love-spoons which were presented as a token of affection to a loved one *(Welsh Folk Museum)*

machine parts used in the early days of factory mechanisation, particularly in the North of England, such as cog-wheels, pulleys, wheels and shafts.

Today's craftsmen must be versatile to stay in business. Most of them make furniture to commission, restore antique furniture and are able to turn their hand to fitting up shops, offices and kitchens with fitted furniture. Arthur Wells of Ross-on-Wye in Hereford and Worcester, a county with a great tradition in all types of woodwork, served his apprenticeship forty years ago as a carpenter and joiner in a workshop where practically everything was done by hand. Over the years he gained experience in all types of woodworking, including making patterns for industry, exhibition stands and bank fittings—he was able, in fact, to turn his hand to anything required, even if it was far removed from the traditional work of the village carpenter. When the Queen went to Hereford in 1971 he had the honour of restoring a very old oak chair on which she was to sit. The chair is now in the Conningsby Museum in Hereford. Although wood turning has always been somewhat of a sideline for Arthur Wells—the main part of his work today being furniture-making to order and restoring antiques—he finds he is more involved with it as the years pass. He demonstrates bowl turning at many of the larger agricultural shows, selling his work there and at craft fairs and markets, as well as in his workshop/showroom.

Another wood turner from this county who started by making furniture is John Piepereit of Ledbury. He bought himself a small lathe in 1951 and in six months became entirely fascinated by wood turning. He then bought a bigger lathe, on which he could turn any shape. He works alone and everything he makes bears his initials. His wood is carefully selected and wax finished to show his customers the beauty of the grain to the fullest extent; no stain or filler is used. He sells his work to private customers and at exhibitions. At the age of 72 he has a lifetime of experience behind him, for which he is convinced there is no substitute and which he is happy to pass on to others. He still gets great pleasure in seeing the beauty in the grain of a piece of wood gradually revealed as it is turned on the lathe, a piece, perhaps, that might have seemed dull and uninteresting on first appearance. The skill is in knowing when to stop turning for the work to be seen at its best. He is in the happy position of having achieved the ambition he has held from the age of 4—to be a worker in wood all his days.

11

METALWORKERS

When we think of traditional metalworkers it is difficult to imagine any other than the blacksmiths, the mighty men, standing at their smithies under chestnut trees, in almost every village in the land. It is true that they were the most indispensable of all the craftsmen to village life, for while many might have been able to make their own woodwork or provide their own clothes, the forging of the numerous articles of iron needed in the everyday life of a village, particularly when horses were the sole means of transport, required special skills and the expertise of heating and shaping red-hot metal.

It comes as something of a surprise to learn that about 300 years ago these skills were practised by women. In small workshops and cottages around Birmingham, Worcester and Sheffield, many women and children were engaged in the manufacture of small metal goods, such as locks, nails, nuts, bolts, screws, buckles, bits and stirrups—a purely domestic cottage industry which was well established by the beginning of the eighteenth century. They were outworkers engaged in piecework for a small employer known as an undertaker, as he in turn worked for a larger manufacturer and undertook to get materials supplied to him 'worked up'. Much of this work was done at home or in small workshops. Of Sedgley, near Wolverhampton, in 1824 it was said that it 'might appropriately be termed the district of female blacksmiths. They are its most prominent characteristic'. It is estimated that some 50,000 women were engaged in this employment, mostly in producing nails.

A visitor to Birmingham in 1741

> was surprised at the prodigious number of blacksmiths' shops upon the road; and could not conceive how a county, though populous, could support so many people of the same occupation. In some of these shops I observed one or more females, stripped of their upper garments, and not overcharged with their lower, wielding the hammer with all the grace of the sex. The beauties of their faces were rather eclipsed by the smut of the anvil.

The picture of little forges attached to cottages and small farmhouses may give an illusion of a pleasant cottage industry, but this is far from the truth. The small brick workshops were very primitive, with little ventilation, and when the fire was not alight gave 'the appearance of a delapidated coal-hole'. The work would be carried out in such a place by a man, his wife and daughter, perhaps with a boy and a girl hired by the year. There were often one or two forges in a room 10ft (3m) by 9ft (2.7m) which would be filled with hot smoke, ashes, water and clouds of dust. In an article written at the end of the nineteenth century these workers were referred to as 'the white slaves of England'.

The children started work as soon as they could walk, first blowing the bellows, mending the fire when necessary, and at 7 or 8 learning to make the easiest type of nail. After two years' training, a child of 10 or 12 could turn out a thousand nails a day, heating the iron and forging every part of the nail, having changed tools to make the head during the process. Even when education became compulsory children were still expected to help in the forge on their return from school. One of their tasks was to blow the blacksmith's bellows at the back of the fire, that had to be constantly pumped to keep up the heat. For the nails for the hobnail boots that everyone wore, the iron was supplied in 6ft (182cm) lengths, which the children brought home from their employer in a home-made cart. The mother would put three bars in the fire at a time to get hot; as one bar was used so another was put in to keep a continuous flow of metal. Gloves were not worn as they slowed up the work and speed was essential for the job to pay.

Where workshops employed about eight individuals, or in the larger factories, about twelve hours a day were worked, with a two-hour break for meals. At weekends the women, children and apprentices worked even longer hours 'sometimes all night on Friday' to get their work completed by Saturday, when the nails were taken to their employer.

At the Avoncroft Museum of Buildings at Bromsgrove, a place once famous for its nailmaking, two workshops with a wash-house between have been reconstructed. The iron was heated in a central hearth and then fashioned into a great variety of sizes and types of nails, using a treadle-operated hammer known as an 'oliver', in conjunction with specially shaped dies set into a block or base. The washing on a Monday was done in a boiler in the corner of the wash-house, which was also used for brewing home-made beer. The wash-house was sometimes known as the brew-house.

The oliver had a springy pole to raise the hammer into position again and was used to point and head the nails. Both large and small nails were made in this way, ranging from those used to fasten sleepers on railway tracks, known as 'rose head spikes', down to tiny nails for fixing glass into window-frames, known as 'sparrow bills'—country names that seem out of place in industrial surroundings, but many women had taken to nailmaking when work in the country, such as spinning moved to the town.

The same oliver was used for making small chains, which had also been organised on cottage-industry lines. These were made in small forges, mostly by women, although many women were also engaged in the larger workshops on factory lines making larger chains. Girls were usually taught to make both nails and chains so that when there was a slump in one industry they could take to the other.

Even when steam power was introduced and larger factories were built, they were organised at first on the lines of several small workshops together, each run by a master who rented his area from the larger owner.

A larger number of very young children were employed, a fact of life so taken for granted in the eighteenth century that debating societies could discuss the motion in 1774 'Is the custom so much practised of sending children to the shops to work as soon as they are well able to walk, injurious or advantageous to the inhabitants in general?' Pinmakers at Birmingham and Warrington started work as early as 5 years, as it was stated that pin heading 'can be done by a child as soon as it acquires the use of its arms and legs'. This state of affairs passed unnoticed much longer in the many small workshops and forges during the growing protests against the use of child labour owing to the fact that many were situated well out of sight down narrow passages and courtyards.

Having started work at such an early age many of the girls were independent by the time they reached their teens. It was said of them that 'They often enter the beer shop, call for their pints and smoke their pipes like men'. Many were married at 16, often to workmen in the same trade, and continued their trade at home after marriage, working there with their own children. To keep the smallest children quiet while their mothers worked they were given 'Godfrey's (or Gregory's) Cordial', a well-known mixture containing opium and treacle, freely used, and dispensed from a large jug which stood on every chemist's counter. It was usually given to the child from the age of 3 weeks, but a coroner in Nottingham knew it to be given on the day of birth, and it was even prepared before the baby's birth. He stated that as a result a great number of infants died, either suddenly from an overdose, or more slowly over a period, the rest often becoming sickly children, their health ruined for life. Women still worked in the metal trades when all the work was eventually done in factories; the last of the women chainmakers, Lucy Woodall, died in 1979.

In the eighteenth century girls and women were also at work in a cottage industry around Christchurch in Dorset of making fusee chains for watch movements.

The village blacksmith who continued to work in rural conditions after the Industrial Revolution probably had a better life than those who moved nearer the centres of coal production. In his own village, especially in the days of horse transport and simple farm and household requirements, the blacksmith was one of the most important members of society. In Wales in medieval times the smith had been one of the most honoured craftsmen at court, on a par with the priest and the poet. With his skill in shaping metal he supplied all the needs of the community in war and peace. He held this vital position until the Industrial Revolution was well under way. In the early days of mechanisation he made the first machines that were used both in the factories and on the farm. The farmer would explain his requirements and the blacksmith would produce the necessary tools. One of his tasks was the modification of ploughs to suit the soil where they were used.

The first record of a blacksmith taking out a patent for making iron chains for the shipping industry was in 1634. Robert Flinn, a blacksmith, made the first recorded chain cable for a ship at his shop in North Shields. Local blacksmiths made the first machines and tools used in the textile and knitting industries. The skills and traditions learned by the blacksmith over centuries enabled him to turn his hand and hammer to the manufacture of anything made of iron; gradually, however, firms specialising in making machines and tools took over the production of the larger quantities of machinery needed in the nineteenth century as mass production replaced the cottage industry. This left the blacksmith with that part of his work connected with horses and horse-drawn vehicles and the repairs to domestic and farm items. When horses were the only means of transport this aspect of his work was often carried on by a farrier, a specialist in horses and the skills of shoeing. In a small district, however, it was usual for one man to be both smith and farrier.

Before coal replaced wood for fuelling the forge, the most important areas for the production of fine ironware were in the great forest areas of Wales, the Forest of Dean and the Weald of Sussex. These were the great industrial centres, particularly during the Tudor period, for the production of instruments of war and domestic goods. Some of the most creative and ornamental ironwork can be seen in the domestic equipment made by local blacksmiths for kitchen and hearth, much of it unchanged in its basic shapes for hundreds of years. It was not necessary to change the design of objects made for a specific district and its needs, when these had proved satisfactory for so long. The craftsman might add some artistic touches of his own to fire implements, to the fire dogs, for instance, which kept the fire in place and held the spits for roasting meat, or to the pot cranes from which the cauldron hung over the fire. As can be seen from the number of repairs to these items and by the fact that they were bequeathed to other members of the family, the housewife did not cry out for a new improved cooking pot every week, but was quite happy with the one which had served her well for years.

It would be interesting to know whether the suggestions for additions or improvements to basic items came from the housewife or the blacksmith, for example the holders to warm a drink found on some fire dogs. No doubt in the case of farm implements the farmer had definite ideas about his requirements, but the variety of decorations on fire cranes were probably the result of the smith's own creative skills.

This artistic ability is shown effectively in the range of designs on the firebacks which were made in large quantities from the sixteenth to the eighteenth centuries. The central fire in the middle of the medieval hall was replaced by fireplaces on a side wall, with chimneys to take away smoke, these early fireplaces were built of brick or stone, but this was shown to be insufficient to stand up to the heat of a fire. Iron firebacks, the earliest dating from 1548, originally known as 'plates for chimneys' were made to keep the heat from the wall. At first they were merely large, thick, heavy slabs of cast iron. When fireplaces became smaller and were contained in an iron firebasket the firebacks gradually became thinner and narrower. The mould was prepared by pressing a wooden board into well-compressed sand, and before the molten iron was poured into the mould and allowed to cool, it could be decorated. A favourite pattern at first was made by a piece of twisted rope pressed into the sand, but soon the wooden board itself was carved with fleur-de-lis and Tudor roses, the workman eventually making a large variety of patterns. With a carved board many firebacks could be made with identical patterns and skilled woodcarvers were called in to make moulds with tops of different shapes, many with the coat-of-arms of the persons for whom they were made, from royalty downwards. Great events of the day were depicted, scenes from the religious persecutions of Mary Tudor, the Civil War, through to the restoration of Charles II, and the classical designs of the eighteenth century. A large collection of firebacks from the sixteenth and seventeenth centuries may be seen in the Museum of Local History in the Anne of Cleeves House at Lewes, East Sussex. The Sussex Wealden iron industry was of great importance during these centuries, when it was powered by water. Besides firebacks, a vast quantity of all types of domestic and farm implements were produced, many of which may be seen in the museum at Lewes. Set out in historical order, these give a complete picture of the production of iron goods before the Industrial Revolution, the introduction of coal power and the transfer of the industry to the coal-producing areas.

Much of the blacksmith's work until comparatively recently was connected with transport; horse-drawn vehicles needed springs, iron tyres and all manner of harness parts. After the invention of the motorcar, many a blacksmith became the local garage-owner, and agricultural and motor engineer. A good example of what happened to many village blacksmiths can be seen in the development of the firm of E. Martin & Son of Closeburn, Thornhill, in Dumfries and Galloway, which was founded in 1854. Edward Martin, who started his career in the village smithy and still practises the traditional skills of the blacksmith and farrier, is now part of a firm that are motor and agricultural engineers using electric and oxyacetylene welding equipment as well as a portable welder and mobile crane.

Today, with the increase in the popularity of horse-riding, some blacksmiths are again busy, shoeing horses and making parts for horse-drawn carriages that are popular once more. Others are supplying fire implements, fire-tongs, pokers and firebaskets for the grates that have been reopened in country homes; the open fire is again popular and cast-iron firebacks and all their appurtenances are being made.

Many modern blacksmiths are producing decorative ironwork, such as gates, and other items often more works of art than useful. Metal sculptures are made by artists who have learned their metal skills in art schools rather than by working as a blacksmith's assistant for years; in any case, with modern fuels and bellows worked by motor most blacksmiths can work without an assistant.

Little else has changed in the blacksmith's workshop. The forge is still the centre of activity, although usually made of iron rather than brick. Water must still be at hand to cool the metal, and the iron anvil is still there, mounted on a block of wood, usually elm, on which the metal is hammered into shape. The methods and tools, often made by the craftsman for his own use, have changed little since the Iron Age, the whole process being a combination of experience, a trained eye, speed and accuracy, for which nothing can take the place.

Many of the metalworkers of the past were travelling blacksmiths or farriers, particularly if there was insufficient work for them to stay permanently in one place. One such group of people were the travelling coinmakers or travelling mints. Today, it is possible to have coins struck by a traditional travelling mint based at Kingsbridge in South Devon. Coins and commemorative medallions to mark a particular event are produced by the Bigbury Mint started two years ago by two engravers, David Holland and Derek Andrews. Once they have established the design and made an accurate working drawing, the long process of engraving the dies begins. Using hand tools, chisels and punches, the steel is gradually carved away. The design is continually checked by taking wax or clay impressions. When completed, the dies are mounted on an iron-bound oak anvil and carefully positioned to ensure correct alignment. The bland medallion in copper or silver, whichever metal is to be used, is brought to a red-hot temperature, quickly placed between the dies and struck a solid blow with a hammer. The new medallion is then quenched in water and checked for quality before being packed in its protective wallet or presentation box.

One craftsman who combines all the skills of the agricultural engineer, the travelling blacksmith, and the artist-blacksmith is David Cox of Horndean, Hampshire (see Plate

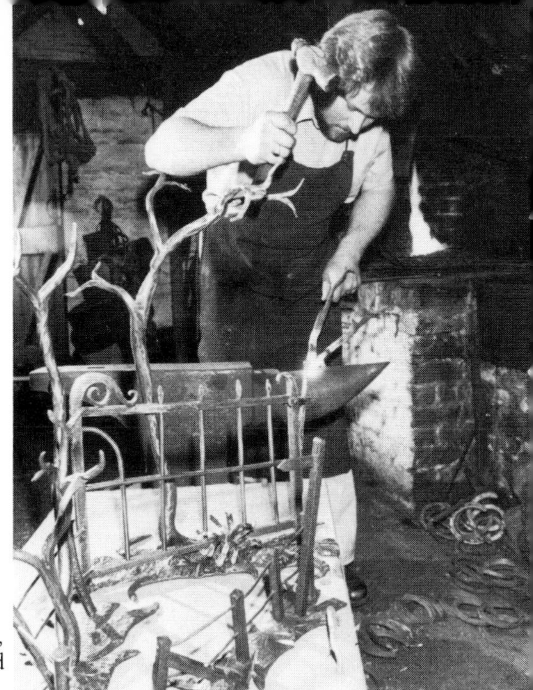

Plate 35 David Cox of Horndean, Hampshire, travelling blacksmith and artist-blacksmith *(Portsmouth News)*

35). Trained at West Dean College, near Chichester, he is mainly employed, working for himself, as an agricultural engineer, travelling in his van from farm to farm with his portable welding equipment. He is able to manufacture any machinery required for a special purpose and to do hand-forged ironwork. Artistic ironwork, for which he has attracted much attention and praise when he has exhibited it at shows, is the part of his work on which he would like to concentrate. This poses a problem for, whereas every village once had a cottage with forge attached, David Cox is having difficulty in finding suitable premises in which to set up his own smithy. Old forges have become modernised country dwellings, often still known as Forge Cottage, but the forge itself having long since disappeared. At present he shares a forge with a farrier friend. Here he produces wonderful hand-forged trees standing by rural gates and fences, and his happiest times are spent demonstrating this aspect of his craft at shows and fairs. He is a member of the Wessex Guild of Craftsmen who hold exhibitions at the Queen Elizabeth Country Park at Petersfield each year.

12

LEATHERWORKERS

In the eleventh century Aelfric, Abbot of Cerne Abbas in Dorset, attributed these words to a Saxon shoemaker:

> I buy hides and skins and I prepare them by my craft, and I make of them boots of various kinds, ankle-leathers, shoes, leather breeches, bottles, bridle-thongs, flasks and budgets, leather neck-pieces, spur-leathers, halters, bags and pouches, and nobody would wish to go through the winter without my craft.

Although modern synthetic materials are used to make all the articles once associated only with leatherwork—shoes, bags, saddles, harnesses—there is no doubt that for quality and durability leather has no match. Today, there are many craftsmen working in leather using traditional methods and making the same articles produced in the eleventh century.

The earliest leatherworker made strictly utilitarian goods—clothing, simple shoes, and carriers for water and possessions. Long ago he was both tanner and craftsman, but the two occupations became separated at any early stage, tanning being a slow process which took up to nine months to preserve the leather.

Prehistoric man may have discovered that one of the earliest uses of flint tools was to scrape the fat and hairs from hides. The large flints which have been found were shaped to fit the palm of the hand and were chipped to give a sharp edge suitable for scraping. He would have softened the hide by rubbing in the fat and brains of the animal, which would have slightly cured the skin. Smoke from his fire would have had the same result, so would the salt used to preserve the meat. The true process of preserving leather by using the tannin content of vegetable matter to cause a chemical change which removes the possibility of putrefaction was probably only discovered over many years. Alum salts which occur in natural deposits may have been accidentally substituted for common salt at some stage. This formed the basis of the production of Cordovan, Cordwain or Spanish leather, a process of preservation that came to Britain from Spain during the Middle Ages, giving the name of cordwainers to early leatherworkers.

By the time the Romans arrived in this country, Britain was already famous for its leather exports, having both the animals to provide the skins and the forests to provide the oak-bark for the tannin process. As well as being used to make cloaks, no doubt as protection against the elements, leather was also used to make garments to be worn in warmer weather, for the remains of the bottom half of what looks like a leather bikini were found at an excavation site near Walbrook, London.

The moulded and hardened leather known as 'cuir bouilli', or boiled leather, was extensively used for parts of medieval armour for both horses and men, such as shields, helmets, shin-guards and knee-caps. The process was probably discovered when stones heated in the fire were dropped into leather water-containers to heat the water. This softened the leather which could then be moulded to shape and left to harden. The process of tanning leather with oak-bark to preserve it must have already been in use for some time before this.

Today, leather is soaked in cold water until it is completely softened or 'sammed', when it is moulded to make cases for all purposes, leggings and saddles. It can be decorated by tooling, incising or punching. When heat is applied to the leather it becomes hard and permanently set. This process was employed in the Middle Ages to cover the enormous trunks or standards and coffers which were loaded up and carried from castle to castle, or manor to manor. The Middle Ages were the age of the traveller and leathermakers provided all the luggage and baggage for their journeys, whether by waggon or horse. The luggage was decorated with elaborate patterns of nails which secured the leather; the waggons were covered with leather sheets to protect the contents from the weather.

Raymond Morris, a leather craftsman and master leather carver—one of only a few in Britain—lives in Scotland, and has the splendid titles of The Chevalier Raymond Morris of Eddergoll and Laird of Eddergoll, among others (see Plate 36). He still makes leather-covered medieval-style boxes, cases, chests and caskets, all handmade, hand-tooled and carved. He specialises in accurate reproductions of seventeenth- and eighteenth-century targes, the circular war shields of the Scottish Highlanders, made of laminated wood covered on both sides with leather. The shields are about 20in (508mm) in diameter and have two straps on the back for hand and arm. The fronts have traditional designs, ranging from simple patterns of brass studs, to added tooling, raised brass bosses

Plate 36 The Chevalier Raymond Morris of Eddergoll, leather craftsman and master leather carver, shown here tooling leather on a reproduction seventeenth-century targe (war shield)

and brass plates, some of which are pierced. Some have 6in (152mm) spikes in the centre which unscrew and can be kept in a sheath on the back. These shields are made in over fifty designs, all found in museums, and all original and authentic.

This combination of woodwork covered with leather is traditional and in Raymond Morris's case probably stems from the fact that one of his grandfathers owned a sawmill and wood-turnery business and the other was a master harnessmaker. He himself spent three years working and studying in tanneries and currying workshops, followed by spells on farms, in agricultural college and forestry. By this time he was ready to go into business on his own as a professional leather craftsman. He started in an old watermill in Perthshire, which he converted into a house, workshop and showroom, where he remained for eight years. Then he moved to the county of Fife, to the royal burgh of Cupar, about 12 miles (19km) from St Andrews, where he lives in a Georgian merchant's house, with a two-storey row of seventeenth-century houses next door, which have been converted into a workshop, studio and showroom.

Another interest of this gifted craftsman is the study of heraldry and he produces personal coats-of-arms on leather. They are usually made as wall panels; sometimes they are painted, or carved and painted, and sometimes built up in separate pieces moulded to shape to give a 3-D effect. They look more effective than a wood carving and although they cost less will still last for a few hundred years.

Raymond Morris also does a small amount of wholesale work in pressed leather—coasters, tablemats, key-rings and 9in (228mm) miniature targes and reproduction historic seals. He produces all this work single-handed and has a metal die to use under a hand-operated press. He uses the heavier leathers, 1/8in (3mm), 1/4in (6mm) and up to almost 1/2in (12mm) thick, for his reproductions. Most of his work is commissioned and some exported. It has been exhibited in America and Sweden.

The tooling is done by pressing blunt tools by hand into slightly dampened leather. The carving is done by cutting all the drawn lines with a very sharp knife. Then the background is counter-sunk by mallet and various shaped metal punches, which do not remove any part of the design (as is done in wood carving). If any part of the design was lost the mass of fibres under the smooth grain of the leather would be exposed and look extremely untidy. Some of the heraldic carved leather designs over circular wood are made as coffee-table tops of about 21in (53cm) in diameter.

Raymond Morris's wife Margaret teaches and demonstrates tapestry-weaving and metal-thread embroidery at their studio and at evening classes. She specialises in the production of miniature tapestries of traditional Fife architecture of white rough-cast walls and red pantile roofs. The cottages which now house their business premises are in this style. The seventeenth-century pantiles were originally brought back from the Low Countries as ballast in the ships which exported the wool of the area to those countries.

Over the centuries leather has been used extensively for making black-jacks (drinking mugs), bombards (beer jugs) and water-bottles. By Saxon times the technique of moulding leather and forming it into rigid vessels for everyday use was already highly developed. They were in general use in medieval times in palaces and taverns; the rich man's black-jack might be lined with pewter and rimmed with silver while those for everyday use were lined with pitch. They were made of oak-bark tanned leather from cattle hide which was moulded over wooden moulds after samming and removed in sections; the recessed bottoms were made separately. The pieces were hand-stitched before the leather hardened so that the stitches sank well into the leather. The hemp used to sew them was made up by an apprentice or a member of the family by twisting together a number of strong linen strands, which were well waxed to make sewing easier. Today, linen thread is still preferred, but it is now possible to buy from a wide range of both natural and manmade fibres. Sometimes, wet sand was used and poured out when dry. The interior of the jack was lined with pitch, or resin poured in whilst molten to make the leather water- or ale-proof. The outsides were stained black and wax polished.

Jacks, bombards and other medieval vessels are made today in traditional manner by Tony and Dawn Dennis at St Eval Leather Crafts, near Wadebridge, Cornwall. They still use oak-bark tanned leather which they obtain from Grampound. Tony Dennis studied the making of these vessels at the Northampton Museum of Leathercraft, where can be seen displays of all the wares made in leather from ancient Egyptian times to the present day. Tony and Dawn Dennis also make modern handbags, purses and bellows, all handmade and hand-tooled. Visitors to their workshop buy the pitch-lined black-jacks and a variety of other medieval leather goods either for use or as unique ornaments for their homes.

There were so many leatherworkers in the Middle Ages—cordwainers, leathersellers, pouch-makers, pursers, cofferers, bottlers, saddlers—that a number of different craft guilds were set up to control the standard of work. The chief wares of leathersellers were laces or thongs needed in large quantities for fastening leather clothing, for lacing shoes and bags and for joining parts of armour.

Leather armour was in use by the end of the fourteenth century and leather tunics and jerkins were extensively worn in the seventeenth. The latter were made of buff leather, so called as originally it was made from the hide of the European buffalo, preserved by an oil-dressing process similar to that used in the production of chamois leather. The pale yellow colour which we call buff was also the colour of the finished buff leather. This leather is so tough that reputedly it could turn the point of a sword. A fine collection of the buff coats worn by the opponents of Charles I during the Civil War may be seen hanging on the wall of the Great Hall of the Manor of Littlecote in Wiltshire, where there is also a guardroom, reputedly haunted by Cromwellian guards, examples of whose armour and buff leather coats are on display. Infantry equipment prior to World War I was still made of buff leather. Leather hats and gauntlets were also worn by the army. Highly ornamented buff leather hats and gloves had been worn since Elizabethan times; one such hat was embroidered and the leather slashed to reveal a salmon pink lining beneath.

In medieval times most men and women wore a leather belt or girdle, often highly decorated and worn with purses, bags or books attached to them for safety.

Fashionable leather belts for women are produced at Graeme Ellisdon's Osprey Belt Company, which operates from Kimpton, near Hitchin, Hertfordshire. This very successful enterprise is run in true cottage industry style: the belts are designed by Graeme Ellisdon, who organises the materials and markets the belts, which are made by sixteen outworkers in the village. About fifty varieties of belts are produced, which are sold mainly by the big London stores, who order from designs and samples. Twice a year the Osprey Belt Company have a stand at the Prêt à Porter exhibition of fashion in Paris and the business owes much of its success to Graeme Ellisdon's experience of designing belts and marketing them in Europe before starting up on his own. He buys the brass buckles in England, where the best buckles are made, and the finished leather from London. He is now starting to buy the leather at an earlier stage in its production to have greater control over the colours produced in the dyeing, so important in fashion today.

Unlike many of today's country leatherworkers, the village leatherworkers of the past would not have specialised in one particular kind of work. He would have been the village saddler—an important part of his work—but he would also have made, among other leather goods, belts, cases for guns and binoculars, and leather aprons for other craftsmen. The work of the village shoemaker, or cordwainer as they were known, was usually a separate enterprise and a busy one, too—many large villages could support up to three and market towns up to ten. In many families the craft of shoemaking was passed on from father to son. In towns the various leather guilds were often called upon to settle disputes as to which jobs were to be done by the tanners, the cordwainers and the saddlers, but in the village the saddler dealt with most of the work unopposed. Before the advent of the motorcar and the tractor he was as essential a member of the community as the wheelwright and the blacksmith.

Apart from saddles, he made harnesses and horse collars in a large variety of sizes and patterns. When horsepower was at its height a village could support individual craftsmen in the different categories of leatherworkers. Horse collars, although of the same basic construction, varied in design in different parts of the country. They were as varied as the breeds of horses for which they were made, the type of countryside in which they were to work, and the jobs they had to do, whether in towns or on the farms. For the efficient working of a draught horse the collar must be well fitted and well made. Tougher leather was chosen to stand hard wear and the more supple leather for greater comfort where needed. The saddler and horse-collar maker used a great variety of leathers in their work, which they obtained from the local tannery.

Oak-bark tanneries were common in Britain until the middle of the nineteenth century, many villages and country towns having their own tanneries. Wales had a flourishing leather industry producing oak-bark tanned leather from the skins of Welsh cattle and sheep which was exported to all parts of the country. They had the oak trees for tanning, tallow from their sheep for dressing the leather and pure water from mountain streams that would not discolour the skins.

The last oak-bark tannery to operate in Wales was at Rhayader. Dating from the eighteenth century, it was mainly concerned in producing heavy leathers for boots and horse harnesses. The hides dealt with at this tannery took at least eighteen months to convert into leather. The craft of currying or leather-dressing was also carried on at this tannery, although it was more usual for it to to be a separate craft. When the tannery closed down it was re-erected at the Welsh Folk Museum at St Fagans, near Cardiff. The visitor can see the clean-water pit where the hides were initially washed and three lime-pits where the raw hides were immersed for several days before the hair and flesh were removed. There are also three 'mastering pits' where hides, such as calf skins, were softened in a mixture of hen and pigeon dung, dog excreta and water. There was also a pit where unwanted items and remains were put, later to be sent to the glueworks. There is a room where the hides were cut up before tanning and a cellar where horse hides were stored in damp conditions to produce a white leather popular for footwear in the nineteenth century.

There is a series of pits in the tanyard, some open-air and some covered by the main tannery building. Most were oak-lined for the actual making of the tanning liquors of oak-bark mixed with water. The bark from Welsh oak trees was ground into a fine powder before use. The remaining pits were used for the immersion of the hides in this liquor for the actual tanning process. This took several months, the hides being transferred gradually from weak to increasingly strong solutions so that the leather tanned evenly all the way through. It would have been disastrous to the production of good leather if strong tannins were used in the early stages because the surface on both sides would tan quickly and it would then be impossible to make the tannin penetrate the hide, resulting in half-tanned leather of poor and brittle quality.

The tanned leather was next scrubbed and washed on stone slabs and dried on racks on the first floor of the building. The currier then took over the leather to make it more supple. He worked on a large mahogany table, first scrubbing and washing the leather with soap and water, then shaving off a thin layer and adding oil and grease with a brush to the surface. The leather was dried slowly and polished with glass, mahogany, stone and steel polishers, after which it could be dyed. The grease was often dubbin, a mixture of tallow and cod-liver oil.

All the processes of tanning were lengthy, requiring much space and labour. Although the earliest leatherworkers may have done all the jobs of tanner, currier and saddler when there was only a small amount of hide to work, these functions became separated early in the history of leather making.

Little change in tanning methods took place until the latter part of the nineteenth century when the chrome method of preserving leather was introduced. This produced leather with quite different characteristics from any previously made. It resulted eventually in leather that could stand up to heat and acids and was washable. It played a greater part in industrial uses, for which oak-bark leather could not be used, and also in the development of modern footwear. The new methods reduced the time needed for tanning leather from months to days.

Most modern saddlers buy their leather ready for use. The types of saddles with which we are familiar date from the eighteenth century, when riding was increasingly enjoyed as a sport by the gentry. The origin of the Saddlers' Company that kept a close watch on the quality of saddles produced went back much further. The foundations of early saddles were made entirely of wood and the saddlers made frequent complaints about the quality of the workmanship of the joiners who supplied them. In the seventeenth century the guild reprimanded many saddlers for poor work, punishing one for making a saddle with 'naughtie' straps and another for making a side-saddle 'very faulty beside evil workmanship', which was eventually burnt outside his door.

The high standards set by the guilds over the centuries are practised by many saddlemakers today, kept busy by the increase in popularity of horse-riding. Sally Barnes is a saddler who has her workshop in one of the old farm buildings on the Lockinge Estate. After training at the Cordwainers' College in London and for a further three years with a harness-maker, she has been running her own saddlery business for two years. She specialises in hand-made and made-to-measure saddles and harnesses, the customers either bringing their horses to her workshop for measuring, if they live near enough, or she supplies a measurement form for them to complete. Obviously, a made-to-measure saddle or harness will be more comfortable and safe for both horse and rider than one bought off-the-peg.

Although first and foremost a saddler, Sally also makes handbags, belts and wallets, all under the name of Buckingham Leathergoods. Among the items on sale at her workshop are fire bellows, leather- and wood-made articles of the type used for centuries. The latter are craftsman-made by John Jones of Pewsey from ash-wood which is stained and french polished or teak oiled; they are finished with top quality leather and solid brass nozzles and decorated with brass studs.

13

OUR DAILY BREAD, BUTTER, CHEESE AND PIES

> The dairy was certainly worth looking at: it was a scene to sicken for with a sort of calenture in hot and dusty streets—such coolness, such purity, such fresh fragrance of new-pressed cheese, of firm butter, of wooden vessels perpetually bathed in pure water; such soft colouring of red earthenware and creamy surfaces, brown wood and polished tin, grey limestone and rich orange-red rust on the iron weights and hooks and hinges. But one gets only a confused notion of these details when they surround a distractingly pretty girl of seventeen, standing, on little pattens and rounding her dimpled arm to lift a pound of butter out of the scale.

This picture of Mrs Poyser's farmhouse dairy, with Hetty the dairymaid packing the butter in dock leaves ready for market, comes from George Eliot's *Adam Bede* and gives a good idea of what such a dairy was like at the end of the eighteenth century, when the making of dairy products in the home was at its height.

From Elizabethan times until the last century all the butter and cheese consumed in this country was produced in farmhouse dairies by farmers' wives, with the help of the daughters and dairymaids. Dairy production was well established in Anglo-Saxon times in homes all over the country. Its history may extend to the days of Roman Britain—perhaps even earlier. Castles and manor houses were probably the first to have specially built dairies, but until the eighteenth century when farmers learned to provide fodder to keep cattle all the year round, milk production had been a fairly seasonal business. However, from the eighteenth century onwards, improved farming and cattle-breeding methods enabled a steady growth in dairy products. Even the wives of well-to-do farmers, who left the cooking and kitchen work to their servants, never thought work in the dairy beneath them and superintended it themselves at all times. They took great pride in the cleanliness of their surroundings and utensils—most dairies were whitewashed twice a year—and in the quality of the butter and cheese they produced which was sent to market.

This had always been classed as women's work, probably because this high standard of cleanliness had to be maintained if the products were to keep well, and also because of the patience needed to churn by hand and the constant attention to detail and concentration required for cheese production.

During the nineteenth century it was important for the business to be successful for many farmers' wives depended on the sale of their dairy produce to buy the extra items needed in the home, which they were unable to produce themselves, such as sewing materials, cottons and needles—'pin money' in fact. These items increased in number as more manufactured goods appeared on the market.

The whole process of dairying was surrounded by superstition. In the North a 'dobbie' stone with a hole in it hung by cow-sheds to protect the cows and their milk from witchcraft; or the berries of the rowan tree, a sacred tree of Scandinavian countries, were hung round the churns for the same purpose. In the Highlands of Scotland a hollow stone was kept near the cow-shed so that a little milk could be poured into it as an offering to the brownie who looked after the cattle.

The process started by the milking of cows by hand, often as they stood in the fields or in dimly lit cow-sheds. Milkmaids did this work in the early hours of the morning or in the dark evenings, balancing on the traditional milking stool. The milk was carried back to the dairy in wooden pails hanging from a wooden yoke over the milkmaid's shoulders, or in the North sometimes in a 'back can' made to fit like a rucksack on her back.

The milk was poured into large pans or crocks which stood on stone or slate shelves or into slate-lined troughs to allow the cream to settle until churning time, which often took place only once a week. The pans or crocks made by the local pottery were glazed on the inside only, which was thought to help keep the milk cool and sweet and also to give more cream. It was very important that the dairy should be a cool place so that the cream would not turn sour before churning. It was usually situated therefore on the north side of the house, with a white flagged floor and small slatted windows, netted against flies, to keep out the sun. There was often an elderbush near the dairy door, where the butter muslin and dairy cloths were hung to dry, to keep away flies and evil spirits.

The cream was skimmed by hand from the milk with a wooden skimmer or fleeter, a flat round utensil with a wooden handle with holes in it to enable the whey to drain out. Near coasts scallop shells with pierced holes were used. Later skimmers were made of brass, copper or tin. Sometimes the trough into which the milk was poured had holes for the skimmed milk to drain away to pans below, leaving the cream behind. It took a quart (1.1 litres) of cream to make a pound

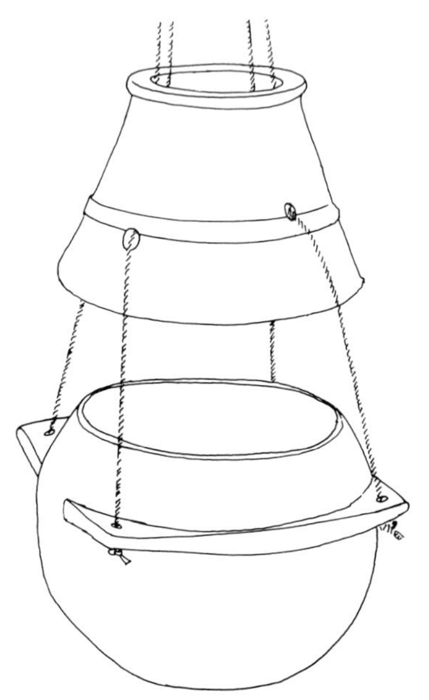

Fig 43 Medieval swing churn

Plate 37 Plunger churn for making butter. It was held in one hand, while the plunger was pushed up and down. The photograph was taken in Brechfa, Carmarthenshire, *c* 1900 *(Welsh Folk Museum)*

Plate 38 A churn turned by a dog pawing the strips of wood on a wheel *(Welsh Folk Museum)*

(450g) of butter and in the early days of dairying this was a fairly energetic process. The earliest method was to swing the cream backwards and forwards in a type of two-handled staved wooden bucket, or in the type of swing churn illustrated in Fig 43 which dates from medieval times.

Whether it was less tiring to work a churn up and down rather than swinging it from side to side is doubtful, but the type of churn next in use, which could make a larger quantity of butter, was the plunger churn or stand churn, made by the local cooper (see Plate 37). This was held in one hand while the plunger was pushed up and down, although never right to the top or the cream might splash out. The plunger had a perforated wooden or metal disc on the bottom and passed through a central hole in the churn lid.

A rocker churn was probably easier to work, being a rectangular box mounted on a stand, with slats fixed across the inside, which was rocked up and down (Fig 44). There were other box-shaped churns with handles which, when turned, churned the cream through a fan inside the box. As late as 1940 box churns still existed on the larger Welsh farms which were turned by a dog running round a wheel (see Plate 38). There

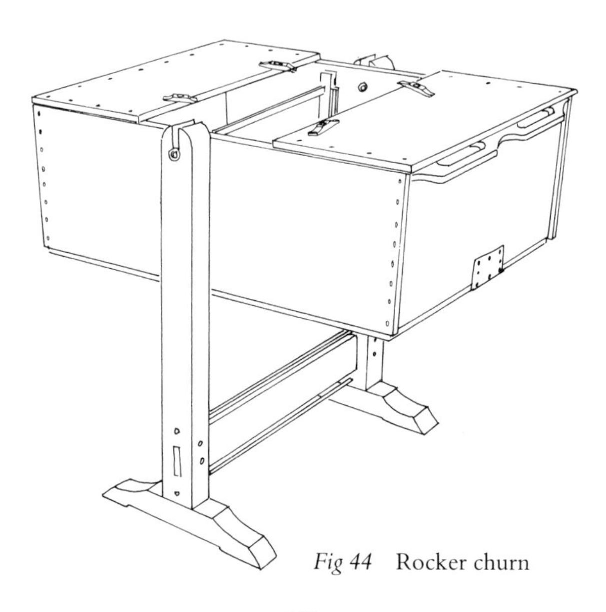

Fig 44 Rocker churn

were strips of wood on the wheel so that the dog could turn it without slipping as it pawed the wheel round; the fan inside turned so quickly that butter was soon produced. It was said that dogs enjoyed this work.

Rotary churns where the whole barrel was turned over repeatedly were the latest in this succession of wooden churns in use until the modern commercial churns made their appearance.

The sound inside the churn told the experienced dairymaid when the butter was ready, even before she looked inside. Churning was a laborious process and accompanied by the muttering of charms to hasten the making and to keep witches away. After the buttermilk was drained off the butter was washed in cold water and then worked to remove all surplus water so that it would keep well. Salt was added at this stage.

Fig 45 Butterworker or clapper with which water was pressed from the butter

The butter was worked either in a shallow staved bowl with a butterworker or clapper (Fig 45 and Plate 39), constantly pressed to remove the water, or it was rolled by hand with a grooved butterworker, a rolling-pin with grooves, or in a butterworker as shown in Fig 46. This device on a stand had a shallow wooden trough about 3ft (1m) long, 18in (457mm) wide and 5in (76mm) deep which sloped gently to one end. The grooved wooden roller, with its spindle connected to the handle, moved up and down when the handle was turned, its tiny wheels fitting into runners on the outside of the trough. The remaining water was squeezed from the butter and drained down a hole at the end.

Plate 39 Mrs Thomas of Arwel, Cardiganshire, preparing butter with a butterworker or clapper in 1968 *(Welsh Folk Museum)*

The dairymaid quickly shaped the butter into rounds or oblongs with the aid of two wooden butter platters or 'Scotch hands', hardly needing scales, knowing by experience the weight of each pat. Some dairymaids made as much as 170lb (77kg) butter in a day. Wooden scales like the ones shown in Fig 47 were in use from Elizabethan times until the end of the last century, and, like so many of the utensils once found in every home, were the products of the village turner. The central stand of these scales would have been turned on a pole-lathe and carries a wooden cross-piece which swings on a round iron peg; the suspended bowls are of wood.

It was in the dairy that from Elizabethan times at least the housewife was at her most productive. There is a tiny dairy in the farmhouse where Mary Arden, the mother of William Shakespeare, lived before her marriage in 1557, at Wilmcote, Stratford-on-Avon. Today it is open to the public and in the cool dairy with its whitewashed walls and small window can be seen some of the wooden utensils that were once used. There are scales, a skimmer, the ridged butter roller and a

Fig 46 Butterworking table
Fig 47 Wooden scales used in the dairy

butter print. These prints were carved in a variety of patterns which, when pressed on the finished pats of butter, decorated it and also identified the butter of a particular farm when it was taken to market; many farms had their own special print (see Plate 40). Prints of cows, swans, flowers and birds were especially popular. Large quantities of butter were taken to market stored in butter casks or kegs.

Plate 40 Butter prints used both for decoration and for the identification of the butter of a particular farm *(Welsh Folk Museum)*

Keeping these wooden utensils clean was a perpetual problem. Most were made of sycamore wood which stood up well to a great deal of washing, necessary if the milk and butter was not to turn sour. Sycamore also had no smell and did not taint the food in the articles made from it. Ashes were often used for scouring. Housewives were well aware of the need for absolute cleanliness in the dairy. In many districts, such as the Highlands of Scotland, hot water in great quantities was not easily obtained. The containers were scrubbed with brushes made of heather and then filled with cold water into which pebbles heated in the fire were dropped to heat the water. In many old examples the marks of burning caused by these pebbles can still be seen. After scouring and scalding the utensils were put out in the fresh air and sunshine to dry and sweeten them.

The whey from butter-making was usually fed to the pigs or calves. In many cases, however, cheese for domestic consumption was made from it, although, judging by the names by which it was known in various parts of the country—'old peg cheese' or 'wangy cheese', that is, tough enough to make wangs or thongs from, or 'Suffolk Bang' which needed to be softened in front of a fire before being eaten—it was not at all savoury.

Ewes as well as cows were milked during the Elizabethan period, a tradition that continued for some time in certain areas. The sheep were milked after lambing in the spring and cheese made from their milk mixed with skimmed cow's milk in the proportion of 1 gal (4.5 litres) ewe's milk to 4 gal (18 litres) cow's milk.

Cheese varied from district to district not only owing to the different pastures on which the cows fed and the various methods of cheese production, but because there were variations within a particular area in cheese produced at different times of the year. The cheese made in the Yorkshire Dales in the spring when the cows first went out to grass was known as 'grass cheese'; 'fog cheese' was made when the cows were feeding on the 'fog', the aftermath of the hay; and the tough, hard cheese made in winter when the cows were fed on hay was known as 'hay cheese'. Cows fed on the herby grass of limestone areas were thought to produce the best milk for cheesemaking.

In Wensleydale in Yorkshire a continuous record of cheesemaking extends for eight centuries. At the end of the eighteenth century large quantities of Wensleydale cheese and butter were sent to York before despatch to the London markets. One person alone exported between 700 and 800 firkins of butter a year, a firkin being 56lb (23kg). A special business existed making butter boxes for this trade. The cheeses varied from 5lb (2.2kg) to 15lb (8kg) in weight. All the farms in the area made cheese even if they only owned as few as three cows. A farm with only seven cows could produce two cheeses a day.

Large quantities of Double Gloucester cheese were made on dairy farms in the Severn Valley and the Vale of Berkeley and sent to markets in many large cities both in this country and abroad.

Before cheese was made, the milk from the evening's milking was poured into the pans and troughs and the cream removed for butter-making. Some of the remaining skimmed milk was heated and all of it added to the next morning's milk to bring it to the required temperature before the rennet was added. Sometimes the whole of the milk was heated; the temperature varied according to the season. When the milk had coagulated the curd was broken either by hand or with a

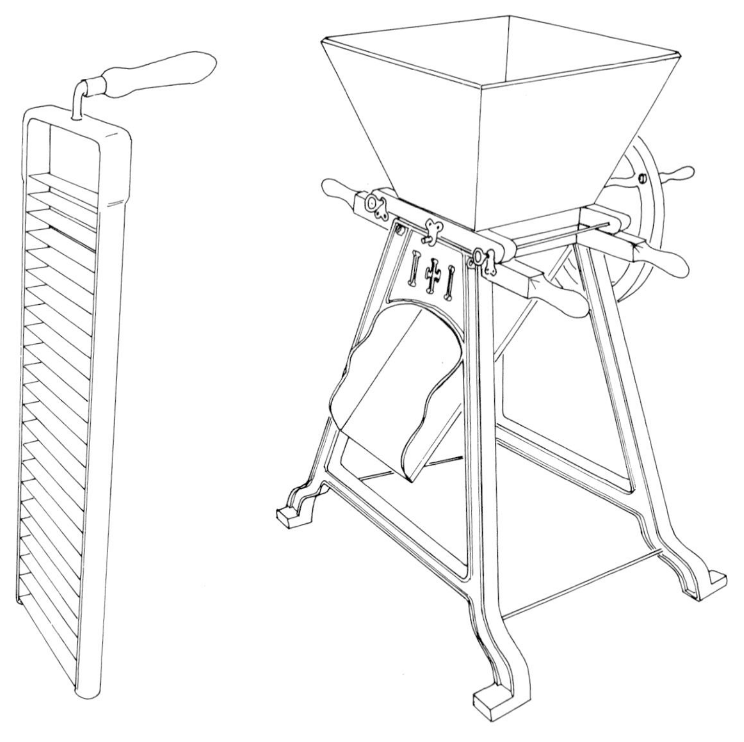

Fig 48 Curd knife with which the curd was broken
Fig 49 Curd mill used to break the curd

type of curd breaker or curd knife (Fig 48). On large farms a curd mill was used (Fig 49). The broken curd was put into a tub to drain, salt was added and the curd piled into a cheese vat, sometimes wrapped in a cloth. The curd had next to be pressed for some hours to remove any surplus moisture. Several types of press were in use (Fig 50). Considerable physical strength was needed to manage these cheese presses and a farmer would take this factor into consideration when choosing a wife. An early form of cheese press was kept outside under a tree with the great stone weight hanging from it. Presses became more sophisticated during the nineteenth century.

Some of the cheese vats were circular wooden frames or rims without top or bottom in which the curd was pressed. A heavy weight or piece of wood would be placed on top of the

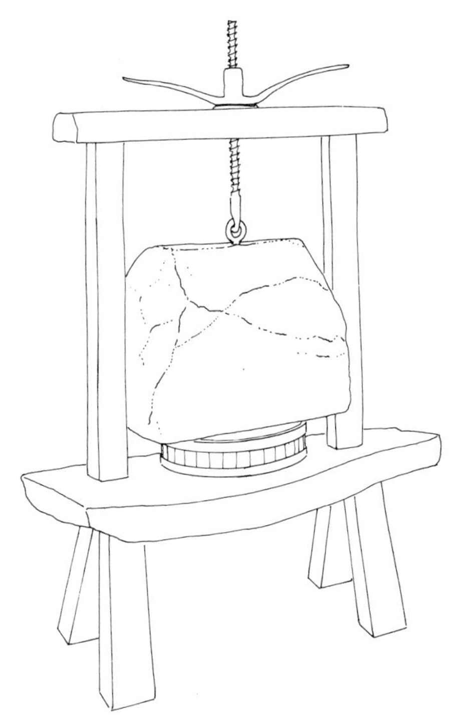

Fig 50 Cheese press used to extract surplus moisture from the curd

frame and a heavy stone placed on top of that. Some vats had two compartments, a partition with holes about two-thirds of the way down; the curds were pressed in the top half and the whey drained beneath.

Many farms had a cheese-room with racks on which the cheeses could be left to mature after pressing. The cheeses needed turning at intervals, often several times a day, and this was where the experienced cheesemaker showed her skills if the finished cheeses were to be of good quality. The cheeses made at Cheddar were left to mature in Cheddar caves, used for this purpose for hundreds of years. In small farms a dark loft or attic was used. The temperature of the storage room was carefully watched and windows opened and shut as necessary.

The cheeses were taken to market or to the many special cheese fairs held around the country in straw-lined waggons.

Many purchasers bought a year's supply of cheese at these fairs.

Dairy production increased in Victorian times, but as more land was enclosed during the nineteenth century the cottager no longer had a place to keep his cow on the common land and milk production became centred more and more in the larger farms. Many Victorian farmers built beautifully tiled dairies. One of these can still be seen at the Home Farm on the Lockinge Estate. The dairy is now the shop where the pottery produced by Les and Brenda Owens at the centre is sold. Their pottery is shown to great advantage against the beautiful hand-painted tiles on the walls and the marble-topped shelves where the butter was once made.

Milk was taken round in churns by pony and trap to those who no longer kept their own cow. Before this, cows and goats were led from door to door and the housewife could buy milk as it was taken straight from the animal on her doorstep; or it could be purchased from a milkman or maid who carried the milk in pails hanging from yokes. Some of the churns had brass taps from which the housewife's jug could be filled. Bottled milk did not come in until after World War I.

The amount of milk sent from rural areas to the towns by train increased after 1850, and by the beginning of the twentieth century there were many large cheese- and butter-making firms established in country areas. Metal buckets, pans and churns were mass produced and replaced the wooden ones. Machines were introduced to speed up production. By 1890 a milk separator was introduced to replace setting the milk in pans to obtain the cream; iron-framed cheese presses with a powerful spring to apply the necessary pressure, made weights obsolete. By 1920 most cheese was produced in large commercial dairies; by the 1930s the price for farmhouse cheese was so low that it was no longer viable to make it in this way, and farmers concentrated solely on milk production.

The village baker was one of the first tradesmen to take over a method of food production traditionally done at home. Baking bread had never been as great a home industry as might be imagined, as large areas of Scotland, Wales and England, especially in the North, lived on a variety of oatcakes which were easily produced on open fires. Bread, when it was eaten, often included such ingredients as peas, beans, barley and even turnips, owing to poor harvests or just plain poverty. In the Middle Ages pure wheat bread, known as manchet, was eaten only by the wealthy. The most common bread was made of rye, or rye and wheat mixed together.

Bakers' guilds were among the earliest guilds formed, but their influence was not as wide as that of the early weavers' guilds. The bakers' guild in Coventry has an unbroken record of existence from the reign of King John. By the time of Henry II regulations established a sliding scale fixing the proper weight for a farthing loaf, depending on the price of corn.

The baker was one of the first tradesmen to set up in the village—baking the daily bread in difficult conditions and obtaining the supply of fuel needed was never easy in cottage and farmhouse homes. Before the kitchen range with its oven at the side became more general in the nineteenth century, bread ovens were often built into the wall at the side of open fireplaces. Faggots or furze were burnt inside until the oven was hot enough, then the ashes raked out and the loaves placed inside, sometimes in tins, sometimes directly on to the oven floor. The latter were said to be the sweetest bread of all. They were put in and removed from the oven with a long-handled flat shovel or oven peel. Pies, cakes and meat were also baked in this way. Where there was no bread oven in small homes the bread could be baked on the floor of the hearth under a bake-iron, a type of lid, which had hot ashes or peat packed round it. Many bakers would bake pies for a few pence and housewives would mark their own pies for identification.

One of the most successful home industries producing traditional home-cooked pies has been run for the last twelve years by Mrs Kathleen Thomas from her country home at Hemyock in East Devon. After twelve years as cookery editor of a national farming journal she has built up a successful business producing country pies made from traditional farmhouse recipes, some of which go back 200 years. The business was run from a converted cow-shed on her husband's farm, using local housewives as part-time helpers. The pies were sold under the label 'Devon Larders' and were supplied to local shops, large stores, hotels and public houses—the latter particularly delighted to have her pies to serve for the ever-growing popularity of the pub lunch. Before long, like so many successful small businesses, she was under pressure to expand. Large food manufacturers wanted to take over the business and she was offered grants and loans to expand. She rejected all these offers for her cottage industry would have soon become just another mass-produced pie factory, entirely defeating the object of the home-made label.

As it happens, Kathleen Thomas has greatly expanded the business, but in her own way. She has granted franchises, for which she takes a small royalty on the profits, to twelve other housewives in all parts of the country from Cheshire to Cornwall; each exclusive franchise covers an area of up to 30 miles (48km) around them. All these housewives make pies to the same recipes as those of Kathleen Thomas and sell them at the same wholesale price to stores, hotels and public houses in their area; at the same time employment is given to local housewives as the businesses expand and extra help is required.

Kathleen Thomas selects her potential clients with great care as the high standard of her products has to be maintained. They come to her home for a four-hour explanation of what running a cottage cookery industry from their homes entails. She gives them advice, where needed, on how to obtain planning permission to alter existing buildings or to build an extension to make a suitable kitchen for home production on a large scale. Many have converted old farm buildings no longer in use on their land. They learn what equipment they will need and how to purchase it, secondhand if necessary, how to keep accounts and how to market their pies and distribute them to their customers. This advice has enabled all those who take up one of Kathleen's franchises to make a great success of their business. She gives them a further three-day training course on how to cook the pies. She has adopted most of the traditional recipes to suit modern palates and digestions, as some would have been too stodgy and fatty in their original forms.

The most popular of the pies is turkey pot, which is either baked in a 6lb (2.7kg) oblong size, making easy cutting in a restaurant or pub, or in a 5lb (2.2kg) round. It contains turkey, bacon and sausage meat—a good solid meat filling. Also made are stuffed chicken pies, the home-mixed stuffing made of sausage meat with herbs, onions and egg; Clovelly Chicken, a pie with chunky pieces of chicken in a white sauce with peas, carrots and pimento in it; Country Pork Pies, all made in large and small versions; Game and Duck pies; cheeselets made with cheese sauce and onion; and a sweet pastry recipe containing mixed fruit, walnuts, dark brown sugar and chopped figs known as Figgy Sly.

All the pies have a shelf life of at least eight days and are made only with the purest ingredients, usually obtained from local producers; no preservatives are used and the pastry is home-made and glazed with egg. Such wholesome home-made food is appreciated increasingly today.

If these franchises are to remain successful businesses, the cooks must also learn how to buy the ingredients cheaply while at the same time maintaining the high quality they must keep up if they are to sell under the Country Larder label. Kathleen Thomas therefore also provides facilities for the bulk buying of many of the ingredients and packaging, such as flour, turkeys, boxes and brochures.

Country Larders also have a connection with a well-known mail order firm from Crediton. Country Larder pies are exported as far afield as Czechoslovakia. At a time of life when many women would sit back and relax, Kathleen Thomas is about to embark on a new venture. Plans are well under way for a Country Larder bakery at the new Coldharbour Mill Museum complex at Uffculme, a few miles from Hemyock. From this they expect to supply visitors to the museum (which will be the only museum of wool in the country) and also to expand the mail order business with speciality lines which will also be sold in the mill shop.

APPENDICES

1 Craft Guilds and Associations

The craft guilds of the Middle Ages had wide powers to control the trade and work of their members. Wardens had the right to search to check that the best quality materials were used and that the goods were properly made. They made rules for the training of apprentices and employment of workers. Their aim was to ensure the public that work was executed by qualified craftsmen who were adequately remunerated.

In the last few decades with the great revival in the making of goods by hand in traditional ways, many guilds have been formed covering a particular craft or county. These are a great help to those who wish to find out where they can obtain a certain craftsman-made article or perhaps watch the work being made. Many of the guilds require their members to submit their work for approval before they are accepted as full members, which gives the public some guidance as to the standard of work. Some of the more enterprising guilds publish maps showing where their members are at work and what they make—a great help as so many work and live in fairly remote areas. Most of the guilds hold exhibitions of their members' work and craft markets where the crafts are demonstrated and are for sale. Some offer a full membership to practising craftsmen and women whose standard of workmanship and design has satisfied a selection committee of craftsmen of the highest repute. All craftsmen may become associate members and ordinary membership is available for anyone who wishes to support the guild, but who is not necessarily a craftsman.

Some of the guilds receive aid from the Tourist Boards for the publication of their lists of members and maps, and also from the councils who help industries in rural areas.

The help given to craftsmen and women as well as to small businesses of all kinds in rural areas by COSIRA (Council for Small Industries in Rural Areas) in England is invaluable. COSIRA is the main agent for the Development Commission whose prime objective is to help the rural parts of England support viable and prosperous communities, especially in deprived areas. The council has county organisers all over England (a list can be obtained from COSIRA) who can give information and assistance backed by committees of local volunteers. About 12,000 small firms are already being helped by professional advice, covering business management and accountancy to engineering, woodworking and plastics; courses in a wide range of skills either locally or in COSIRA workshops; and finance.

Normally, small manufacturing and servicing businesses are eligible provided that not more than twenty skilled people are employed and the business is located in an English rural area or country town of not more than 10,000 inhabitants. Similar services are offered by the Welsh Development Agency and the Scottish Development Agency. COSIRA has been able to help find suitable buildings for sale or rent where small businesses can be carried on and advise on their conversion. Using exisiting buildings, often old farm buildings no longer needed, is much favoured today and supported by the Development Commission with grants in counties with special needs for the revitalisation of their rural areas. Many of the craft centres and craftsmen mentioned in Appendix III have been helped in this way.

The following selection of craft guilds, councils and associations may be helpful to those who run cottage industries and to those who wish to buy their goods:

Council for Small Industries in Rural Areas (CoSIRA)
141, Castle Street, Salisbury, Wiltshire, SP1 3TP
The Scottish Development Agency (Small Business Division)
102, Telford Road, Edinburgh, EN4 2NP
Welsh Development Agency (Small Business Division)
Treforest Industrial Estate, Pontypridd, Mid Glamorgan, CF37 5UT
Basketmakers' Association
Mrs Olivia Barratt, Millfield Cottage, Little Hadham, Ware, Hertfordshire, SG11 2ED
The Cornwall Crafts Association
Anna Luuk, 3 Lower Shaptor Cottages, Henwood, Liskeard
Craftsman Potters Association of Great Britain
Stephen Brayne, William Blake House, Marshall Street, London, W1V 1FD
Crafts Council
Ann French, 12 Waterloo Place, London, SW1Y 4AU
Devon Guild of Craftsmen
Mrs Helen Hull, Bramblemoor Cottage, Leusdon, Poundsgate, Newton Abbot, Devon, TQ13 7PS

Dorset Craft Guild
Mrs Mavis Hollingworth, Contenbury, Mill Lane, Chideock, Bridport, Dorset, DT6 6JS
Guild of Gloucestershire Craftsmen
Mr G. W. Brotherton, Hambutts Barn, Edge Lane, Painswick, Gloucestershire
Guild of Herefordshire Craftsmen
Miss Vera Lockyer, 43 Somers Park Avenue, Malvern Link, Hereford and Worcester, WR14 1SE
Guild of Lincolnshire Craftsmen
Mr A. G. Mitchell, 6 Broadway Close, Lincoln, LN2 1 SW
Guild of Sussex Craftsmen
Mr Michael Pryke, 8 High Street, Ditchling, East Sussex, BN6 8TA
Guild of Yorkshire Craftsmen
Ms Trisha Briscoe, Duncan Craft Workshops, Ilkley Road, Otley, West Yorkshire, LS21 3JP
Highland Craftpoint
Mr David B. Pirnie, Beauly, Iverness-shire, 1V4 7EH
Norfolk Rural Craftsmen's Guild
Mr A. D. Schaay, 131 Middleton's Lane, Hellesdon, Norwich, NR6 5SQ
North West Craftsmen
Ms Brenda Morrison, Lantern Gallery Workshop, 3 Worsley Road, Worsley, Greater Manchester
Somerset Guild of Craftsmen
Rev R. D. F. Wild, The Railway House, Stogumber, Taunton, Somerset
Wales Craft Council
Ms Carol Lloyd, Box 8, Ladywell House, Newtown, Powys, SY16 1 EH
Western Isles Crafts Association
Mrs Meg Thompson, 5 Rathad na Muilne, Stornoway, Isle of Lewis.

2 Museums

The following is simply a selection of the many museums which have displays relating to local industries and history, where much of the equipment mentioned in the book can be seen.

Abbey House Museum, Kirkstall, Leeds, West Yorkshire
Abbot Hall Museum of Lakeland Life and Industry, Kendal, Cumbria

Angus Folk Museum, Kirkwynd Cottages, Glamis, Tayside (National Trust for Scotland)
Anne of Cleves House, High Street, Lewes, East Sussex
Arlington Mill Museum, Bibury, nr Cirencester, Gloucestershire
Aston Hall, Trinity Road, Aston, Birmingham
Avoncroft Museum of Buildings, Bromsgrove, Hereford and Worcester
Bewdley Museum, The Shambles, Load Street, Bewdley, Hereford and Worcester
Bishop Hooper's Lodging, Gloucester
Black Country Museum, Tipton Road, Dudley, West Midlands
Bradford Industrial Museum, Eccleshill, Bradford, West Yorkshire
Breamore House Countryside Museum, Fordingbridge, Hampshire
Bridewell Museum of Local Industries, Norwich, Norfolk
Bridport Museum, Bridport, Dorset
Cambridge and County Folk Museum, Cambridge
Castle Museum, York
Dorset County Museum, Dorchester, Dorset
Framework Knitters' Museum, Ruddington, Nottinghamshire
Gladstone Pottery Museum, Longton, Stoke-on-Trent, Staffordshire
Hereford City Museum, Hereford
Highland Folk Museum, Kingussie, Inverness
Honiton Museum, Honiton, Devon
Horsham Museum, Horsham, West Sussex
Luton Museum, Wardown Park, Luton, Bedfordshire
Maritime Museum for East Anglia, Great Yarmouth, Norfolk
Museum of Costume and Textiles, Castlegate, Nottingham
Museum of East Anglian Life, Stowmarket, Suffolk
Museum of English Rural Life, Whiteknights Park, Reading, Berkshire
Museum of Leathercraft, Bridge Street, Northampton
Nidderdale Museum, Pateley Bridge, North Yorkshire
Norfolk Rural Life Museum, Gressenhall, Dereham, Norfolk
North Cornwall Museum, Camelford, Cornwall
Oxfordshire County Museum, Woodstock, Oxfordshire
Pennine Farm Museum, Ripponden, West Yorkshire
The Piece Hall, Halifax, West Yorkshire
Quarry Bank Mill, Styal, Cheshire (National Trust)
Red House Museum, Christchurch, Dorset
Rye Museum, Rye, East Sussex
Ryedale Folk Museum, Hutton-le-hole, North Yorkshire
Somerset Rural Life Museum, Abbey Farm, Glastonbury, Somerset
Souter Johnnie's Cottage, Kirkoswald, Strathclyde (The National Trust for Scotland)

Staffordshire County Museum, Shugborough, Staffordshire
Tiverton Museum, St Andrew Street, Tiverton, Devon
Tolson Memorial Museum, Huddersfield, West Yorkshire
Truro County Museum, Truro, Cornwall
Truro Pottery Museum, Chapel Hill, Truro, Cornwall
Uffculme Woollen Museum, Coldharbour Mill, Uffculme, Devon
Weald & Downland Open Air Museum, Singleton, West Sussex
Weaver's Cottage, Kilbarchan, Strathclyde (National Trust for Scotland)
Welsh Folk Museum, St Fagans, Cardiff, South Glamorgan
West Yorkshire Folk Museum, Shibden Hall, Halifax, West Yorkshire
Wycombe Chair and Local History Museum, Castle Hill, High Wycombe, Buckinghamshire

Opening times can be checked in *Museums and Galleries* published by ABC Historic Publications.

3A Craft Centres

Many craft workshops today are in centres where several craftsmen work under one roof or in a group of buildings, such as those on the estate at Lockinge in Oxfordshire. This estate was flourishing in the mid-nineteenth century when its owner Lord Wantage built model cottages and farm buildings for his employees. A century later these buildings were no longer needed; the farming scene had changed and the present owner of the estate, Christopher Lloyd, and his manager decided to turn the surplus buildings into workshops and let them to craftsmen and women wanting to set up in business on their own. COSIRA helped them with their plans and put them in touch with suitable craftworkers. At present some of them are working in the old dairy, the watermill, grain shed and stables, as well as a silversmith and jeweller in the old school building and small electrical firms in other parts of the village. The life of the village has thus been greatly enhanced by the creativity taking place in buildings that might otherwise be deserted.

The village of Llanaelhaearn in Wales with its knitting co-operative described in Chapter 3 is another example of how work helps to revive a village that might otherwise have declined.

Having served for 200 years as a granary, wheelwright's shop and wine cellar, the Old Granary at Bishop's Waltham in Hampshire has at last found itself as the workplace for a number of craftsmen who can be seen at work. Their goods are on sale to the public who can also enjoy a meal in the adjoining restaurant. Among the craftsmen are knitters of hand-dyed garments, fashion and textile designers, a silk-screen printer and leatherworker. The craft shop also sells goods produced by other cottage industries in the area.

At Styal near Wilmslow in Cheshire the National Trust has leased Quarry Bank Mill to a trust who are developing it as a working museum illustrating the development of the cotton industry. The mill and village are the most complete and least altered factory colony of the Industrial Revolution, cotton spinning having been established at the mill in 1784. A fine long room built as a weaving shed in 1840 has now been converted into Styal Workshop where courses are held in the skills of spinning, weaving and dyeing. Craftsmen come from the United States of America and Europe as well as from this country to learn in these inspiring surroundings. Visitors to the mill can watch craftsmen at work spinning and weaving and the apprentice house contains a social history of the village.

An ambitious scheme is under way at present at the old Coldharbour Mill at Uffculme, near Cullompton, Devon. This mill had been in production since it was bought by the Quakers Thomas and Sarah Fox in 1797 until its closure in 1981 as a result of the recession. At its peak production period, it employed up to 300 people and its closure was a great blow to the village in an area with little alternative employment. In the eighteenth century the West of England was a flourishing area for the production of cloth. Thomas Fox was one of the foremost manufacturers in the area, both at his mill at Wellington in Somerset and later at Coldharbour Mill where water power was used (the mill stands on the River Culm). Now the mill is to have a new lease of life. It is owned by the Coldharbour Mill Trust, consisting of local trustees and representatives of local authorities, the education authority and the Science Museum, who have all been instrumental, along with many others, in helping this ambitious project to make a start. The project co-ordinator is the Vicar of Uffculme, the Rev Geoffrey Fraser. It is to be a working wool museum employing people to produce knitting wools and woven material on historic machinery, illustrating the whole process of cloth production from the raw wool to the finished product. Other craftsmen will be accommodated in some of the smaller buildings and eventually some of them will be housed in cottages near the mill with workshops attached. There will also be a restaurant serving food created in the bakery at the mill under the supervision of Kathleen Thomas, and a shop. The whole will form a large complex and tourist attraction for this part of Devon.

Antur Aelhaearn, Llanaelhaearn, Llŷn, Gwynedd. Tel Llithfaen 698.
Village co-operative

Ardington, near Wantage, Oxfordshire.
Estate buildings housing saddlery, potters, farrier, furniture-makers, vintage-car workshop, upholsterer

Balbirnie Craft Centre, Balbirnie, near Markinch, Fife, Scotland.
Situated in Balbirnie Park. Craftsmen in furniture, pottery, leather and knitwear

Bickleigh Mill, Bickleigh, near Tiverton, Devon. Tel Bickleigh 419.
Potters, wood turners, leatherworker, corn-dolly maker, spinner, weaver at work. Farm, shop and restaurant.

Cirencester Workshops, Cricklade Street, Cirencester, Gloucestershire. Tel Cirencester 61566.
Leatherworkers, potters, weavers, basketmakers, knitters at work. Craft shop and coffee-house

Clevedon Craft Centre, Moor Lane, off Court Lane, Clevedon, Avon. Tel Clevedon 872867.
Pottery, leatherwork, spinning, weaving, wood turning. Craft shop, museum and restaurant

Coldharbour Mill, Uffculme, near Cullompton, Devon.
Working wool museum; other crafts. Shop and restaurant

Maes Artro Craft Village, Llanbedr, near Harlech, Gwynedd. Tel Llanbedr 437.
Village made up of a collection of workshops, woodworkers, knitters, handloom weavers, potters

The Model Farm Folk Collection, and Craft Centre, Wolvesnewton, near Usk, Gwent.
Museum and craft centre in eighteenth-century barn, shop and restaurant

The Old Granary, Bank Street, Bishops Waltham, Hampshire. Tel Bishops Waltham 4595.
Knitters, fashion and textile designers, silk-screen printer and leatherworker at work. Restaurant and shop on premises

Ruthin Craft Centre, Ruthin, Clywd. Tel Ruthin 4774.
Fourteen independent craftworkers in separate units under one roof, with restaurant and shop

Styal Workshop, Quarry Bank Mill, Styal, Wilmslow, Cheshire. Tel Wilmslow 527468

The Viables Centre, Harrow Way, Basingstoke, Hampshire. Tel Basingstoke 3634.
Former cattle-breeding farm, now craft workshops for pottery, leatherwork, wood turning, knitting

The Village Craft Centre and Forge, 3 Hungate Lane, Hunmanby, near Filey, North Yorkshire. Tel Scarborough 890453

Workshop Wales, Lower Town, Fishguard, Dyfed. Tel Fishguard 2261.
Workshops for craftsmen; craft shop

3B Craftworkers

The following is a small selection of craftsmen and women working alone or in small cottage industries. Those who are specifically mentioned in the text are marked with an asterisk. The number of people working in this way is increasing all the time and fuller lists may be obtained from the organisations listed in Appendix I. Many of these craftsmen welcome visitors, but as so many live in remote areas a telephone call to check that they are at home is advisable.

Lacemakers

Gwendoline Bristow, Hayes Barton, 10 Vicarage Road, Stoke Gabriel, Devon. Tel Stoke Gabriel 436

The English Lace School, 42 St Peter Street, Tiverton, Devon. Tel Tiverton 253918

★June Hunt, Hartshill, Bewley Down, Axminster, Devon. Tel South Chard 20343

★Isobel Kennet, 34 Rise Park Gardens, Eastbourne, East Sussex. Tel Eastbourne 764717

★'Papillon', 24 Flambard Avenue, Christchurch, Dorset. Reproduction Victorian underwear

★Jean Pegg, 90 Kimberley Road, Southbourne, Bournemouth, Dorset. Tel Bournemouth 429416

Ann Woodward, 9 Shrublands Road, Berkhamstead, Hertfordshire. Tel Berkhamstead 2723

Lace bobbin maker

Tim Parker, 10 Newcombe Road, Tuckton, Bournemouth, Dorset. Tel Bournemouth 429455

Spinners and Weavers

Cambrian Mills (Velindre) Ltd, Drefach, Velindre, near Newcastle Emlyn, Dyfed. Tel Velindre 370209
Tweed manufacturers and museum of the Welsh woollen industry

★Church Farm Weavers, Kingston St Mary, Taunton, Somerset. Tel Kingston St Mary 267

Joyce Coleman, Speen Weavers and Spinners, Speen, Aylesbury, Buckinghamshire. Tel Hampden Row 303.
Handwoven rugs, silks, linens, wools and cottons

Dulverton Weavers, The Studio, Dulverton, Somerset.
Dresses, waistcoats, skirts, etc, from their own cloth woven on the premises

Grewelthorpe Handweavers, Grewelthorpe, Ripon, North Yorkshire. Tel Kirkby Malzeard 209
Fine worsted cloth handwoven by Malcolm McDougall. Craft shop

H. Griffiths & Son, Tregwynt Woollen Mill, Letterston, Haverfordwest, Dyfed. Tel St Nicholas 225.
Traditional Welsh tapestry, 100 per cent pure wool, tweed and brushed woollen fabrics

*Lachlan Macdonald, 'Cnoc-ard', Grimsay, North Uist. Tel Benbecula 2418

John M. Macgregor, 27 Garenin, Carloway, Isle of Lewis. Tel Carloway 257.
Handwoven Harris tweed

Malvern Weavers Ltd, The Country Weaving Workshop, Stone Hall, Colwall, near Malvern, Hereford and Worcester. Tel Colwall 40660.
Small company of weavers making ties, head squares, scarves, fabric lengths and shawls

Geoffrey Peppler, Closewood Farm, Ammerham, Winsham, Chard, Somerset. Tel Winsham 289.
Rugs made from undyed fleece of Jacob Sheep

*Russell Gurney Weavers, Brae Croft, Muiresk, Turriff, Aberdeenshire. Tel Turriff 3544

Doreen Sanders, Pippin Cottage, Woodditton, near Newmarket, Suffolk. Tel Stetchworth 357.
Handwoven rugs, cushions, curtaining

Stoney Park Weavers, Stepaside, Narbeth, Dyfed. Tel Saundersfoot 813868.
100 per cent wool tweeds and flannels handwoven by David and Linda Noon for dress and light furnishings, individual designs in ties, travel rugs and tabards. Weavers loft in small converted grain store

Spinning-Wheels and Looms

John Brightwell, Crinkle Birr Cottage, Higher West Hatch, Taunton, Somerset. Tel Hatch Beauchamp 480548
Spinning-wheels, needlework chests

H. Pouncey, The Stables, Craigdarrock, Moniaive, Thornhill, Dumfriesshire. Tel Moniaive 230.
Stable workshop in former home of Annie Laurie making spinning-wheels in traditional designs

*Jacqueline and James Sheriff, 'Monks', Shaftsbury Road, Child Okeford, Blandford, Dorset. Tel Child Okeford 860086

Whim Looms, Whim Square, Lamancha, Peeblesshire. Tel Penicuik 77474
Tapestry and weaving looms made

Knitters

*Antur Aelhaearn, Llanaelhaearn, Llyn, Gwynedd. Tel Llithfaen 698

*Cambridgeshire Knitters, (Mrs A. Farmer), 27 Madingley Road, Cambridge. Tel Cambridge 357752

Betty Francis, 3 Chapel Square, Deddington, Oxford. Tel Deddington 38400.
Handmade, knitted in pure Aran wool, sweaters, hats, scarves, shawls

*Little London Spinners, (Fran Benton), The Hand-spinning and Weaving Studio, North Lodge, London Minstead, Near Lyndhurst, Hampshire. Tel Cadnam 3425

Muileann Beag a' Chrotail, Sgoil Dhuisdeil, Camascross, Isle of Skye. Tel Isle Ornsay 271.
Knitting workshop producing traditional jerseys, scarves and hats

Smocks, Gloves, Buttons

*Diana Illingworth, 59 Milton Abbas, Blandford, Dorset. Tel Milton Abbas 880489.
Dorset Buttonmaker

*Beverley Marshall, New House Farm, South Perrott, Beaminster, Dorset. Tel Corscombe 516

*The Old Button Shop, Lytchett Minster, Dorset

*Jean Plisner and Dobrila Jenkins, 26 Haslingfield Road, Harlton, Cambridge, Tel Comberton 2855

*Peggy Tuck, Horsington Hill Cottage, Templecombe, Somerset. Tel Templecombe 70794

*Woodstock Leathercraft (H. A. Napier), Harrisons Lane, Woodstock, Oxfordshire. Tel Woodstock 812368
Glovemakers

Printed Textiles

Caroline Bailey, 44 Woburn Drive, Hale, Cheshire. Tel 061 980 8455.
Printed textiles

Hugh & Sophia Blackwell, The Chapel House, Pancake Hill, Lower Chedworth, Cheltenham, Gloucestershire. Tel Fossebridge 626.
Fabric designers and printers specialising in quilts and bedspreads

*Claire Chambers, The Granary, Bishops Waltham, Hampshire. Tel Bishops Waltham 4595.
Hand-printed fabrics

*Pin Linni Prints, 23 Chapel Street, Camelford, Cornwall. Tel Camelford 212733

*Mary Potter Studio, Laughton, Lewes, East Sussex. Tel Halland 438

Mary Tinker Designs, 4 Corporation Street, Aberystwyth, Dyfed. Tel Aberystwyth 612673.
Silk-screen printer

Wendy Todd Textile Workshop, Corn Mill Galleries, The Old

Town Mill, Ulverston, Cumbria. Tel Ulverston 55456.
Workshop in seventeenth century cornmill. Hand-printed Wendy Todd dresses, fashion and furnishing items. Galleries and museum

Baskets

Tony Allen, 43 Cambridge Villas, Godmanchester, Cambridgeshire. Tel Huntingdon 56636.
Willow and cane baskets; rush and cane chair seating

Eric Boon, Bodafon, Penmachno, Betws-y-Coed, Gwynedd. Tel Penmachno 251.
Cane and willow slips and baskets made and repaired; rush and cane chairs reseated

*David Buck, 2 Cherwell Way, Gorleston, Norfolk. Tel Great Yarmouth 61749.
Cane turner and framemaker; willow basketmaker

Alex Coates & Sons Ltd, Willowfields, Burrowbridge, Bridgwater, Somerset. Tel Burrowbridge 227.
Cane and basketware

*Keith Colsell, Ervdale Cottage, Sourin, Rousay, Orkney. Tel Rousay 351.
Rush and straw coil baskets

David Drew, 5 Higher Hare Farm, Hare Lane, Buckland St Mary, Somerset. Tel Buckland St Mary 597.
Traditional English willow baskets, including Somerset apple pickers and washing baskets

*W. Gadsby & Son (Burrowbridge) Ltd, Burrowbridge, Bridgwater, Somerset.
Basket manufacturers and willow growers

*Thomas Smith (Herstmonceux) Ltd, Herstmonceux, East Sussex. Tel Herstmonceux 2137.
Trug baskets

Corn Dollies

J. A. Myers, Wolvesnewton Folk Museum and Craft Centre, near Chepstow, Gwent. Tel Wolvesnewton 626.
Large selection of corn dollies, strawcraft, corn-dolly kits, Welsh corn-dolly folk dolls

Meg Pettitt, 2 Southgate, Lydford, Okehampton, Devon. Tel Lydford 239.
Maker of traditional and modern corn dollies and fine straw work

Nerys Smith, Ruthin Craft Centre, Unit 11, Ruthin, Clwyd.
Traditional corn dollies and kits containing all materials and full instructions for making traditional dollies

Ropes and Nets

*Bridport-Gundry, Bridport, Dorset.
Netmakers

★Albert Kirby, 42 Fernhurst Close, Hayling Island, Hampshire. Tel Hayling Island 4768.
Craftsman in ropework

★W. R. Outhwaite & Son, Town Foot, Hawes, North Yorkshire. Tel Hawes 487.
Ropes made by traditional methods

Potters

David Ballantyne, Avon Group Gallery, 5 Bridge Street, Christchurch, Dorset. Tel Highcliffe 4196.
Pottery and porcelain, building elements, industrial products

★Susan and Alex Blair, Stornoway Pottery, Borve, Isle of Lewis. Tel Borve 345

Clive Bowen, Shebbear Pottery, Shebbear, Beaworthy, Devon. Tel Shebbear 271.
Wood-fired red earthenware clay tableware, oven dishes, storage jars

Breanish Pottery, (Diana and Ian Sutherland), Breanish, Uig, Isle of Lewis. Tel Timsgarry 349

★Burley Pottery, 3 Ringwood Road, Burley, Hampshire. Tel Burley 3205.
Hand-thrown stoneware; handmade figures and cottages

Peter Clough, Poole Cottage, Poole Green, Cheshire. Tel Nantwich 64919.
Hand-thrown reduced stoneware, including tea and coffee sets

Cromarty Design Workshops, Fishertown, Cromarty, Ross-shire. Tel Cromarty 254.
Hand-thrown earthenware pottery decorated with coloured slips, white slips hand-painted and sgraffito work

Jacky Duncan, Closewood Farm, Ammerham, Winsham, Chard, Somerset. Tel Winsham 289.
Terracotta garden pots, hand-dug clay and wood fired

David Eeeles, Shepherds Well Pottery, Mosterton, Beaminster, Dorset. Tel Broadwindsor 68257.
Handmade stoneware, porcelain and earthenware, oil and wood fired

Michael Emmett Stoneware, Higher Slade Farm, Sheldon, Honiton, Devon. Tel Broadhembury 254.
Hand-thrown stoneware and porcelain

★Ewenny Pottery, Ewenny, near Bridgend, Mid Glamorgan. Tel Bridgend 3020

★The Leach Pottery, St Ives, Cornwall. Tel St Ives 6398

John Leach, Muchelney Pottery, near Langport, Somerset. Tel Langport 250324.
Handmade stoneware, domestic pottery, wood fired

Pennine Pottery, 16a Holmes Street, Heanor, Derbyshire. Tel Langley Mill 67409.
Medieval-style pottery, goblets, pitchers, platters, English slipware

Peter Robinson, Menston Pottery, Four Lane Ends, Menston, Ilkley, West Yorkshire. Tel Menston 77985.
Hand-thrown slip-decorated earthenware, anything from bread crocks, 2ft (60cm) diameter plates to small mugs

Rye Pottery, Ferry Road, Rye, East Sussex. Tel Rye 3363.
Hand-thrown tableware, decorated by hand using seventeenth century Delft or majolica technique

*Truro Pottery, Chapel Hill, Truro, Cornwall. Tel Truro 2928

Furniture-makers

Grahame Amey Ltd, Standard Street, Crickhowell, Powys. Tel Crickhowell 810540.
Craftsmen making solid wood furniture in ash and oak in thirteenth-century granary

*Edward Barnsley, Froxfield, Petersfield, Hampshire. Tel Hawkley 233

Ralph Farrer, Stogumber Woodwork, Wayshill, Stogumber, Taunton, Somerset. Tel Stogumber 205.
Handmade furniture and turnery

Peter Hall Woodcraft, Danes Road, Staveley, Kendal, Cumbria, Tel Stavely 821633.
Solid oak or mahogany furniture made to order

Hamlyn Lodge Cottage Industry, Welbeck, Worksop, Nottinghamshire. Tel Worksop 85252.
Family home workshop and showroom, cabinet-makers and antique restorers

Gerald Hitchcock, Mill House, Powderham, Exeter, Devon. Tel Starcross 890548.
Cabinet-maker

*Maurice Leach, Sandpits Hill, Curry Rivel, near Langport, Somerset. Tel Langport 250750

Nicholas Partridge, Church Farm Workshops, Sutton Mandeville, near Salisbury, Wiltshire. Tel Fovant 388.
Furniture designer and maker

*Peter Pike, Grove House, Tutts Lane, West Wellow, near Romsey, Hampshire. Tel West Wellow 23105.
Cabinet-maker and antique restorer

Jasper Shackleton, Derwen House, Hill Brow Road, Liss, Hampshire. Tel Liss 3448.
Specialises in in-lay work

*Treske Ltd, Station Works, Thirsk, N. Yorks. Tel Thirsk 22770

Woodcarvers, Turners and Chairmakers

Cecil Colyer, Orchardene, Candys Lane, Shillingstone, Blandford Forum, Dorset. Tel Child Okeford 860252.
Furniture, silverwork and wood turnery

Jenny Daniel, Gisla Woodcraft, Gisla Lodge, Uig, Isle of Lewis. Tel Timsgarry 371.
Wood-turned items

Dennis French, Rock House, Brimscombe Hill, Stroud, Gloucestershire. Tel Brimscombe 883054.
Comprehensive range of hand-finished domestic woodware

★Nigel Griffiths, The Old Cheese Factory, Grange Mill, near Matlock,.Derbyshire

★Rupert Griffiths (Monastic Woodcraft Ltd), Saracen's Head Coaching House, Brailsford, Derbyshire. Tel Brailsford 429

Charles Jones Woodcarving Workshop, Criccieth, Gwynedd. Tel Criccieth 2833.
Over sixty different designs of hand-carved Welsh love spoons in fruitwood, elm and sycamore

★J. Peipereit, 5 Blenheim Drive, Parkside, Ledbury, Hereford and Worcester. Tel Ledbury 2092.
Wood-turner

Richard Raffan, Star House, Sandford, Crediton, Devon. Tel Crediton 4627.
Wood turnery, bowls, platters, boxes made in English and foreign hardwoods

★Robert Thompson's Craftsmen Ltd, Kilburn, Yorkshire. Tel Coxwold 218

★J. Arthur Wells, Gatsford, Ross-on-Wye, Hereford and Worcester. Tel Ross-on-Wye 2595.
Wood-turner

Rush Seats and Caning

Bedfordshire Rushwork (L. M. Waller), 6 Bedford Road, Pertenhall, Bedford. Tel Kimbolton 784.
Rush baskets, mats, etc

★Country Chairmen, Home Farm, School Road, Ardington, near Wantage, Oxfordshire. Tel East Hendred 614 and 362

Rebecca Hitchcock, Mill House, Powderham, Exeter, Devon. Tel Starcross 890548.
Caning, sea-grassing and upholstery

Jim Ingram, 3 Hanson Drive, Loughton, Essex. Tel 01-508 0930.
Chair caning

Alison Leslie-Jones, The Old Vicarage, Stourton Caundle, Sturminster Newton, Dorset. Tel Stalbridge 62453.
Cane and rush seating

Mrs P. M. Morgan, Ousel Cottage, Mill Lane, Pavenham, Bedfordshire. Tel Oakley 2393.
A wide variety of rush baskets, mats, etc. Rush seating

Metalworkers

★Bigbury Mint, The Coach House, Bigbury, Kingsbridge, Devon. Tel Bigbury-on-Sea 426.
Medallion and coin designers; travelling mint

★David Cox, 13 Mobile Homes Park, 133 London Road, Horndean, Hampshire. Tel Horndean 591932

T. D. Davies, The Smithy, Ystrad Meurig, Dyfed. Tel Pontrhydfendigaid 248.
Village smithy; agricultural repairs; wrought ironwork to order, gates, fire-baskets, etc

Harold Geatch, Exwell Cottage, Powderham, Exeter, Devon. Tel Exeter 832132.
General blacksmith and ornamental ironwork

Michael Malleson, The Blackmore Vale Forge, Bishops Caundle, Sherborne, Dorset. Tel Bishops Caundle 404.
Domestic and architectural hand-forged ironwork

★E. Martin & Son, Closeburn, Thornhill, Dumfriesshire. Tel Closeburn 267

John Roger Thomas, The Forge, Bethesda Road, Tumble, Llanelli, Dyfed. Tel Cross Lands 841612.
Hand-forged wrought ironwork

Trapp Forge, Simonstone, near Burnley, Lancashire. Tel Padiham 71025.
Wrought ironwork of all kinds, including gates and staircases, fire-grates, fire-irons, made at family forge

Wing & Staples, The Forge, Motcombe, Shaftesbury, Dorset. Tel Shaftesbury 3104.
Practical and decorative ironwork of all descriptions

Leatherworkers

★Sally Barnes, Buckingham Leathergoods, Ardington, Wantage, Oxfordshire. Tel 0235 88 719.
Made-to-measure saddlery and harness. Handbags, belts, wallets

Candles in the Rain, The Old Smithy, Nantglyn, near Denbigh, Clwyd. Tel Nantglyn 389.
Leather workshop and showroom in eighteenth-century Welsh smithy. Wide selection of handmade heavy hide goods in top grain bridlehide. Hand-carved designs.

Joyce Daniel, 5 Coppice Hill, Bishops Waltham, Hampshire. Leather goods, belts etc, all hand-tooled in finest English leather. Can be seen at The Old Granary Craft Centre, Bishops Waltham

★Tony and Dawn Dennis, St Eval Leathercrafts, Downhill, St Eval, Wadebridge, Cornwall. Tel St Mawgan 357

W. E. Garrett, Master Saddler, Back Lane, Draycott, near Cheddar, Somerset. Tel Cheddar 742367

S. W. Halford & Son, 10 South Street, Crowland, Peterborough, Cambridgeshire. Tel Peterborough 210605.
Saddler, harness-maker, all riding work. Driving harness and heavy show harness

★John Jones, 35 Milton Lilbourne, Pewsey, Wiltshire. Tel Pewsey 2696.
Bellows

John Willie's Saddle Room, 2 Ringwood Road, Burley, Hampshire. Tel Burley 2386.
Saddler and harness-makers

McCoy Saddlery, High Street, Porlock, Somerset. Tel Porlock 862518.
Handmade saddlery and leather goods

Ben Morris, Inskin Leather, West Street, Fishguard, Dyfed. Tel Fishguard 872510.
Handbags with Celtic designs; embossed hide products, such as belts and wine mats

★Raymond Morris of Eddergoll, Eddergoll House, 29 Bonnygate, Cupar, Fife. Cupar 54757

★Osprey Belt Company (Graeme Ellisdon), The Studio, Cutts Lane, Kimpton, Hitchin, Hertfordshire. Tel Kimpton 833350

Jon Richards, Bailey Hill, Castle Cary, Somerset. Tel Castle Cary 680.
Hand-crafted leatherwork in high-quality cow hide: shoulder bags, belts, purses etc

John Wood & Son (Exmoor) Ltd, Linton, Old Cleeve, Minehead, Somerset. Tel Washford 40291.
Sheepskin processing, from raw to finish: moccasins, hats, gloves

Home Cooking

Highland Fine Cheeses Ltd, Blarliath, Tain, Ross and Cromarty. Tel Tain 2034.
Highland cheeses, such as 'Crowdie', 'Caboc', Hramsa and Galic

★Mrs Kathleen Thomas, Devon Larders, Whitehall Mill, Hemyock, Devon. Tel Hemyock 680347

A most useful booklet giving details of craft fairs, as well as much additional information of interest both to craftsmen and the purchasers of their wares, is contained in *The Craftsman's Directory* published annually by Stephen and Jean Lance, Brook House, Mint Street, Godalming, Surrey, GU7 1HE (Tel Godalming 22184) for £3 (1982).

FURTHER READING

General

Brander, Michael, *Scottish Crafts and Craftsmen* (Johnston & Bacon, 1974)

Brill, Edith, *Life and Tradition in the Cotswolds* (Dent, 1973)

CoSIRA, *Craft Workshops in the English Countryside* (1979)

Countryman, The, *Rescuing the Past* (David & Charles, 1973)

Grant, I. F. *Highland Folk Ways* (Routledge & Kegan Paul, 1961)

Hartley, Dorothy, *Made in England* (Eyre Methuen, 1939)

Hartley, Marie and Ingilby, Joan, *Life and Tradition in the Yorkshire Dales* (Dent. 1968)

Hill, Jack, *The Complete Practical Book of Country Crafts* (David & Charles, 1979)

Jekyll, Gertrude, *Old English Household Life* (Batsford, 1975)

Jenkins, J. G., *Life and Traditions in Rural Wales* (Dent, 1976)

–. –. *Traditional Country Craftsmen* (Routledge & Kegan Paul, 1965)

Jobson, Allan, *Household and Country Crafts* (Cedric Chivers, 1970)

Lansbury, Angela, *See Britain at Work* (Exley Publications, 1981 [factories and workshops in Britain open to the public])

Manners, J. E., *Country Crafts Today* (David & Charles, 1974)

Peate, I. C., *Tradition and Folk Life* (Faber, 1972)

Rollinson, William, *Life and Tradition in the Lake District* (Dent, 1974)

Wales Tourist Board, *Guide to Craft Shops and Workshops Open to Visitors* (1980)

Welsh Craft Council, *Welsh Buyers Guide* (1981)

Lacemakers

Freeman, Charles, *Pillow Lace in the East Midlands* (Luton Museum, 1980)

'Lacemaking in Oxfordshire', leaflet from Oxfordshire Museums (1980)

Wright, Thomas, *The Romance of the Lace Pillow* (Olney, 1919; reprinted 1971)

Spinners and Weavers

Fox, Hubert, *Quaker Homespun* (Allen & Unwin, 1958)

Jenkins, J. G. *The Welsh Woollen Industry* (Welsh Folk Museum, 1969)
Leadbeater, Eliza, *Spinning and Spinning Wheels* (Shire, 1979)
de la Mann, J., *The Cloth Industry in the West of England* (Clarendon Press, 1971)
Thompson, Francis, *Harris Tweed* (David & Charles, 1969)

Knitters
Harvey, Michael and Compton, Rae, *Fisherman Knitting* (Shire, 1978)
Traditional Fair Isle Knitting Patterns (The National Trust for Scotland, 1981)
Wells, F. A., *The British Hosiery and Knitwear Industry* (David & Charles, 1972)

Smocks, Gloves and Buttons
Bright, Mervyn, *Buttony, The Dorset Heritage* (Old Button Shop, Lytchett Minster, 1971)
Hall, Maggie, *Smocks* (Shire, 1979)
Leyland, N. L., and Troughton, J. E., *Glovemaking in West Oxfordshire* (Oxfordshire Museums, 1974)
Marshall, Beverley, *Smocks and Smocking* (Alphabooks)
Nichols, Marian, *Smocks in Luton Museum* (Luton Museum, 1980)

Printed Textiles, Country Furniture-makers, Woodcarvers, Metalworkers, Leatherworkers, Home Cooking
Filbee, Marjorie, *Dictionary of Country Furniture (The Connoisseur,* 1977)
Fogg, Charles, *Chains and Chainmaking* (Shire, 1981)
Ingram, Arthur, *Dairying Bygones* (Shire, 1977)
Robinson, Stuart, *A History of Printed Textiles* (Studio Vista, 1969)
Thompson, James, *The Mouseman of Kilburn* (Dalesman Books, 1980)
Waterer, John, *Leather and Craftsmanship* (Faber, 1950)

Basketry
Bagshawe, T. W., *Basketmaking in Bedfordshire* (Luton Museum, 1981)
Freeman, Charles, *Luton and the Hat Industry* (Luton Museum, 1976)

Pottery
Algar, David, *Verwood and District Potteries* (Newsome, 1979; obtainable from Red House Museum, Christchurch)
Barton, K. J., *Pottery in England* (David & Charles, 1975)
Leach, Bernard, *A Potter's Book* (Faber, 1976)
Medieval Pottery and Metal-ware in Wales (National Museum of Wales, 1978)

INDEX